DIGITAL IS DESTROYING EVERYTHING

DIGITAL IS DESTROYING EVERYTHING

What the Tech Giants Won't Tell You about How Robots, Big Data, and Algorithms Are Radically Remaking Your Future

Andrew V. Edwards

ROWMAN & LITTLEFIELD
Lanham • Boulder • New York • London

Published by Rowman & Littlefield
A wholly owned subsidiary of The Rowman & Littlefield Publishing Group, Inc.
4501 Forbes Boulevard, Suite 200, Lanham, Maryland 20706
www.rowman.com

Unit A, Whitacre Mews, 26-34 Stannary Street, London SE11 4AB

British Library Cataloguing in Publication Information Available

Library of Congress Cataloging-in-Publication Data

Edwards, Andrew V., 1956–
Digital is destroying everything : what the tech giants won't tell you about how robots, big data, and
algorithms are radically remaking your future / Andrew V. Edwards.
pages cm
Includes index.
ISBN 978-1-4422-4651-5 (cloth : alk. paper) — ISBN 978-1-5381-2175-7 (paperback) — ISBN
978-1-4422-4652-2 (electronic)
1. Automation—Social aspects. 2. Technology—Social aspects. 3. Internet—Social aspects. 4. Electronic data processing—Social aspects. I. Title.
T14.5.E385 2015
303.48'3—dc23
2014048145

Printed in the United States of America

This book is dedicated to my wife, Luchy, and my children, Adam and Siena.

CONTENTS

FOREWORD

When *Digital is Destroying Everything* was published in hardcover in 2015, our president was Barack Obama. At that time we were surprised to hear, via Edward Snowden[1] , that the NSA secretly had been collecting our data. Amazon had already been a digital juggernaut for a decade or more. Driverless cars had yet to make much news. Robot bombs (aka "drones") were deployed in a number of military theaters with remarkably destructive results.

In that world, I tried to describe the way digital technologies were impacting us. Many industries, some of whom had laid themselves open to attack, had been "destroyed" by digital already: music, newspapers, cable television, bookstores and the like. I also suggested that the pace of such change would accelerate and tried to give some examples of where the impacts might be most strongly felt.

Today it is surprising to me that some of it has come to pass so quickly! I had suggested that "nation will hack at nation" with digital armies and especially that elections could be affected; and that political outcomes could be distorted so as to set back the notion of democracy. I would not have predicted that Russia might have succeeded, largely via social media, in helping a particular candidate win the presidency. I would not have predicted that the candidate might win at least partly because he knew how to fascinate everyone with his tweets.

There were few kind words for Facebook in my book, but I would not have predicted that one of the top stories of 2018 would be that Facebook might have been a supplier of data to a company like Cambridge Analytica as they helped the Russians target American voters in certain critical swing districts.[2] I had noted how digital enabled people to enclose themselves inside of self-reinforcing data bubbles that would seem multidimensional while really being very closed and small—but I would not have predicted that this might generate a phenomenon rooted in hate that we now call the "alt-right."[3]

I had noted that finance especially might be vulnerable to digital distortions, but I would not have predicted that cryptocurrencies like Bitcoin would become for a certain type of day trader/computer nerd a leading source of speculative wealth. Nor that "blockchain" (simply a list of linked lists) would become a magic word to raise billions of dollars of venture capital.

When I looked at data as it might be used by government, I did not like what I saw: increasing surveillance and official observation of private individuals. But I did not predict that, for instance, the Los Angeles Police Department would soon use artificial intelligence to target and retarget certain types of communities for increased police intervention.[4] I did mention that cell phone videos might act as a deterrent to abuse. And while I don't know if it's been a deterrent, it has certainly recorded its share.

Finally, I had wanted to make sure we might also appreciate all the fine and enjoyable things digital has brought us. These things continue to multiply and improve. We are never lost, with GPS on our phones. We can order anything we want and have it delivered to our front door, and we can do this from anywhere, at any time of day. We can send and receive money over the phone, instantly. We can see almost any television show or movie we want, anywhere, any time, on any number of devices. We stand in line much less, because we can do so much more *on*line. Computer gaming in particular is more spectacular and more engrossing than ever—and so it shall continue to improve.

As I had suggested in 2015, the only cure to any digital ill is to put down the smartphone and look around you. The analog (physical) world is far richer in detail and dynamic than anyone can comprehend. It's likely to be more rewarding than what you might see on even the best-engineered flat-screen. Today I would want to emphasize this with even more urgency.

Enjoy digital for what it's worth! But only for what it's worth to you.

A NOTE ON THE USE OF THE WORD "DIGITAL" IN THIS BOOK

The word "digital," in the context typically assigned to it in the current era, has been used more or less as an adjective ("digital marketing," "digital domain," "digital expertise") as a stand-in for descriptives like "computerized" and "information-technology-related." I've decided to turn the adjective into a noun. Thus, in this book, "digital" conveys a meaning similar to "all disciplines, practices, and products relating to the information-technology industries." Using it thus makes for an encompassing locution that provides clarity and simplicity at once, and also makes for a briefer and more incisive volume.

I

DIGITAL IS DESTROYING EVERYTHING

Digital—the combined power of Internet Protocol–enabled devices, the World Wide Web, cloud computing, cheap storage, algorithms, "social media," massive data collection by marketers and governments, mobile apps and wireless connectivity—is destroying everything. And yet a new and rather eye-catching garden is sprouting on the blasted heath, often with a suddenness that appalls the unprepared. Much of the culture we've known until recently is already destroyed, and some of what's been toppled has seen us refreshed and reinvigorated by digital, but some has not. And some things we thought would be forever, things we've admired and held dear, are soon, before the march of all things digital, likely to be no more.

When I began working "in computers," I regarded the information-technology industry a most amenable way to make a career for myself—indeed, it allowed me to "go out on my own," which was fortunate, as I had demonstrated but little skill at working for others. Digital was absorbing, and there was a scent of revolution in the air. It was scrappy, and nobody, including some very large organizations that ought to have known better, thought it would amount to anything, and for several years it seemed as if it might not. I devoted many years to proving the doubters wrong.

Now digital has gotten spooky. We used to hope for the wonders we have today, but we always had thought it would also involve an egalitarian multiverse of independent voices and views; that it would do more to level the field than foment volcanic ranges that smoke out the sun. We had scarcely imagined that governments might even be interested, never mind mastering it the more to master us.

This book will examine specific industries and familiar ways of life that have been, or are soon to be, altered, in ways that few have been able to predict, and fewer still able to contextualize or fully comprehend.

This book is not, despite its title, a dystopian rant against all things digital (I would be remiss in pretending digital has not provided me a good living since the 1980s). Nor is it a false-flag attack on digital designed to set the stage for its apotheosis. Instead, expect to find a lively investigation into the ways digital has opened us to new and sometimes quite wonderful experiences, driven down costs for consumers, and given information a chance to be free. But we will also take a clear-eyed look at many of the good (and sometimes bad) things—businesses and behaviors—digital has destroyed, and how the world that ensues may be diminished, compromised, sapped, and subject to an amount of oversight that mocks the notion of individual empowerment that is perhaps too often touted as the exemplar of digital's salutary effect on the human domain.

CREATIVE DESTRUCTION?

The reader may be forgiven for suspecting this book might largely treat of a phenomenon known (especially in the information technology [IT] industries) as "creative destruction," but this would be a misapprehension. "Creative destruction" is a term coined in 1942 by Austrian economist Joseph Schumpeter and later popularized in the United States by Harvard professor Clay Christensen as he approached a related subject in his landmark book *Innovator's Dilemma*. But while Schumpeter may have examined the phenomenon as an example of what would eventually destroy capitalism, Christensen argued that the driving force behind destruction was innovation. Based on his business-school prescription, the term was, in popular usage, deployed to describe ways that large, stable industries could be disrupted and sometimes destroyed by smaller, more nimble players in the same market.

Both Schumpeter's and Christensen's were neutral concepts, and neither "creative" nor "innovative" were meant to zero out the potentially deleterious effects of "destruction" or "disruption." That said, digital entrepreneurs, especially those associated with the Darwinistic ethos of Silicon Valley, have bowdlerized the term as a way of congratulating themselves. They seem to believe their achievements approach a condition of natural law.

Digital entrepreneurs . . . seem to believe their achievements approach a condition of natural law.

They have taken the "creative destruction" term and turned it into a creed, and in doing so can admit no flaw in the belief system, to wit: what has been destroyed must have been bad (because it could not survive!); what destroyed it, for whatever reason, and regardless of any collateral result or circumstance, must be good. While we do not intend to disagree that creative destruction is a legitimate phenomenon, it is the hagiography of all changes wrought by digital that we intend to deal with incisively and without fear or favor.

ASSESSING THE IMPACT OF DIGITAL

Digital has come of age and is ready for its close-up. Some thirty-five years after the advent of the first personal computer (an interval roughly analogous to my working life), we can now appreciate the scope and depth of what this revolution of bits and bytes has wrought. And while the ubiquity of information (and its easy manipulation) is laudable in theory, there are too many unhappy displacements, too much slavish conformity, and too much centralization of power to suggest we are anywhere near the utopia that digital entrepreneurs love to suggest they're creating.

Instead, what the lords of digital seem most excited about is not the benisons they've bestowed on the yearning masses at Overstock.com; it is rather the astonishing height of their own stacks of gold that seems to drive their enthusiasm.

The most recent generation of digital masters seems driven much less by such early idealism as was apparent in the likes of the (Insanely) Great Jobs and even, to his credit, Gates the Lucky, and more by the amount of money they can make without producing discernible benefit. Many of the best minds today are dedicated to trivial pursuits like building apps that match paint colors to pop music (as recently was done for the Dutch Boy brand), while structural challenges to the nation and the planet (poverty, public transportation, or the environment, for example) remain largely unaddressed. The worst seem driven not just by money but also by an unseemly desire to see how much data they can gather about their fellow citizens and sell to the highest bidder. In the summer of 2013, this trope leaned toward a distinctly infernal helios when it was revealed that digital behavioral data was being mainlined by the American spy network in such completeness and volume as to astound even the cynical. Since then we have seen an outcry from across the political spectrum but no real change. Powerful liberals and conservatives seem to agree the government must be able to spy on its citizens in order to continue fighting an endless "war on terror" (more on this subject later).

Having made a living in the digital industries for so long, and as a specialist in digital analytics, I cannot hypocritically denounce data collection as inherently disreputable. But the 2013 revelations about the National Security Agency's *very* disreputable spying on every American has made any defense of data collection suspect, especially with revelations that some of the technology industry's giants have either been getting paid or been forced (depending on which narrative you accept) to deliver your data to cloak-and-dagger operatives deep inside their black ops bunkers. Despite that desperately unpleasant aspect of data collection, however, nearly every marketer collecting data today is honestly (and only) looking for better ways to connect with its customers and constituents. What they are doing with the practice known as "digital analytics" really could not be further in scope or intent from the dragnet thrown by a government in its overweening search for evildoers and miscreants. By way of comparison, it's as if a shopkeeper looking at folks perusing items on the shelf of her store were somehow bunked in the same iniquitous den as a truncheon-bearing gendarme looking for dirt on characters unpopular with the regime.

But let us not get too distracted with the subject of privacy, which, while it shall be duly treated in this book, really deserves a shelf of volumes.

THE MACHINE AGE THEN: THE DIGITAL NOW

If the original impetus of the Machine Age was the diminution of hard, agrarian labor, its result was the tyranny of the assembly line. And if the dawn of software was the beginning of the end for data blindness and sleeve protectors, its result has been the widespread disappearance of human contact; an expanded acceptance of media (much of it "home-made") of a type that, arguably, is increasingly shallow and undistinguished; a false sense of belonging where no such thing exists; and massive data-collection systems that enable command-and-control structures of almost unimaginable power and complexity. Such complexity also suggests the eventuality of near-unimaginable failures, and as nation hacks at nation, we have perhaps only begun to encounter the tip of this particularly icy berg.

One example of a massive digital failure, now receding in memory, was the disastrous launch of the websites associated with the Affordable Care Act that its detractors love to call Obamacare. Putting any merits or demerits of the ACA aside, we must grapple with the fact that within three weeks of its launch, the digital platform upon which the ACA seemed perhaps too heavily reliant had been a near total washout, and for too long, the news of its maladroit launch suggested it was actually endangering health care for millions. In the following months the website improved, but the notion that digital would almost automatically be the best possible solution was shaken.

The ACA launch failure illustrates that digital, when relied upon too heavily, and when deployed too widely, can create as much damage, or even more, as any other method of information architecture.

By every indication the site is now much improved, a new tech leader has been appointed to run it, and the ACA in general has proved itself successful enough to become an asset to the party that championed it. But the technology rollout could not have been worse.

In a similar vein we are now seeing what I believe to be the beginnings of a bandwidth crisis that may prove difficult to master. Streaming video and a general upsurge in connectivity is clearly straining the infrastructure. In August 2014 Comcast had a massive outage across much of its network. More locally to me, and in the same time period, Fairpoint Communications had an e-mail outage (the cause of which has not been disclosed), and Mid-Hudson Cablevision, often down and oftener slow, regularly plays a brand of infomercials on TV that features the president of that company saying how tough it is to keep up with demand for bandwidth. One shudders to think what might happen if a truly massive breakdown were to occur somewhere among a thicket of fiber-optic cables critical enough to take down all digital communication across a generous cross section of the American spectrum. There is no evidence to suggest we are even remotely prepared for such an event, and the results could be especially catastrophic for business.

At the same time, we now have, according to a *New York Times* article on September 5, 2014, the unlikely burg of Kansas City equipped with Google Fiber with speeds so fast no one can think of what to do with it. [1] So far the chief accomplishment seems to have been the downloading of more than six hundred cat pictures in about a nanosecond. Perhaps more troubling news comes from a *Wall Street Journal* article of October 2014, [2] wherein it is reported that middle, upper-middle, and wealthy households have signed up for Google Fiber in high percentages, while renters and "the poor" have signed up almost not at all.

IF CHAPLIN COULD HAVE KNOWN . . .

In a generation we have gone from a handy error-correcting typewriter *cum* home organizer (with a sanitized Charlie Chaplin vouching its lovability in a series of early IBM PC commercials) to remote drone strikes. From WYSIWYG on the desktop to the delegitimization and wholesale destruction of print media; from a simple file storage system on insubstantial floppy disks to a surveillance state where one's every keystroke is made upon a network-aware machine in which the network is more aware of you than you are of the network.

In a generation . . . we have gone from WYSIWYG on the desktop to the delegitimization and wholesale destruction of print media.

Digital has brought uncountable benefits to us all—from instant blood-sugar readouts to teller-free banking to movies (often free or nearly free) almost anywhere at almost any time—but digital has also left us with what may be permanent underemployment, a near-total loss of privacy, and a further retreat behind the flatscreen of our choice. Far from heralding an era of fellowship and equality, arguably it has contributed instead to the alarming and widening gap between those who have and those who wish they had.

The Doors's Jim Morrison, in his typically portentous manner, once sang of the future, and how it is uncertain, and that "the end is always near."

And so it may be as regards our selfless love affair with all things digital.

2

CRAZY TRAIN: HOW DIGITAL DROVE BIG MUSIC OFF THE RAILS

The destructive onslaught of digital ranges far and cuts deep. Some types of destruction have had a more obvious, or perhaps a more widely known, impact than others.

We can start with something easy for us to grasp: the music industry as we had come to know it circa 1955 to circa 2010. Much ink has been spilled and tears mixed with jeers in relation to this subject. I imagine nothing noted in this chapter will be entirely unexpected. But I do expect to lay out the example of a pattern (in an industry already well impacted) that shows how digital can be utterly transformative. Despite a quaint resurgence of vinyl for aficionados, the music industry such as it has long been known does not exist anymore. It has been destroyed by digital technologies that have made music virtual, untethered to a physical unit, and very easily appropriated.

NO MORE GRAVY TRAIN

Gone are the blockbuster albums, supergroups, record deals, Pink Floyd's infamous "gravy train" for lucky musicians, any noticeable song rotation on the radio, the notion that we pay for music to listen at our leisure, the notion that record companies ought to be paid, or even that *musicians* ought to be paid. Except for a very few (entrepreneurial) top stars—Gwen

Stefani in spring 2014 launched her third line of clothing,[1] while the redoubtable Taylor Swift in 2014 removed her music from Spotify so that she could be paid better—musicians have nearly all been reduced to the condition of buskers on the sidewalk: *hear my madrigal in passing and toss a coin if it please ye.*

There remain ways to make money in music, and the likes of Gwen Stefani seem to have cracked the code: use music as a base and expand your offering much as any brand might. It isn't new, of course (remember Beatle wigs?), but now it becomes more critical as album sales plummet and live attendance fails to make up all the difference. And you don't have to be a superstar in order to supplement your income through merchandising. According to *Fortune,*[2] plenty of fairly esoteric musicians participate in the merchandising bonanza, and the more bizarre the "merch," the better: the Flaming Lips offer a "silver trembling fetus Christmas ornament," while DJ deadmau5 sells headphones—for cats.

DYING CULTURE?

In 2011, Robert Levine, author of *Free Ride*, said that "digital piracy and greedy technology firms are crushing the life out of the culture business," according to an article in the UK *Guardian* from August of that year.[3] And things have only gotten worse in the years since. *Music Business Research*, citing data published by the Recording Industry Association of America, claims there has been an 83 percent decrease in CD album sales in the US between 2000 and 2013.[4] A top-selling album today might reach 1.7 million units, down from 5.6 million in 2000. The trend continues down as we write this.

According to the same source, 10.5 million people have stopped buying music in the US and UK entirely since 2008. The implication is that they are now downloading music without paying for it. To be fair, Music Industry Blog also posits that iTunes and other services like it represent a possible lifeline to the industry. I remain skeptical of this notion, as, given the preponderance of what music-industry folks call "piracy," it seems iTunes may simply be a gateway drug to non-payment downloading. Nor has Spotify's subscription model made for any appreciable change of fortune in the music business.

Musicians today work day jobs, sell T-shirts, and tour until the wheels fall off. And if you're like most listeners, you probably own much more music today, and at much, much lower cost, than you might have hoped when the Recording Industry Association of America (RIAA) towered like a T-Rex over the auditory landscape.

The RIAA says, "Music theft is a real, ongoing and evolving challenge. Both the volume of music acquired illegally without paying for it and the resulting drop in revenues are staggering. Digital sales, while on the rise, are not making up the difference."[5]

But aside from the league of lachrymose recording-industry executives, who's crying?

Almost no one.

That's because music might be the perfect case for why it might be okay that digital can be so destructive. One of the most fascinating developments in the age of digital is to witness how many besieged industries may in fact deserve the death-by-hacking to which they succumb. Among these is the bloated, oft-despised enterprise we still insist on calling "the music industry."

DOWNBEAT

Big Music—apart from (in my opinion) its diminishing and now rather paltry serving of good music itself—had long been a sink of corruption,[6] well known and long derided as hypersexualized, price-gouging, abusive of the consumer, abusive of the musician. It was mired in a swamp of deceit, thievery, and excess that could hardly fail to disgust all but the most insensitive observer. Perhaps the only part of the industry more egregious than the vaunted superstar structure upon which it still attempts to sup is the rapacity of the record labels themselves.[7] In what may have been a final paroxysm of misbehavior, they took to the courts, suing the Ugg boots off of Debbie Downloader and extracting thousands of dollars from her workaday mom.[8] That was a spectacular public relations failure, and they gave it up.

At least since Elvis Presley shimmied shamelessly and girls screamed, the music industry has profited from a sense of hormonally infused danger, if not outright lawlessness. Mick Jagger cannily sought sympathy for the devil. AC/DC offered dirty deeds, done dirt cheap. The Sex Pistols wanted anarchy (at least in the UK). Axl Rose of Guns N' Roses sneered he'd watch us bleed. With the advent of hip-hop, an entire musical genre seemed to celebrate a thug lifestyle freighted with ropes of jewelry, gyrating females, and large-caliber weapons. Having thus sown decades of disregard for even a modicum of decency, Big Music now reaps the whirlwind: massive, free, digital music downloads. With little (if any) moral authority to fall back upon, they now must witness the pillage of their assets by a generation of digitally sophisticated music lovers (the above-referenced "pirates") that has learned not to pay for its listening pleasure.

There is no reliable estimate as to how many individuals have illegally downloaded music, but certainly it is a number well into the millions and very probably in the tens of millions. According to *The Independent*, in 2010 alone there were over a billion songs downloaded, with over seven million individuals downloading. And anecdotal evidence suggests many of these have amassed libraries of music that would have rivaled, in an earlier era, that of a good-sized radio station.

DOWN THE RABBIT HOLE WITH DOWNLOADING

While it may be tempting to frame digital downloading as a David vs. Goliath equation (with the music industry playing the heavy), it is important to note a certain churlishness on the part of some downloaders. Generally, "young folks" today seem relatively untroubled by illegal downloading, and most of that may be because it just seems normal to them. One study by the American Assembly at Columbia University found that more than 70 percent of people between eighteen and twenty-nine had downloaded music for free.[9] Microsoft Research found that young Internet users "became angry when peers used their works without permission, but didn't see a problem in lifting images from shows or movies for use in their own work."[10] This may reflect a remarkable tendency toward lack of introspection, and the manner in which digital oversharing has blurred the difference between *thine* and *mine* may be a contributing factor.

But those who actually facilitate nonpaid downloading arguably ought to know better. Witness Hana Beshara, formerly of NinjaVideo,[11] who went to jail for her part in founding and maintaining a site that encouraged illegal uploads and downloads of video content. In a statement she made to the *New York Times*, Ms. Beshara seemed to believe that because "the [movie] business is so big . . . skimming a little doesn't hurt anybody." According to the same article, Ms. Beshara made more than $200,000 via the NinjaVideo venture (which she is now paying back to the Motion Picture Association of America). The irrationality of her argument can be demonstrated by comparing it to the sale of a small amount of hot dogs, having offloaded them from a huge truckload of hot dogs, arguing that the lifted hot dogs really wouldn't be missed. On the face of it, this would probably be the case. Yet in every state in the nation, that hot dog heist would still be a crime.

And here we approach the rabbit hole of the argument, where the notion of digital breaks down traditional boundaries between production, ownership, physicality, virtuality, and the legitimacy of expectations. For in fact, the counterargument to the hot-dog-theft example is that even as hot dogs (movies) were sold without authorization, no "hot dogs" were ever "missing from the truck." These putative hot dogs were not simply "not missed" but actually "not missing."

Downloaded music, legal or not, never decreases inventory. Downloading never deprives a shopkeeper of physical property he has paid for and which, if stolen from his premises, might well result in punishment for theft. Moreover, the mechanics of illegal downloading almost invariably involve the notion of "sharing," in which (at some theoretical point in time and space), a legitimate "owner" of the music *uploads* it to a location where others can then download it. Almost certainly it cannot be illegal to upload music, and, again, the upload does not *decrease* inventory anywhere but in fact only *increases* it somewhere.

Here is where claims against illegal downloading get mired in a swampy lowland. After all, if half of the sharing is okay, then why not the other half? We like to think that copyright laws are unambiguous about this, and the music industry is hard at work to suggest they are—but they are not. We know that there are laws set clearly against using copyrighted material without permission—such as in performing for an audience or distributing physical copies. But here we are really not talking about *using* (certainly not for money) but about *hearing*, which the copyright owner will want to call "listening," the hearing having been predicated upon a deliberate act (such as hitting the "play" button on an MP3 player). Yet when has listening to something ever been held illegal in and of itself?

Let me propose to turn this argument on its head and see if anything falls out of its pockets. Even if you grant the copyright owner a form of proprietorship that includes some control over the manner in which the owned item is experienced, you still fail to satisfy a basic objection that the item in dispute is ephemeral, cannot be subject to any outright claim of depredation (because it is spurious to state *a priori* that the downloader might arguably have purchased the item in another context), and does not actually deprive anyone of anything except an ephemeral expectation of market success in lieu of prevailing circumstance.

So are we talking about illegal listening? If I hear a song that I know was illegally downloaded, am I then party to a criminal act even if I have not downloaded the item myself? Some legal scholars might argue that this act is some distant cousin of "possession of stolen property." And if we are going to try to claim damages from people who willfully listen to something they did not pay for, how far are we then from listeners making claims that they had been deprived of their right to peaceful enjoyment of their own home and property by, say, a passing car with very loud music unpleasant to the listeners? Does the law then contemplate liability on behalf of the musician, having been a proxy participant in a disturbance of the peace? And what if that music continued to play during the commission of a robbery—a soundtrack, as it were, to a heinous act? Does the right of free speech trump the right of free hearing? If an illegally downloaded song played in the woods and nobody was there to hear it, did it actually play at all?

No small number of musicians today not only accept downloading but also are genuinely okay with it[12] as a way of getting people to hear their music—much as radio might have done in earlier days.

Digital brings us to places "curiouser and curiouser," as Lewis Carroll once said of the adventures of Alice in Wonderland.

UPBEAT

In response to the destruction of Big Music due to digitization and non-payment for music on a global scale, a new paradigm of music has emerged. Energized by a love of music itself and the power of digital technology, countless indie labels have sprung up. Forced to sing for their supper, musicians are playing everywhere, and live performance has perhaps never been more accessible. Crowds of music enthusiasts pack clubs like the Bluebird in Denver (the Lumineers) or the Bowery Ballroom in New York (the White Stripes)—not far, by the way, from the site of the old CBGBs. And yes, the Troubadour in Hollywood, dating from 1957, continues to help launch careers. In the unlikely town of Hudson, New York, Club Helsinki is a noted outpost for satisfying musical acts: in 2014, its set list included Shawn Colvin, Black Francis of the Pixies, and Chuck Prophet and the Mission Express.

STADIUMS FULL OF EMPTY

This new music world is much more congenial than that which may have been characterized by the besotted roar of a great stadium concert. Before the onslaught of digital, these dehumanizing shows had reigned supreme. Like many of my generation, I have some rather hazy but nonetheless searing memories of bad stadium concerts. At a rundown minor-league stadium lost in the swamps of Jersey, it rained hard, the guards stole all our bottles and broke them, and the Dead never showed. At another, I saw a security guard throw my friend against a wall for "not sitting down." After a Stones concert, a drenching rain fell, and in the middle of the night no transportation back to the city was to be had, and I was soaked and unhappy and ended up in an awfully expensive taxi that never quite got me home.

But digital downloads have atomized the industry, and the stadium show is, perhaps to our collective benefit, going the way of the passenger pigeon. It's true that some acts can still draw big numbers and fill the ballparks—the Stones, of course, and Springsteen, and certain newer acts like Jason Aldean (as well as established acts like George Strait)—but in 1994 there were more than two hundred stadium shows and in 2004 there were forty-six. Perhaps indicative of the state of Big Music today, 2014 was considered a banner year, with less than half the total stadium concerts of 1994. [13]

MICRO-FANS

The power of digital music dissemination has led to a vast increase in musical choice. No longer subject to the melodies forced upon them by Big Music, fans today congregate in micro-fan bases, avidly seeking the latest from bands that you've never heard of—thousands of them. And many of these bands, by releasing songs themselves or through tiny labels, have happily found an audience through digital technology. Where once they might have been stymied by the arduous and often futile process of sending a demo tape to an A&R guy in Hollywood who would as likely stub out his cigar on it as listen to it, these musicians—many of them quite dedicated and quite good—have seen their communication with an audience become much more frictionless and successful.

At labels like Captured Tracks in Greenpoint, Brooklyn, hopeful interns regularly ship out boxes of vinyl records, CDs, and download keys for bands like Beach Fossils, Dinner, and Naomi Punk. Captured Tracks even has its own retail store, and just as in the stories of old-time rock-and-roll, often enough the bands show up and hang out with the staff. An inside source tells us it's a great place to work, enjoy good music, and hang out with musicians.

So there is music. And there are musicians and those that seek out their sounds. But today there is much, much less cash extraction. Hence, I feel comfortable saying the music industry we knew has been destroyed by digital—destroyed, replaced by a simulacrum that calls itself the music industry.

3

THE BEZOS BAUBLE: DIGITAL IS DESTROYING THE NEWSPAPER INDUSTRY

Another timely example of the power of digital destructiveness regards an industry I shall refer to as "newsprint." In May 2013 the *Washington Post* reported massive losses at its print division. Until it was bought by Amazon founder and billionaire Jeff Bezos, a casual observer might have been forgiven for speculating that its future was in doubt. Its future *remains* in doubt, since it exists only at the will of its new owner, who seems to have purchased it as a sort of desk ornament.

That said, Mr. Bezos does demonstrate commitment to the success of the brand, trivial as it may be in comparison to his larger goals at Amazon. According to an article in the *New York Times* in October 2014, the *Post* has added one hundred people to its newsroom after years of layoffs and has created a "national tabloid edition" offered as a supplement to newspapers in the United States.[1] While this attests to perhaps brighter prospects for the *Post*, the implication of the "*Post* supplement" for all the other newspapers is less clear. What does it say about the *Dallas Morning News* that they are selling an insert from a competitor? Does this suggest a brighter future for the *Sacramento Bee*, the *Cleveland Plain-Dealer*, the *Albany Times-Union*? I believe it does not. If anything, the notion that other papers would be forced to use *Post* content to lure readers underscores a persistent weakness in local newsgathering and reporting.

In the same edition of the *Times*, another article points out that another entrepreneur who bought another paper (Aaron Kushman, the *Orange*

County Register) is encountering strong headwinds and recently was forced to close a five-month-old newspaper he had begun to publish in Los Angeles. The above-mentioned headwinds consist, in the main, of lawsuits brought against Mr. Kushman regarding unpaid bills. The article says that "despite Mr. Kushman's love of newspapers, he has struggled to keep up with the bills of running them."[2]

The Great Grey *Times*, the print edition of which went full color in 1997 (it was the last big city paper to do so), is now distinctly a shade of blue—and we find it hard to tell if it's because of sadness, asphyxiation, or some of both. Recently the *Times* has sold off nearly all of its assets not related to newsgathering and has refocused on the *New York Times* product itself. They offer limited free views of their information and strongly encourage payment. According to *International Business Times*, the *New York Times* today has about eight hundred thousand paying subscribers to its digital version, a not insubstantial number.[3] But ad revenues continue to sink, and one can only assume they have needed to make up the difference by directly selling things like very fancy, high-minded hejiras to Tuscany and the Galapagos[4] and "unique" collectors' items like antique radios.[5]

They have also recently launched *NYTimes International*, which presumably replaces the old *International Herald Tribune* that ex-pats assiduously sought, and which also puts them on a footing to compete with the BBC as a powerhouse across the globe. While the *Times* certainly has a robust digital subscriber base, the *Wall Street Journal*, perhaps predictably, resides profitably behind a paywall that has been in place for a much longer time than that of the *Times*, because their readers—primarily businesspeople—tend to make money by knowing things and, we may safely assume, are quite willing to pay for the information.[6]

Print news media in general seems recently to have been relegated to an anteroom that leads directly to the dustbin. Witness Time Warner spinning off its print empire[7] in anticipation of a potential merger with Comcast, the connectivity giant. Once-proud names like *Time, People, Sports Illustrated, Fortune,* and *Money* were (metaphorically, of course) put into a lifeboat by the corporate ship, given a few cans of sardines, and set adrift (there had been talk of a merger with rival publisher Meredith, but those plans were scrapped).[8] It's anyone's guess whether those publications will ever recover their readership and, more importantly, their advertisers, though I would place heavy odds they will not. Illustrative of a resounding fall from a media pinnacle, magazines—including many that once bestrode the land like Titans—with their week-old (or month-old) data and broad (unfocused) appeal, have lost so much advertising they've become more like pamphlets; more like ephemera than the authoritative tomes overspilling with cultural dictum they once represented.

Newsweek ceased publication in 2012 and now is digital-only. *Time*, now disassociated from the conglomerate that carries its name, seems as if it cannot be far behind (it now concentrates on "special issues," more like perfect-bound books of memorabilia). *U.S. News and World Report* is now known not for news at all, but for an influential college survey. And it is a striking phenomenon indeed that a visit to the newsstand today reveals the faces of female models on the cover of almost every publication, no matter how tenuous the connection to any actual content inside the covers. They all seem like the same magazine! Even a cursory study of older magazine covers shows this not to have been the case in years past. Arguably there is an air of desperation about the newsprint industry overall, and sometimes it seems the choices made in panic only worsen any chance at survival.

Meanwhile, the small-circulation *Anytown Advertiser* (my stand-in name for that legion of small-town newspapers covering hyper-local news) is now not much more than a charity case—in all likelihood worth less as an enterprise than the pulp upon which it is printed.[9] Many have become mere wrappings for ever-thickening shopping guides and coupon books. The *Register-Star* of Hudson, New York, prints a weekend edition that appears to be thick with news, but upon inspection, the bulk is almost entirely of circulars, coupons, and the funnies.

In his article "Death of a Small Town Newspaper," journalist Christopher Marcisz says that one of the local papers in his Berkshire-region community had become "almost comically anemic," "not viable," and that "if I was a local newspaper mogul, putting [it] to sleep would have been the first thing I did."[10] According to an article in the *Washington Post* in 2014, the *Manassas News & Register* ceased publication after 143 years when its owner (BH Holdings/Berkshire Hathaway) said it was "no longer viable in a digital world."[11] The same article states that investment in news sites has focused much more on national or "borderless" news sites like *Huffington Post* and *Politico*; furthermore, while these ventures and others like them account for more than 60 percent of new journalism hires, they do not come close to making up for the jobs lost at local newspapers.

GOOGLE VS. ALL PRINT MEDIA

In December 2012, *The Atlantic* (digital) published an article that cited a study by the Economist Group about the decline of print journalism. It said that, since 2006, print had lost $20 billion in ad revenue and that digital ad revenue had erased no more than 2 percent of the loss.[12] The article went on to say that most of the missing money went to Google: in other words, instead of advertising in a newspaper, brands bought keywords so they would come up near the top in a Google search, or they outright paid for space at the top of the list. According to the same study, today Google takes in more ad dollars than all of US print media does, and currently it has 41 percent of total online ad spending!

Many are now questioning whether Google advertising continues to be a smart play for advertisers, as Googlers have become skeptical of the results—partly because of too much "targeting" (a related topic we will discuss later in this book).

Guessing the Customer

Not very long ago the great newsprint enterprises did wield spectacular influence. Their columnists decided what might succeed and what would be ignored. Advertisers, hardly knowing whom they reached with their copy (except that they knew there were lots of them), would forklift crates of cash each day to the press to pay for precious print inches. They lived in mortal fear of invisibility—and irrelevance.

There was a certain abstruse science in use back then, and many knew it as "market research." Print media owners pretended to "know their audience" and spent more time convincing advertisers of same than on actually trying to know anything (except on the most rudimentary level) about the folks who got inky fingers from reading newsprint. But they could not be blamed entirely for owning but a foggy notion of their customers. There were very few ways to know what people really did once they bought the paper (or the "book," as magazine publishers fondly called their publications).

Print media owners pretended to "know their audience" . . . but they could not be blamed entirely for owning but a foggy notion of their customers. And then came digital.

And then came digital. And with digital came trackability. Web analytics. Click-throughs. Usability tests. The customer journey. Conversion events. And so on.

We have not the space here to detail the frenzied years of dotcom hype—to tell of the naïve efforts of the savvy media giants as they uploaded their precious content to the web for free. They did it because this was a new publishing paradigm, and they were not about to be left out. Who gave a fig if no one had figured out how to charge money for it? It was a brave new world, it was like going to the moon, it was exciting, it was all for tomorrow's profit. And then the bills started falling due. And already they had trained a generation of customers to believe they weren't going to pay for anything inside a browser. Apparently, in the digital domain, it was the customer's attention that was valuable. And the publisher would gladly resell those "eyeballs" to the advertiser just as they had always done.

There were at least two awful problems with this plan. The first was that with digital trackability came the realization that eyeballs probably were not eyeballing the dreadful banner ads, and users certainly were not clicking on them (an article in *Smart Insights* from 2013 indicates that banner ads get about 1 click per 1,000 impressions and calls it—deservedly—"shocking!").[13] The second was that the myth suggested by the phrase "the cover price doesn't pay for much" really was mythical. If we can draw any conclusion at all from the decline of the newsprint industry as it is affected by a steep decline in "newsstand" sales, it is that publishers[14] really needed you to buy that sheaf of paper at the newsstand. They needed you to allow them to drop their stapled masterwork in your mailbox month after month. They needed the cash. And they needed those circulation numbers such that they might then shill to the brands that you had indeed seen in the ad, even when you most likely had not.

Worse, the advent of ad networks meant that even high-minded online publications might be peppered with tacky ads featuring dancing monkeys and lots of "weird tricks" (a phrase that must have tested quite phenomenally well in someone's SEO effort) that seem to come from everywhere and anywhere and generally seem to have no relation to the ethos of the publication itself. Recently launched is Ghostery, a service for users and enterprises that (a) tells users who exactly is watching them while they browse and (b) tells the publisher how many ad networks are hooked up, who they work for, what they show, and how they share information. Perhaps it will be a way for publishers to better understand what their users are seeing in their advertising slots. My guess is that this knowledge won't change a thing, given that online publishers today are in no position to start blockading "incorrect" ads lest they lose even more money than at present.

Some say there is hope for print in that there may be an uptick in the reading of "long-form" articles especially on mobile,[15] and I can attest to a sense of focus and attention when reading on a small device that is, to me, entirely counterintuitive. One summer I read *Moby-Dick* on—yes— a Palm Pilot and found it quite absorbing. But the long-term impact of long-form reading on small devices does little to save the inkier enclaves of the industry.

Digital stripped newsprint of many conceits enjoyed by that industry over decades of dominance, not least of which were the conceits that newsprint saw itself as somehow essential, that advertisers could not get along without it, and that digital was an unworthy competitor. It may be difficult to tag the multitude of ways that digital destroyed print, but in light of its overwhelming success in this media battle, we ought to try.

Ads Move to Pixels

Advertisers jumped to digital because they could get a better understanding of their customers via digital tracking. This took their ad dollars away from print and at first this seemed okay as long as CPMs (cost per mille— the price per thousand views) for digital remained high. But then came ad networks and the truth that had long been known about direct advertising: the very, very low response rate. The web was determined, perhaps sagely, to be a form of direct marketing, and the rates for digital advertising started to drop. And they kept dropping. They are now at historic lows. Media venues are begging for ads. Digital ad wizards have gotten much more adventurous in the type of ads they serve: images float across the content, banners roll down and then back up like window shades, while if you hover your mouse in the "right" (wrong) spot, you induce a sudden video stream and more.

Despite the pixelated gimcrackery, advertisers today pay comparatively very little to be visible on digital domains. The dilemma is even more confounding where apps are concerned, because very few can claim to have gotten a handle yet on what "in-app advertising" really means, or what benefit it provides. Overall, the near-catastrophic drop in CPMs may be a reflection of the actual value of advertising, rather than the value pumped historically by newsprinters and ad agencies.

THE SUNDAY PAPER?

At a certain point—a few years back now—folks just stopped buying the paper. This is good for trees but bad for newsprint publishers and certainly bad for newsprint manufacturers, or "mills," as they are commonly called. After decades of rising prices, newsprint itself (the actual roll of paper) is getting cheaper due to low demand.[16]

Recently I moved to a home rather distant from my long-time New York City neighborhood, and I decided to reward myself with regular purchases of the hometown paper, that being the *Times*. Since getting an iPad I had not regularly read the *paper* paper and had noted its shrinkage in size and rise in price as proof of my good instincts toward the flatscreen rather than wood pulp. But when I went back to reading the now-diminutive *Times*, I experienced a newsprint epiphany: it was so much better than the flatscreen version! It unfolded like a gift; it was crinkly and smelled kind of fresh in an inky sort of way. The articles seemed somehow more literate, though I am certain this was pure illusion. Most important, I read the articles often enough for mere adjacency rather than their relevance to the advertising beacons that (usually ineptly) guessed at my "persona." Serendipity crept in where only ad planning and content targeting had been before. I found myself reading about the same awful massacres, of course, but then about a book I'd never have heard of because the review was on the page where the bad-news article ended. And then I would follow that to the next page and find an article about goat cheese, a subject I absolutely would have passed by on my digitally blinkered way to what "interested me."

I spent much, much longer reading the paper than I had done online.

Can't Share Woodpulp

And then I noticed something peculiar and kind of unsettling about the newspaper. I noticed I could not tweet from it. Tweeting articles had become so reflexive that I felt it was almost a diminished experience to read a great article and *not* post to my followers.

The next day I spent some time online looking for articles to tweet. I could not help it. Digital had destroyed my ability to enjoy a newspaper without the ability instantly to blurt my admiration for a story that might appeal to my absurdly tiny but somehow still worthwhile public.

So people don't buy the newspaper—maybe because we have grown accustomed to instant sharing online. We can, if we feel nostalgic about both media consumption and outmoded dietary regimes, still buy the weighty Sunday edition and drink coffee and eat bagels with cream cheese. But we used to do it every week. Now we do it almost never. And the newsprinters, because we're not buying the paper, are falling by the wayside like starvelings on a long march to nowhere.

All the News That's Fit to Blog

We're still getting the news, and it may be from the tree-killing method of information dissemination or, more likely, the free online version of our favorite newspaper.

Or it may be from somewhere else online.

Which brings us to a third way that digital has destroyed newsprint.

Digital has destroyed the *legitimacy* of newsprint. Today it takes a feat of the imagination to conjure the busy newsroom of yore, where reporters chased down stories and checked facts, and where reporters and their editors took professional pride in providing important information to an eager public. They were not all paragons of honesty, to be sure, but most of them cared about what they wrote and whether it was true. And they knew how to write and how to write a news story. Apart from that, you wouldn't know anything about them. You didn't know their sports teams; you didn't know if they had kids or if they were married or if they liked barbecue. You just had the news, and for the most part you had it well written and carefully researched.

Not so much anymore.

Yes, we can still read that kind of reporting. But often enough, we don't bother. We go to Reddit or Imgur or 4chan (recently where nude pictures of celebrities were on offer until complaints from the violated celebrities forced them to take them down), or we hear it on Twitter or Facebook or on any one of what seem like a trillion blogs where no holds are barred and where stick aliens march next to climate-change deniers. And all of them carry exactly the same weight, which is practically nothing. Except it all gets tossed into the ether like an information salad and rains down a big mess where you can't tell fact from fancy. Where every story seems based on another story, which is based on a rumor that no one checked, but which supposedly was based on something somebody overheard in a diner not far from Area 51.

But here again we find ourselves wondering if this could have happened to such a powerful industry had not that industry somehow laid the rails for its own ride out of town.

When newsprint was big, it was awe-inspiring. It was arrogant. It was cut-throat. And much of its influence was baleful. For every muck-raking, truth-telling idealist in the news business, there were as many playing on the pipe of racial prejudice, or scandal-mongering, or beating the drums of war, or scapegoating, or pandering to power. After all, they had to sell copies of their rag in a tough business, and often enough in a tough town. It isn't hard to see how this evolved. But it's also easy to see how it became tiresome and then became suspect and then became useless and even contemptible. And when the locals discovered they could open a magic window into any news source anywhere, anytime, for no money, and get a not-dissimilar level of discourse (give or take a fact or two), then the game was over for newsprint.

Decline seems to beget decline. Newspapers have responded to falling revenues by cutting resources, including their ability to report the news, and the results have been fairly consistent with what one might have expected. A recent study from the Pew Research Center's Project for Excellence in Journalism suggested that as many as 31 percent of readers had abandoned a news source because they had noticed a difference in the quantity and quality of the news being reported by that news source.[17]

Digital took away the ad dollars; newspapers took away the news. No more of the Walter Winchells, or the William Restons, for that matter.

Digital Democracy

After a few years of this, it got to where anyone with a login to Blogspot became a "citizen" journalist (as if, formerly, professional journalists were a privileged class of information wizards). And every citizen journalist had a right to have her say even if nobody but a few wiseacre pals and *au courant* netizens would ever be aware of the effort. By this method we saw the birth of stars in the news firmament. Buzzfeed and Wonkette and Alternet and Gawker all had their start as self-publishers. Even the *Huffington Post* was a startup at one time—though now it is owned by a company few even remember from the very earliest dotcom days: AOL. Talent and luck have always needed each other, and they needed each other in what once was called "the blogosphere" as well. But they found each other, and we now have a great many news sources that would never have found an audience had digital not democratized journalism.

There Are *a Lot* of Blogs . . .

The total number of blogs is unknown, but Wordpress, a popular, open-source content management tool, recently said it had been used by 42 million blogs, with half a million new posts per day. This is an enormous amount of information sharing, and that's from just one source that happened to know its own domain. As you read, this number has probably already been superseded by a new and even more shocking number—such is the rapid evolution of digital.

According to a recent study by BlogHer, "the largest community and network of women influencers on the web," 81 percent of US consumers trust information from blogs[18] and 37 percent watch online videos about someone's experience with a product they are considering purchasing.[19] And, as reported by inbound marketing automation company Hubspot, 57 percent of companies with a blog acquired a customer through their blog.

This is not to say there are spectacular dollars being generated by citizen journalists. For most, it's a labor of love and therefore insidious to the professional newsprinter. Blogging.org created an infographic that indicates upward of 80 percent of bloggers never earn more than a $100 from blogging.[20]

No one can say for sure if the audience for news has expanded to match the explosion of new sources. But it's probably a safe bet that it has not. It's more likely that nearly every reader who spent an hour horsing around on blogs or poking at YouTube was not spending that hour reading a newspaper, or even reading digital newspapers on the Internet. There really are only a finite number of audience members, and they stopped reading the news in the newspaper because of digital media, and they're never coming back. And neither are the advertisers.

Newsprint is over. The recorded declines are staggering, and the decline is only getting steeper. The mighty *Washington Post* has become a toy. Newsprint publication, I believe, is now only a bad habit that needs to be broken by any media company hoping to survive the coming decade.

NOW IT GETS EXCITING

News itself is on a wild ride, and nobody knows where it's heading. There are a hundred million fingers on the keyboards now, telling us in real time about the shooting or the bombing or the wikileak or the guy who did that crazy thing you never would have expected in a tight-knit community.

And it isn't just blogs, of course. It's Twitter and Facebook and Snapchat and Whatsapp and Higgledy-Piggledy and beyond. In the summer of 2014 we saw Twitter and digital video foundational to a national outcry against police militarization in the town of Ferguson, Missouri, during a period of severe conflict over the police shooting death of an unarmed young man. Also in 2014 a certain tribe of Islamist destroyers (commonly known as ISIS) posted videos to YouTube of their beheadings of two American journalists caught in their black-hooded web of terror.

The democratization of news brought on by digital has created a virtual space not unlike a global hangout where everybody tells everybody everything about everything—a mashup of public and private, melody and dirge, as rich and varied as fresh tomatoes pulled wet and tasty right from the plant. Sometimes there's a worm. And sometimes it's not ripe. But lots of it is fresh and fulfilling.

There is no way for any organization of professionals to match the excitement this provides, because this is the real thing. Unfiltered, unexpected, shocking, schlocky, doubtful, weird, passionate, truthful, deceitful—in short, everything. It's a closer approximation of life than "news" ever dared to be or ever could be. The millions of Twitter feeds, YouTube videos, and blogs today are, collectively, a much more direct and unfiltered news product than we've ever had before, and, if we can stand it, this will only keep getting more so with time.

Digital has destroyed newsprint. And replaced it with a hundred million versions of the truth.

4

THE BUSINESS CASE, OR, WHEN DIGITAL DESTROYS DIGITAL

These days, it seems like everybody is measuring everything. The urge to measure everything digital with digital is creating an atmosphere in which, too often, data fails to deliver insights to humans, and in which humans lose faith in data either because they have been insufficiently trained to understand it or because the data really offers far less insight than might have been hoped.

In this context, digital destroys itself.

Our journey through a digitally altered business, cultural, and societal landscape now turns to a place where digital self-replicates—specifically, where digital measures the impact of digital marketing efforts in business and the broad implications of same.

With data piling up at truly viral speed, the heights of these data hills have attracted the intrepid. Who doesn't dream of conquering an Annapurna? And so it is with digital analytics. The very fact there is so much data suggests it must be utilized.

Some of us may not be convinced. There is an argument that the massive amount of data being collected today (Judah Phillips, in his book *Building a Data-Driven Organization*, says there are more bytes than grains of sand on Earth[1]) is really just an artifact of the digital process with limited actual value. And that the obsession with data is a fad that will fade once we see how little living benefit we achieve through its analysis.

VICTORY OF THE QUANTS

On the other hand, we have data master Nate Silver and his kind. Many may recall Mr. Silver from his days at 538.com and how he appeared on the news quite often during the 2008 and 2012 elections with what were regarded as authoritative data analysis of possible outcomes. In both cases, he was right where many other pollsters, using less precise methods, turned out to be either outright wrong or off by several more percentage points than Silver. His work earned him a spot at the *New York Times* for a while, and then he went to work with sporting statistics at ESPN.

With Mr. Silver in mind, let us review what may have been a defining moment in the public's understanding of the importance of data—and especially the importance of *paying attention to data*. This event might fairly be called the Great Republican Data Debacle of 2012. It featured an especially pasty-looking Karl Rove (a senior Republican strategist and frequent commentator on the Fox News network) practically squealing that the quants could not possibly have given Ohio to the other guy and could they please check again? A memorable moment ensued when the back-room analysts nodded their heads and gave Ohio and the presidency to Obama.

The Great Republican Data Debacle of 2012 . . . featured Karl Rove practically squealing that the quants could not possibly have given Ohio to the other guy.

It turned out that Nate Silver, with his poll of polls and his careful, unbiased look at state-by-state data, was right about nearly everything. And the party of Lincoln, having eschewed data in deference to the nominee, was found howling piteously that they could not comprehend how they could have turned out to be so very incorrect about the math. But had they looked at signal instead of noise, they'd have been on the right frequency and seen that Governor Romney hadn't had a chance after he'd bested Bachmann and Perry and Paul.

BIT BY THE DATA BUG

Businesses everywhere seem bitten by the big-data bug: they're running a high fever in the belief that the answers are in the numbers somewhere. The site i-cio.com in March 2014 said that "new research from Oracle and Gartner reveals growing ambition to exploit big data and cloud-based business intelligence" on the part of big business. [2]

I can certainly attest that in my professional life, due to my proximity to data and measurement regimes at the enterprise level, it is clear that a plan to be "data driven" in marketing decisions and beyond has become almost axiomatic. From pharmaceutical companies to big media companies to consumer packaged-goods companies (often referred to as CPGs, an industry term that refers to companies like Procter & Gamble and Pepsico), I have seen no small number of senior marketers in those industries work hard to determine the value of their digital efforts by measuring it and performing analysis on the data they collect about usership. One of the problems for all digital marketers, and a key point I'm making in this chapter, is that while many companies collect data, far fewer know what to do with it, and fewer still act on it in any meaningful way. Therefore, I believe it can fairly be said today that there's an almost universal hunger in business for information, even when methods to utilize it effectively may be lacking.

I won't be the first to note the gap between what digital can offer and what humans can absorb. But I would like to amplify the notion that data analysis can wield a great deal of destructive power within organizations if not properly managed. Indeed, how can it be anything but destructive to base decisions on inaccurate or poorly understood data? If you've ever had movie tickets to a show you thought started at nine when it actually started at eight, you know the frustration of having wasted money and lost an opportunity because of reliance on inaccurate data. In business it's really not so different, only much more costly in general.

CREATIVE VS. DATA: BATTLE TO THE DEATH?

Sufficient budgets for digital analytics and data analysis in general are not in place at most enterprises. Again, there is little documentation on this, but I am relaying it as an artifact of my own personal experience. Lack of budget, such as it exists, may reveal that the need for *good, reliable* data is in too many cases only vaguely apprehended by senior management that grew up on "hunches" and "people I know." Further, analytics' success at the enterprise is often thwarted by big-advertising "creatives" who build digital campaigns and then purport to accurately self-measure as a courtesy. There is little on the record about this phenomenon, but my years in the field have offered me a view perhaps afforded to not that many—and I have seen more than one case where data is derided as "piffle" by creative teams; where they do offer measurement as part of their practice, it can be counted on only to support the greater agency narrative as it relates to its customer, the brand. Based on my personal observations, I can suggest that self-measurement is not quite an oxymoron, but it does set up a natural conflict of interest. Content creators want to measure themselves the same way a ball team would love to call its own balls and strikes. Except there really wouldn't be any game to play if that's the way it were umpired.

Ask any number of in-house agency/web developer analytics specialists, and they will likely tell you they often feel like a voice crying in the wilderness. Facts discovered by agency analysts are, if industry scuttlebutt is to be believed, fungible. They fall victim to the opinion of the senior ad wizard about what worked and what did not. In the end, the enterprise that hired the agency gets little untainted information about how much of its advertising dollar was wasted.

Billions of dollars of misspent marketing and advertising revenue harm not only the enterprise but also the consumer. When the cost of delivering a product to the pantry is driven up by its advertising fee, the buyer pays for it. The extra dollar you spend at the check-out counter, often enough, is passing through the enterprise into the pocket of the advertiser who "measured results" themselves with no objective oversight, and then spent some of that money figuring out how to spin the data, no matter how unhappy, into an example of either success or successful research. The solution to this dilemma is fairly obvious for those who know but too often ignored by those perhaps not willing to look at the built-in conflict of interest engendered by self-measurement. Measurement, I believe it can be fairly suggested, should be performed by a neutral third party—an analytics specialist, if you will (preferably one whose mandate is to find the facts and who has no stake in the success or failure of any particular campaign, content, or other competing factor), for what works in any one type of competition (sports, for example) can be relied upon to work in another (digital marketing).

THE PROMISE OF TRUE MEASUREMENT—
AND ITS BETRAYAL

Digital advertising exploded partly because the public swooned for digital unlike for any new media in history. But it also promised something the old-fashioned type of advertising could not. It promised to be measurable. Verifiable. It was supposed to be the end of guesswork and the beginning of *numerically accurate* advertising science.

Advertising science is not new. We already know that audience acceptance has been measured by industry for decades, and with increasing emphasis on data over guesswork. The recent success of the *Mad Men* series brought the venerable focus group into millions of non-advertiser flatscreens. As illustrated in the series, until the advent of digital, advertising science was of a sociological variety. It was the study of people themselves and what they said, and extrapolation of data was an enormous component of its utility.

Extrapolation of data is required when volume is lacking. The prime example of extrapolation in the delivery of advertising data is the science of television audience measurement developed by the Nielsen company. For decades, its word was law in broadcast media. In television, low ratings meant almost instant cancellation. According to a 2011 article on Splitsider.com, NBC President of Research and Media Development Alan Wurtzel said, "Listen, Nielsen is a monopoly. They're the only game in town. [Their ratings] are the only currency."[3] Arguably this so-called monopoly was possible because Nielsen purportedly "knew" how many millions were tuned in (or not) to a broadcast event.

The method by which Nielsen claimed to "know" was by having installed devices on the televisions (or collected data from paper diaries) of several thousand selected homes—a vanishingly tiny percentage of the general population.[4] From this tiny sample, they deployed extrapolation techniques to "enlarge" the data onto a bigger screen. They created mathematical formulae that would take the minuscule sample and play out a thousand into a million and a million into ten million. For all anyone knows today, it may have been reasonably accurate. Or it may have been wildly incorrect. Without knowing what the many millions of non-Nielsen households were doing, it would be impossible to determine with 100 percent certainty the actual number of households watching any particular show.

I am not in the business of singling out Nielsen as a paragon of inaccuracy. They'd not have been a success for two generations without being able to demonstrate substance and plausibility. And lack of 100 percent certainty does not rule out reasonable accuracy and even the sufficient business utility of the extrapolated numbers.

But I am pointing out that digital made substantial claims to be the anti-Nielsen. It was supposed to do away with the need for data modeling and extrapolation. It was supposed to tell you how "users" were *in fact* interacting with digital media with much, much greater accuracy. This new level of accuracy was to be accomplished by measuring actual behavior in unsampled data packets that would result in verifiable "true" counts. If, as Rand Schulman has said, "Creative without conversion equals zero,"[5] then digital analytics was supposed to provide unadulterated evidence of how creative drove "conversions."

A note on some of the inside-the-beltway terms used above: in a field as esoteric as digital marketing analysis, it's tough to avoid nomenclature that sounds alien to the uninitiated. I have tried to avoid it, but the notion of "conversion," which was popularized by Bryan Eisenberg and Jim Novo more than fifteen years ago, represents the core activity of digital marketing. The definition of conversion roughly can be described as "turning a website visitor into a purchaser," though it can get more complex than that. So when I cite the combination of two instances of jargon, as in "creative without conversion equals zero," it tends to be fairly electrifying stuff for folks who know the code. It means, "You can create beautiful commercials in cyberspace, but if your commercials don't get anybody to buy anything, then at best you've gained nothing, and probably wasted your money."

This concept of non-conversion lies at the heart of any critique of digital analytics. And as we move toward a multi-channel measurement model, it is perhaps an even more potent indictment of the amped-up promises of digital analytics in general.

Why is digital analytics failing its promise? And how does that contribute to its own destruction—and ultimately to an unhelpful distrust of the verity of an entire class of non-financial business data?

Actual Data: Who Really Wants It?

Facts are hard things, and often they're not very popular. Humans are intervening between the facts gathered about actual behavior and its accurate reporting in so many ways that digital analytics itself threatens to become a game of corporate three-card monte. Whoever controls the marketing conversation controls the data. For many large enterprises, the marketing conversation is, if not controlled by, then certainly channeled by the (typically) large agency tasked with finding customers for the product.

The conversation only rarely moves to a study of raw numbers in digital analytics reports. It would be easy to verify the success or failure of an expensive digital campaign by looking at how the intended audience interacted with it. Did they click a lot in the right places and see the things you wanted them to see? Did they buy something? Or did they bounce off to an unknown URL because your campaign—which could include your website itself—failed to engage their interest long enough to make any business difference?

That conversation would be easy to have. But it would be a short one. Those marketers that control conversations tend to prefer long ones, where lots of variables make for near-impossible interpretation. These are the qualified kinds of conversations a certain type of agency tends to have with their customers. Facts have no necessary relevance.

But let's not gaze too long upon Madison Avenue. It would be unfair to say that agencies *never* share the facts with their customers, just as it would be unfair to say transparency is common. There are others also damming the flow of information from data collection to its proper use.

If I Don't Understand It, Then It Must Be Useless

Healthy deployment of analytics is halted by internal functionaries who know too little and talk too much about how hard it is to get digital programs working properly—never able to admit it's because they themselves may not have the right skills to meet the demand for better insight through data.

Often with only a modicum of technical understanding and a stingy awareness of the statistical sciences, the roadblocking staffer will pounce on small inconsistencies to distract from broader understanding of trends.

Not appreciating the significance of data collection and attempting to trivialize it as an accounting system, they urge further refinement before anyone might attempt an insight. Often they expect not to have any insights themselves, since they don't quite understand what they are looking at. And if they cannot obtain insights, they must make sure no one else does, either.

They may get discovered as data blockers at some point, but they are legion, and they go about their work quietly and consistently. Their job is to keep analytics from working—mainly because they do not know what to make of it and are too hidebound to learn.

Vendor Misdeeds

An especially counterintuitive indication is that the proper use of data is disrupted by digital analytics application vendors themselves. Too many of them pretend they have a product that solves every problem all on its own, while *ignoring the expertise* needed to make their tools perform useful work. They distract their customer from the facts about expertise and process requirements. Too often they try to make the case that their data-parsing product is all that stands between the prospect and insight. Unfortunately, their products tend to be of sufficient complexity as to require a great deal of technical expertise in order to properly implement them in the robust types of digital environments in which they must function. Once the technology is properly implemented and results begin to arrive, these applications require an additional dose of business/analytical expertise in order to make any use whatsoever of the reporting.

Simply put, the application vendor needs to move boxes (or, in a SaaS [Software as a Service] environment, new accounts). Any conversation that slows down the sale—pesky details like "Hey, you need to know how to drive if you want this car not to smash into a tree"—is anathema to too many product vendors. By taking this attitude, they do a disservice to their customers and ultimately shorten the odds against their own long-term success. They impair their own product's lifetime by creating a league of underwhelmed, unhappy customers who don't know how to get value out of the application they just bought. Those customers don't re-up for the next round of SaaS, and they go around badmouthing the product. But the salesperson, perhaps, has already got the commission. And, often enough, that makes up the fate of digital analytics at the enterprise level.

Struggling to Cope with a Data Onslaught

The promise is clear. If we could all be Nate Silver for a day—if we can all hope to solve the unsolvable with the data our companies collect from a variety of channels—we would gladly give up a month's worth of kale chips to feel the warmth of that glow. Our enterprise would finally understand the behavior of users on its various digital channels. Used properly, analytics, coupled with an action plan to fix impediments, would deliver results to the bottom line. More customers. More conversions. More sales. More dollars. All because you knew what people wanted by watching their behavior as they interacted with your properties.

As businesses become increasingly dependent on data they cannot understand, the misuse of digital analytics has the potential to be enormously destructive, for there are few creatures more dangerous than those convinced by "facts" that are, in fact, fancy. Computer-aided error, or the digital product of misconfiguration multiplied by misunderstanding, can lead to catastrophic miscalculation. Just as costly is the undermining of faith in the accuracy of data, so that accuracy becomes the cry of the boy beset by wolves. Repeated failures in data accuracy, coupled with misuse or misunderstanding of accurate data, leads to data apathy and data mistrust. And in an era where "gut" is in relatively short supply, the lack of data to support one's postulation will make for sleepless nights, especially when accuracy is ignored and the danger is real.

THE DISENCHANTMENT

Digital analytics today is burdened by disillusionment and disappointment. Let a hundred vendors shout from the battlements that they have successfully overcome the gap between raw data and useful information. Let them next point to their success stories. At once the air grows silent, and you can hear the crickets. Not that there are no success stories with digital analytics. There certainly are. But they are comparatively rare.

Digital analytics today is burdened by disillusionment and disappointment.

Much more common are legions of valiant but frustrated marketers continuing to struggle with the basics, who are likely to be troubled by the following doubts:

Is data collection accurate? Once we learn what the data tells us about our business, are we in a position to do something about it? What happens when our agency tells us they've taken care of measurement and, behold, the campaigns are "all good" (or at least not a total waste)? What does change really look like, and can we make it happen in time to matter? How do we do that without automation? And where are the successful predictive models that drive automated responses?

The unanswered questions don't stop there, but for the sake of brevity we shall.

Having spent a working lifetime helping companies grapple with and overcome these challenges, I can say that the struggle is mighty and the solutions are difficult to master, even for the most eager organizations. Many businesses do get to a place where they are comfortable measuring with accuracy and understanding. Many fewer end up being able to fix any but the most egregious "disconnects" between themselves and their customers. The vast majority settle for knowing what happened, with a moderately strong determination to do something about it "in the next release."

In this context, data, at least for folks who rely on it to improve their business, can seem a singular failure. Think of the dollars and the effort and the expertise spent, and then think of the tangible benefits won, having gone through the exercise. Too often, the balance does not leave analytics on the upside of the see-saw.

How Digital Can Deliver for Marketers

Many of the most dire threats to success in digital marketing can be overcome by adhering to a process. The process is not very mysterious and, in fact, can, with some adaptation, be applied to almost any endeavor requiring rigor and results.

For digital analytics, the process, which I call eBusiness 5 Step Optimization (or e5o), looks something like this:

1. Determine Key Performance Indicators

2. Implement Data Collection and Reporting
3. Review and Analyze Reports
4. Make Content Changes
5. Measure Again to Prove Success

Following these steps will go a long way to avoiding disappointment and marketing paralysis, but often it proves devilishly hard to get through the process.

Making the Worst of a Bad Situation

Today we are at the foothills of a Himalayan range of data that changes our weather and keeps us isolated in valleys because we haven't the tools and we certainly haven't enough of the expertise needed to make sense of any of it. So digital presents a tantalizing prospect. It promises both clarity and velocity. But too often it delivers a muddy cup that goes down sluggish without much savor. When too many drink too many muddy cups from the same old coffee house, they usually stop going to that coffee house.

Digital is making its own worst case in the arena of analytics. Technology vendors (some but not all) make ever-grander promises while their SaaS products are barely delivering the basics of what they claim. They try to fill the gaps without enough expertise. And customers end up with a big bill and a small result. Eventually, the practitioner begins to think the stuff is just not for them.

Not Too Late . . . Maybe

I believe in the data-driven business model. But I am also concerned that it might not pan out. We are confronting the very real possibility that human mendacity and human error might defeat the clear purpose of the exercise. And if that happens, then digital will be a long time sleeping in the barn before being invited back in for a hot meal.

In its place we'll have "gut" and "brand voodoo" and "the people I went to school with." And maybe we'll be more comfortable with that. But we're here to talk about digital, and in a scenario where we go back to what "feels right," digital is just a lap dog. If that happens, it will be at least partly because a battalion of smart businesspeople will have given digital a chance to prove itself in the rough-and-tumble, and digital will have wandered off to sit in the weeds. And that's how digital will have destroyed itself in business.

5

UNDIGITAL, UNEMPLOYED: DIGITAL IS DESTROYING THE JOB MARKET

Many things more vital than music and newspapers are in disarray or on the way to diminishment or total destruction because of digital. Many of the effects of digital are long-term, energy-sapping, depersonalizing, psychologically disadvantageous, and economically damaging. Where we might champion a computer-aided map of the genome, we also mourn a cyberbullying suicide. For each YouTube cat sensation, there's most likely a shut-in who imagines she has actual friends on Facebook.

SOFTWARE IS NOT A JOB

Perhaps most dismaying of all the ways digital has wrought destruction is the way it's contributed to what looks like a permanent state of real-wage erosion and, too often, unemployment for even the better-than-average American.

There are exceptions, of course. Some will say digital has recently reversed a trend in outsourcing, and that digital may, in an unanticipated manner, bring all the good jobs back home again.

In 2013, according to a story in the *New York Times*,[1] a textile manufacturer returned his looms to the US, citing quicker turnaround, better quality, and cheaper transport than could be obtained from starvation-wage India. What doubter would not be called cynical for suggesting this could possibly be anything less than wonderful news for the dispossessed American laborer?

Apparently, the cynics would be right. The news about returning looms to the US is not that good for job-seekers, thanks to digital.

Instead of employing lots of loom workers at the loom, the entire operation is now controlled by robots running sophisticated jacquard-weaving software.[2] Every phase of the manufacturing operation is performed partly or mostly by robots—or digitrons, as I like to call them. And the folks who mind the digitrons are perhaps only a tenth in number compared to the amount of millworkers employed in what they now call "the heyday" of the already much-diminished 1970s and 1980s.

Any fair-handed treatment of the mill and its workers, idle or not, must take into account the absolute hell that millwork was and, in places like Madras and Mauritania, is today. In our fair land, it was emblematic of economic oppression to have been called a millworker. The day's labors were long, hot, unrelentingly dull, and dangerous. Limbs were lost to the weaver, and lungs lost to the cotton fibers that eventually filled bronchial tubes like down in a pillow. And the wages were so low as to make a family man desperate.

There is much talk in political circles, and more hand-wringing, devoted to the notion that "high-paying factory jobs" have disappeared while "low-paying service jobs" have been the only replacement. But as pointed out above, many of those factory jobs were never high paying, and if they were, they might also have been dehumanizing and otherwise mighty unpleasant. Further, while a job at Mickey D's may be an economically poor option for workers, at least it is not dangerous, demeaning, and unrelentingly monotonous the way many factory jobs were (and are) today. And many of the new class of jobs have been brought about by digital. Entire industries now employ knowledge workers, client-interface specialists, programmers, designers, marketers, and analysts whose jobs did not exist before the dawn of connectivity and software. The difficulty, as I will point out later, is that there just are not enough of these digital jobs to occupy people who lost their jobs at the plant.

Hard labor lost, first to Asia and now to algorithms, is but one of the ambivalent miseries visited by digital upon the analog among us. Apart from the minimal "success" story where a physical plant returns to a depopulated American industrial tract, it's digital that now plays an ever-increasing role in the otherwise massive amount of outsourcing that idles the unskilled or semi-skilled American. Charlene Lunchbucket may have a smartphone, but she doesn't have a full-time job with health insurance, and because she's on the wrong side of the digital divide (does not work with computers in some way), she may not, some say, have much of a future in a digital society.

Where she might have picked up work as a programmer or software engineer or even a help-desk worker in a new economy, digital's ability to make India or the Philippines functionally as close to management as the cubicle down the hall (combined with very low offshore wages) has driven these anonymous, factory-like digital occupations far from Lansing or Biloxi or Long Beach, California, and they have arrived in the Bay of Bengal instead, or in Manila Bay.

Outsource, Then Digitize

Digital was not the cause of the first wave of outsourcing. Entire factories were packed up and shipped to starvation-wage, no-tax lands of toilers,[3] and all computers did was help figure out the profit. But now digital is outsourcing more high-touch jobs as well (like customer-service jobs) and more jobs that require more technical sophistication than assembling parts on a line or stitch cloth in a Mumbai firetrap.

Vast numbers of administrative positions have melted away into software functions where complex processes take place in a nanosecond, with no person involved at all. Digital claims to make transactions "less sticky" and to "improve throughput." What this really means is that the process itself—tasks ranging from keeping a schedule to booking a hotel to bookkeeping—has been depopulated. Moist, inconstant, overly complicated humans have been replaced with ethereal software. And all the humans who used to do the stamping and the stapling, the phoning and the price-knowing, are now doing something else. Some of them are happy telecommuters working in frisky startups. Some are heavy into anti-depressants with two part-time gigs not close to home and another kid on the way.

Not all administrative functions can be replaced with software, of course—at least not this year. But digital has enabled the wholesale removal of many of *those* jobs from the Developed West as well, as we shall see below. However, instead of burying the functions inside a software algorithm, digital connectivity has instead enabled the jobs to be moved to a place where they speak English and get paid almost nothing. Chiefly that place has been India, but it's not the only place. There are some telephone help centers in some lost towns on the American prairie, as the costs and wages there are so low that they rival in "value" their counterparts in Chittagong.

In large part this "offshore" model relating to the type of jobs that require an ability to be semi-articulate is driven by digital. With e-mail, same-time texting, very-low-cost Internet telephony, robust help-desk databases, and browser-based project management, it has become possible to place in a one-dollar-a-day city the same computing power and the same immediate communications capability of an "onshore" hundred-dollar-a-day city. Which is why Charlene Lunchbucket hasn't got a job today.

Many of these digitally enabled jobs are known to us via the lilting tones of the credit-card helper or the motherboard troubleshooter as they ask us again and again for our names and account numbers without ever seeming to comprehend that we remember when things were different and, in many ways, perhaps, better. They seem to have fake names like "Davey" or "Lani," and you may imagine them at a pleasant cubicle in a pleasant suburban tract somewhere in a pleasant part of the North American continent not part of Mexico. But most likely they have trained extensively to "sound American" and are working the graveyard shift for a proverbial box of pennies in an unimproved industrial hall not far from a herd of goats in Guragon.[4]

You might count it an emblem of churlishness to suggest Davey and Lani in Guragon are less deserving of their jobs than Donald or Pearl in Terre Haute. We're not here taking sides against either team of service representatives, and we know they are but brief players upon a crowded stage. The big show is really about how digital enables fierce campaigns to *reduce cost at any cost*, in the name of what sanctimoniously is called "shareholder value."

Regardless of whether you believe jobs should be transient, it's a fact that the teleportation of jobs overseas has been made possible largely by digital. Without very low cost, connective technologies, and sophisticated management software, administrative functions would have stayed in the ink-stained hands of millions of unnoticed functionaries. Without the same digital connectors, the folks who helped you talk about mundane, bothersome troubles with your accounts, your appliances, or your insurance would very possibly be people in your own community (or one very much like it). They would have bought the same kind of orange juice you bought, they would have been on the same electrical grid, and their children would have gone to schools yours might go to. They might also have been driven to stark madness by having to listen to your complaining nonstop.

There's never been a study as to whether the American polity misses these jobs in particular, or whether they're so underemployed now that they've lost perspective and really would take any job no matter how mind-numbing, no matter how low the wage. Digital has knocked down the "artificial" barriers of geography and the "annoyance" of "middlemen" and sent millions of jobs to the Gray Havens, where they exist in a near-invisible half-life until they can be replaced entirely by human-voice digitrons that will know everything and nothing at the same time.

People Are Friction

Years ago, placing an order for goods in China would have required several phone calls, faxes, possible shipped documents, and even personal visits. It certainly would have included complex order codes, shipping arrangements, translations, and arcane, convoluted currency voodoo to execute. Digital communications make the process nearly seamless, and orders are taken in China without much more red tape than a take-out order at the Chinese restaurant.

Today, almost anyone can set up an account with a wholesaler almost anywhere (often through an intermediate website, an "aggregator" of business and services) and within a few clicks have purchased, say, cast-iron frying pans in bulk from a factory in an Asian province you've never heard of. A prime example of this kind of aggregator is the Chinese site Alibaba, which cleverly leverages the notion of an Arabian bazaar in its choice of name; indeed, it is the digital equivalent of that, as you can buy almost any good manufactured (most often in China).[5] It's frictionless. But it's also (for this country, anyway) jobless, and I don't mean because they are casting the iron overseas.

It's because an appreciable percentage of the middlemen (dealers, representatives, distributors, licensees, franchise holders, freight forwarders, import/export firms) have been turned out. "See your local retailer" has often been replaced by a clickable URL leading to a shopping cart.

For those who want to suggest digital has created uncountable high-paying jobs in this nation, it's important to note that for every programmer involved in setting up that e-commerce software, there is an untold number of those friction-making middlemen—and many others!—that got set free. In an article in the *MIT Technology Review* in 2013, David Rotman wrote that, according to professors Brynjolffsen and McAffee at MIT, "impressive advances in computer technology—from improved industrial robotics to automated translation services—are largely behind the sluggish employment growth of the last 10 to 15 years."[6] *The Economist*, in an article from January 2014,[7] said, "The effect of today's technology on tomorrow's jobs will be immense—and no country is ready for it." The article goes on to say that "for workers the dislocating effects of technology may make themselves evident faster than its benefits. Even if new jobs and wonderful products emerge, in the short term income gaps will widen, causing huge social dislocation and perhaps even changing politics." And when a rational, supply-side source like *The Economist* refers to a "dislocating effect," you can bet what they are suggesting is job loss even as they want to say that "optimism is the starting point" of the entire discussion (which for entrepreneurs—ostensibly who read *The Economist*—is a true statement).

In addition, some of the famous brands in digital field very small staffs compared to their outsized reputation. Jaron Lanier says that "Kodak employed 14,000 people; Instagram, 13."[8] According to website Statistica, Facebook has currently around 7,000 employees[9] and, based on its current stock price, is worth a little less than $200 billion. Meanwhile, Exxon is worth about $380 billion and employs around 75,000 people.[10] If Exxon were like Facebook in this regard, it might employ about one-eighth that number. Etsy (a well-known Amazon-like site for "hand-made goods") keeps a customer-service outfit in an unprepossessing former cannonball factory in a small town in the Hudson Valley. It is not a large facility, and there cannot be more than a couple of hundred people thus employed.

The entire sales pitch deployed by business-to-business software vendors—whether they are selling on-premise versions or SaaS products—has been historically the same as that of other "efficiency" businesses. I know this because my professional life has seen me typically on the efficiency side rather than, fortunately for me, the ill-affected side of the equation. Efficiency claims are simple, and (with few nuances) they're about one thing. They're about firing people and replacing them with automated processes. In the pre-digital age this process was often called "the machine," and it took cotton pickers out of Tuscaloosa, steel workers out of Bethlehem. Now it takes garment workers out of both Madras and Charlotte.

In digital, the job-destroying dreadnought has no name yet. It cruises the market undaunted, cutting through entire industries and sending their workers to the bottom without even the suggestion of a lifeboat. Our American entrepreneurial culture, in which the software industry is rooted, suggests that if you got slammed, too bad. Suck it up and create something fundable. "It's a free country!"

To me it seems too many Americans buy into this hooey. They blame themselves for not being "current" enough, as if digital were some kind of natural force not driven by the designs and foibles of other humans no better, but perhaps more technologically knowledgeable, than they are. Re-education plans sound vaguely Marxist and also have been shown not to work. Entrepreneurs talk about "changing the world" and "creating jobs," but what they are really after is "getting other people to do the valuable work" via unabashed capitalistic methods, and about "getting rid of dead wood" at their customers' businesses when their customers are other businesses. They never have dead wood at their own companies because typically they have no loyalty whatsoever to anyone and ruthlessly chop and change their companies to suit the demands of profit.

DRIVEN BY EFFICIENCY—ON YOUR BEHALF

Every company today is driven madly before the taunts of efficiency advocates. Despite the fact nothing in a global economy is very well understood and certainly not at all simple, it's fair to say the primary driver to efficiency is cost. If you can't deliver goods at a competitive cost, then you are going to dry up and wither like cornstalks after Halloween. And the demand for low cost is driven, at least in part, by the consumer. That consumer is us, as we look for the cheapest offer for the same good. Bananas or digital analytics cloud services: it's all the same in the marketplace. It's either a good banana or a bruised banana, and it's either the right price (cheap) or not.

If it's cheap and good, that's a winner.

And that is what digital tries to help companies deliver. By leveraging computing technology in extreme ways, and because such computing power is now available in bite-sized chunks via "the cloud," nearly every company—large, medium, and small—can now access sophisticated algorithms and advanced, ergonomic interfaces that help them get their work done with a scientifically reduced amount of human intervention. Among the more common uses for distributed digital among businesses are sales-management software, digital-analytics software (measuring the success of digital marketing programs), human-resources software, financial software, and insurance software. And let's not forget the communications software known as e-mail.

Countless hours of human labor are locked inside these software offerings, and the value of that human labor is unlocked for you and for the software company's owner every time you click a button to perform any action inside these programs (nowadays usually on your browser or on a mobile device). The same holds true, of course, if you are buying something from Amazon, but we discuss e-commerce in another section.

Countless hours of human labor are locked inside these software offerings, and the value of that human labor is unlocked for you and for the software company's owner every time you click a button.

SOFTWARE UNSTOPPABLE

Software preserves the value of certain kinds of human activity almost indefinitely. It codifies the activity and then enables the code to replicate and thrive almost as a living thing as it gets deployed by the "end user" via keyboard and mouse a million, a billion times over. The effort that is captured inside software is immense. Who owns the rights to the software sits like a grand panjandrum on a throne directly equal to the market primacy of the software itself. I don't have time here, nor any inclination, to describe the fabulous riches that constitute many of these thrones.

What I do want to point out is that the throne is like Soylent Green. *It's people!*

Like it or not, the efficiency engines of software have taken human endeavor, bound it up behind a paywall, and made it easy to access. The programmer was well paid and is now on to his next efficiency-enablement gig. In the meantime, all those commuters who used to work in skyscrapers have either departed permanently for jobs unknown ("I'll be your server tonight!") or perhaps simply perished off the job market and were reborn into a netherworld of junk-shops, barter, and government programs.

Who really needed those office drones, anyway? They performed so many mindless tasks. List keeping, note taking, phone calling, arranging, remembering, filing, comparing, checking, rule following—all things that had reduced their humanity to a level not much more than that of a machine. And perhaps then it should have come as little surprise that they would be replaced by software, which in the end is a very smart machine that mimics certain types of human activity at speed and with accuracy humans would never have been able to match.

The speed of this revolution is accelerating. Today it's the office functionary thrown off the boat. Next year it might be the lawyer, the accountant, the lab specialist, the physician, or the teacher, as I will discuss in a later chapter. Played out to its logical extreme, the only elements remaining in the economy would be the Owner, the Programmer, the Software, the Digital Marketer, and the Consumer. There won't be many other things to be in the later digital economy, and we are headed in this direction with all due speed.

As I've suggested above, while cheap labor was the first driver of offshoring jobs, now digital (e-mail, texts, document-sharing, collaborative creative capabilities [like Adobe's Marketing Cloud], and e-commerce) takes the friction away from even some of the thorniest challenges faced by those who want to offshore their labor force. And then digital, in the form of robots that entirely replace humans in many industries, may even put offshore markets out of work.

Perhaps digital has—or very soon shall have—destroyed the job market as we know it today. But it has also thrown us back upon ourselves in an almost existential manner. What, if not our work, are we here for? If software can replace nearly all of us, then what is our purpose and what are we doing about that? Perhaps the answer needs to go far beyond the confines of "providing value"; perhaps it leads into realms of the spirit to which digital cannot yet contrive to reach. In any case, we are, in this country and others, free to imagine.

6

THE LONELY SCREEN:
DIGITAL IS DESTROYING HUMAN
INTERACTION

Many aspects of what we thought were timeless elements of human interaction are being shredded by the Internet Protocol and its relative technologies. Perhaps the most glaring example is the not-very-funny running joke that millions now believe they have actual "friends" by virtue of having added value to a privately owned data-logging venture with an ingenious, humanistic/literary name. A couple of years ago it sought funds from the public under the "FB" symbol. And it may be only slightly less unfunny that texting has replaced talking, much as role playing has replaced playing. Much of the domain of human interaction, characterized by long-valued, perhaps sappy notions like "the milk of human kindness" and "brotherhood/sisterhood" has been offloaded (not to say ceded) to the displaced electron inside of a silicon chip.

Our great sporting pastimes may also be at a level of risk they can hardly begin to assess. The old canard that "baseball is too slow" may turn off those who've gotten used to instant gratification, and that isn't really the fault of digital. Football is probably in more trouble than the NFL knows, partly because of a recent spate of ignominious behavior on the part of certain players (such as cold-cocking one's girlfriend in an elevator) and partly because even the great NFL must now admit that brain trauma is a much-too-likely end game for the retired professional.

But what is perhaps more worrisome is the fact there is a growing tide of "sports fans" not interested in watching humans bat balls or flatten quarterbacks. In Seattle, where the Seahawks reigned in 2014 as the Super Bowl champs, recently (August 2014) an indoor arena was packed to the rafters with folks watching a competitive event where humans were interacting, but not in the flesh. Ten thousand instead watched as they battled avatar-to-avatar in video games. There was cheering and booing, and there was the consumption of beverages and bad food, just like at a regular sporting event, but all the action was virtual. Nowhere did an actual human take an actual risk on the field—instead, the stars were busy at their keyboards firing "missiles" or swinging "halberds" at a virtual enemy in a beautifully rendered fantasyland.

WHO IS US?

Perhaps we had been looking for this escape all along. There's an old school of thought that suggests we remain, at our core, relatively unconvinced that anyone else is real in the sense that we ourselves are real. Without delving too deeply into existential philosophy or the politics of identity, let us say that we've long sought escape from the prison of "others" by declaring primacy of the "self." And having achieved a modicum of self, we now seek escape from this cage as well. If some of us can now create separate personae in a virtual space—fairly complete personages, "avatars," as mentioned above—that we can enter and exit; that we can deploy to interact with other personae; that we can utilize as a layer of protection against the slings and arrows we feel as soon as we walk out the physical door of our dwelling—if we can do that, why would we not choose to devote an appreciable amount of energy to making that persona and its connections as real as we might? There is no apparent risk.

In a digital world, we can have relationships and then immediately end them if we don't like them. We can stop worrying about how we look or even how we smell. We can craft a doppelganger, a two-dimensional 'bot that performs as us at our will. And we can sit behind the goggles of our own eyeballs, much as some philosophers posit we have always wanted, totally in control and remote from harm. And we can do it all for free (except for when you pay to watch video gamers)!

At least, this is how it is supposed to work.

But we still have to exist in the flesh, and there's the rub.

Must we feign surprise when we find that we, and everyone else we know, has lost at least some respect for the basic humanity of the next, when all we've seen is a goofy, tiny picture of that human and perhaps a video of their cat knocking something off a table? What happens when the relatively unsophisticated set of younger cybercitizens cannot tell there's even much of a difference between *that* person and *this* (the one we live inside of)? And when heretofore powerless or otherwise chicken-shit sociopaths find they can press a few buttons and torment an innocent neighbor? And when that sad little neighbor-friend decides they cannot face the other real humans in the real world, and they jump from a window somewhere, and everyone spends a day or two lamenting "cyber-bullying"?

It's one more example of what happens when people are removed not just from other people but also from themselves.

The trouble reaches deep inside all our relationships and also into our workplaces.

WORK NOT AT WORK

People have never really liked going to work. We know it's necessary, and some of us really do get paid to do what we love and therefore never "work." But this is another example of the suck-it-up happy talk promulgated by the most capable and least thoughtful among us as if, even if everyone were to follow that edict, it could ever possibly result in anything but anarchy and probable destruction of the race of men and women as we know it. That said, it sure is a great thing when it works.

But for nearly everyone, it does not work.

And where it doesn't work, there's work. And going to work. And getting up and going to work. And being stuck in traffic. And listening to conversations over the wall you wish you'd never heard and which even may haunt you as you lie awake at night wondering what kind of weirdo you work with at work. So you jump at the chance to not go to work.

If you're a smartphone owner, you've got more computing power in your pocket than the Apollo program had for the moon shots. Your desktop has more processing power than the computers deployed during the first space shuttle launch. What wonderful new thing can you do with this power?

First on the list is that you sign up for telecommuting. According to the Society for Human Resource Management, "Forrester Research in 2009 found that more than 34 million U.S. adults telecommuted at least occasionally, and predicted the ranks would reach 63 million by 2016, fueled by technology and growing management experience."[1]

The boon is fantastical and beyond the dreams of your parents and totally unimaginable for any generation before theirs. You are working without going to work! This is transformational; it's the utopia even George Jetson could not fully achieve at Spacely Industries. He may have had a video feed, but he didn't have data input.

We can be there without being there. We can participate in meetings, see another screen, chat, edit, share, write, check off, create content, and manage others remotely. It's almost idiomatic these days to say we can "work in our pajamas," even though we are probably not actually in pajamas while working from home. The larger point is that we have bunkered ourselves away from the office, which, according to the Society for Human Resource Management, has become at least in some instances "dysfunctional."[2] Apparently this is because office workers get distracted too often, and, for some reason, distractions—which I shall for the moment define as "unbidden interaction with other people"—get in the way of what we now call "work." In this context, "work" seems to be something apart from "interacting in real time with other people," and for some of us, the value we deliver may in fact be much about what we do apart from other people.

Not having worked in a communal office for more than ten years, I believe I am one of these people, and when I want to be "heads-down" on something, I do not want distractions. I have worked successfully in hotel rooms, cafes, trains, home offices, my bed, a garage, and a shady spot in the backyard. In many of these locations, it may seem to the casual (or interested!) observer that I am not actually working. And this is one reason why, curiously, telecommuting includes nearly everything except that video feed the Jetsons had. It's not only unnecessary but also scary and intrusive—and it kind of ruins the fun. We don't really want to see each other *en déshabillé.* We're good with text and voice only.

Some may argue that telecommuting has destroyed the heretofore apparently healthy separation of home from office, in the sense that it seems to have encroached meaningfully upon our collective leisure time (which, in most people's lives, is probably not much about leisurely activities but more about getting the kids to bed or cleaning the gutters). According to an article in the *New York Times* in March 2014, Jennifer Glass, a sociology professor at the University of Texas, says that "much of what managers and professionals call telecommuting occurs after a 40-hour week spent in the office."[3] Apparently, folks these days check e-mail, return calls, and create content from home, but it's not during working hours—instead, it is in the evenings and on weekends when they're supposed to be relaxing.

Telecommuting is very strongly associated with information workers, the self-employed, and managers,[4] so as a phenomenon it will at some point run up against natural limits. You can't bolt on a fender or gut a chicken remotely. Those workers have to go home from work to spend time on a computer.

The rest of us don't. Instead, we have abandoned the dubious camaraderie of the cubicle farm for a seat at the kitchen table where we do the same work and maybe even more, except in isolation. We have little opportunity to interact on a personal and perhaps serendipitous level. We have neither the responsibility nor the ability to augment our circle of influence, and it works both ways. We gain release from the commute. We lose the benefit not just of being able to influence others by our personal impression but also of possible influence by others. Who can reach us in our blinkered state? Sure, they can e-mail us and talk on the phone, and some might even say this is not meaningfully distinguishable from actual physical proximity.[5] But according to others,[6] physical isolation may be depriving us of something valuable, much as power-napping is just not the same as a good night's sleep. In telecommuting, we are asking that others provide us only with the abstract "business value" they deliver and nothing associated with their full human presence. Perhaps we just don't want human interaction as much as we would like to think. So we retreat to a digital cavern, a place where we are there but not there. Increasingly, we seem to prefer it this way, as it seems, perhaps, less risky and less trouble in general.

PHYSICAL FADES

In light of all the above, what can we say about factors relating to the real influence of physical presence? What of the long-recognized value of "charisma"—an almost unclassifiable sense that a certain person, based largely upon a combination of their physical presence, appearance, and behavior, can in some way be more influential than another, and that they may be, in a manner that can be spotted rather easily but not so easily articulated, somehow more desirable as a companion, a business partner, a leader. The worthy but uncharismatic among us might have called the whole thing unfair. Why, in a more justly constructed world, would any one person achieve better influence simply because of the way they looked, the way their voice sounded, how they waved their hand, glanced at you, stood before you—in short, because of their "physical presence"? Perhaps we have long been dissatisfied with this native unfairness. And digital has rewarded us by removing this quality from our interactions. Call it "revenge of the nerds," but in many ways the personal advantages of good looks and good comportment are, in a digital world, no longer in play.

Circles of influence today are based on things like Twitter followings and the number of so-called "friends" we have, and on how many other influencers we are linked to on LinkedIn. In many important ways, these are almost entirely illusory accomplishments; they are stand-ins for anything that might accrue from actual popularity or actual influence.

Seen in this light, it can be posited that one of the chief accomplishments of digital—the ability to project personality across a broadband spectrum—has also resulted in a loss of community and a radically reduced set of our sensory experiences. Who is to say that the notion of charisma is not somehow bound to our ability to perceive subliminally something of substance about a person that, minus the experience of their actual presence, cannot be discerned?

While television (or the nickelodeon?) may have begun the substitution of believable experience for the actual, digital's ability to allow the participant to believe they have seen things and gone places they have never in fact seen or gone to or actually experienced is on a level much more stunning and debilitating than television might ever have accomplished.

After all, even the tiny community that would sit around watching TV together has now been scattered—each viewer now with his or her own screen, each "interacting" with tiny sigils on a luminous surface that may or may not remotely connect them to another person somewhere (texting) or to another avatar somewhere on a website, in an app, in a video clip, or anything else that can be reduced to two dimensions and sent through our current broadband network.

To a large extent, we have stopped talking to one another[7] except in public places where we pay to do so, such as bars and restaurants. We rent space there, get fed and watered, and sometimes blab and act as if we weren't waiting for the moment when we could say g'night and go back home to our digital cavern, where we enjoy more mastery over our environment than in any place where other physical entities are vying for primacy. Some say even these sanctioned theaters for human interaction may be threatened by the preferences of a new and perhaps more socially awkward generation. According to an article in *TechCrunch* in June 2014, "The trend of avoiding the emotional risk associated with live encounters has become wide-spread." And, according to a young man interviewed for the article, "nobody talks to anyone in person these days, not even the people they *do* know and like already."[8]

Where we might have gone visiting, or for a walk, or talked on the phone, we now send a few characters to "keep folks updated" as we are half-involved in some other endeavor where our physical body may happen to reside but which likely is not the focus of our attention. Take a look back and be honest about whether you do miss all the visiting and hanging out and punching and plundering that you were part of before there was a Twitter or instant messaging. There was pain and pleasure in there, and our imperative to pain-avoidance has led us to a vacuous place where threats are few and allies fewer.

Digital has destroyed community even as it has created "community." Flash mobs are driven by instant messaging. Revolutions are started in chat rooms. Revolutions are real enough because in places where revolutions happen, people are hurting bad enough to come out and kick some ass in order to save theirs. The rest of us are rather more complacent. We have traded in our birthright membership in the human clan for an account on a privately owned service that can be revoked without cause and without recourse. Digital has allowed us to outsource human interaction.

Living on a Platform

That we have outsourced a significant portion of our human interactions to cost-free services is notable in its profligacy. Too few people even grasp the notion that, while the Internet is not owned by anyone, Google is owned and controlled by a group of people and/or algorithms that care about you not at all. Facebook, despite the sad misapprehension rather too rampant in the land of users, is not a place where you run your own show. According to an article by Jay Rosen in *The Atlantic* in June 2014, "You have (almost) no rights [on Facebook]. You have (almost) no control."[9]

Facebook in particular is emblematic of the kind of genial fascism that began with Apple's "Okay" button back when stand-alone software used to crash and you had only one choice and that was the "Okay" button (which frequently rebooted your Mac). With Facebook, everything is good until it's not. Based solely on personal observation and minus any inside track at Facebook, it can be posited that if the Facebook user-tracking algorithm flashes an alert and somebody from the inner sanctum doesn't like what you're doing, they shut you down. A recent example came to my attention during the run-up to the 2012 elections, when a certain pro-candidate Facebook page gained rapid success organically (i.e., without spending a penny at Facebook). Oddly, it got locked down without explanation for two weeks. Once its momentum had been sapped, it was allowed to continue. But the not-so-subtle message was much less political than cash-hungry: *we wish you success, but not that much success—unless you buy something.*

Entire businesses—in fact, entire *business sectors*—have been built around the Facebook juggernaut. Zuckerberg's mountain is big enough to influence its own weather. It may give the appearance of a real, living community much the way a tribe or small civilization might for a time thrive on a volcanic island. But that tribe is living on unstable ground. It certainly cannot control any of the seismic activity taking place beneath its collective feet, much as Facebook volunteers ("users") cannot control any of the rules that shape their discourse inside the confines of the Facebook ecosystem. And if by chance something happens within the Facebook mountain that corrupts its core, or if by some carefully considered policy move it blasts away a slope or two, and you happen to be there when it does—then you'll be Pompeii'd under digital ash, and you'll have zero recourse. Because by participating in Facebook (and its ilk), you have agreed in principle that, in exchange for lots of "free" stuff (which you pay for with your personal data), you give over an appreciable portion of your personal sovereignty,[10] and arguably your right to digital life or death, to the great gods of the Facebook mountain. They can, if

I am not terribly mistaken about Facebook's terms of use, vote you off the island or explode the island any old time.

By participating in Facebook, you have agreed . . . that, in exchange for lots of "free" stuff (which you pay for with your personal data), you give over . . . your personal sovereignty . . . to the great gods of the Facebook mountain.

It may be hard to imagine building a business around something as whimsical as the above examples, but many have. One can only hope the owners of those businesses have diversified their holdings so that, if and when Facebook decides to terminate them, they've got cash enough to migrate to the next platform owned by somebody else.

They Make the Rules

While outsourcing our humanity to the digital, we put it at still further remove by signing off on the rules of engagement imposed by private carriers. This is much more of a big deal than paying for phone service. Sure, you needed to pay your phone bill in order to not be isolated. But there was nothing you could do qualitatively (aside from something that might involve police and eventual prison time) that might affect your right to have a phone. In addition, telephony was regulated by the government, and the companies that came to be known (and regulated) as public utilities could not just go out of business or unilaterally decide not to serve you.[11] This would have been illegal.

Government has been shoved out of the free market where Facebook founders grow rich. There are almost no laws governing what Facebook can do or not do[12] as regards their relationship with you as a user of their service. As has been famously said elsewhere about online services, "Where you are not paying for the product, you are the product." Upon agreeing to the terms of use on Facebook and many other free online services, you have entered a zone where everything you might do as a virtual person is freely available to yourself (and, of course, to the owners of the platform), except that it is instantly revocable without recourse. There are no hearings at places like Facebook, no trials, no judges, no representatives, nothing. You are playing by their rules and helping them make money, or you are subject to being shut down and banished.

Some people, myself included, would not care one way or the other if Facebook decided not to "like" me. Once, during a brief period of what one might call digital sentimentality, I created a Facebook page for myself but almost immediately took a dislike to it (I knew about their terms of service and have habitually had issues with authority). The only Facebook interaction I can recall with clarity involved siblings, profound and bitterly expressed differences of opinion about immigration, and ultimate estrangement. I have not reviewed, updated, or attempted to delete this page in memory and have no plans to do so anytime soon. But many millions of perhaps more innocent (or less paranoid) users would be shocked and even debilitated if Facebook were to cut them off. It would be as if they were told suddenly to seal their lips and go off silently to a distant exile. In the real world, they would recover, but perhaps at great cost and almost certainly after no small amount of consternation and even grief.

Do you use your smartphone camera at dinner? Imagine a world where you could not post photos of your prime rib at a fancy restaurant. Imagine having to confront yourself as a stand-alone, going to restaurants, attending family events, and enjoying great sunsets more or less anonymously. Somehow it seems most don't want this kind of world anymore, though their kids might look at what we call social media years from now quite differently. Younger generations have a way of not doing whatever their parents thought was fun. It's possible we could see a back-to-basics movement not unlike the "back to the land" movement of the baby-boomer era that turned suburban overachievers into bearded hillbillies for a time before they shaved and got into law school.

Backlash is always a factor in social preferences, and it may be that social media one day will suffer the indignities of an abandoned toy, and people will hope again to connect with other people in real places without the intercession of avatars and supporting documentation. But until the pendulum starts to swing that way, it seems clear digital will have delivered a body blow to what we had, up until recently, called "human interaction."

7

A GOLDEN RING, JUST OUT OF REACH: DIGITAL IS DESTROYING HIGHER EDUCATION

Poorly educated societies tend to be poor societies. Today we may have an acute crisis at all levels of our learning infrastructure,[1] but here I will discuss the way digital may at some point destroy higher education as we know it.

Education is in many ways similar to software, in that its essence cannot be boxed or perhaps even adequately quantified. If anything, it is even more ephemeral than software, since there's no body of work that can be said to constitute the product. Education is experience, exposure, the delivery of information in context. Once delivered, it cannot be removed (though it can be forgotten). The sheepskin is only an artifact. The accreditation associated with a degree is an affirmation that the graduate has been exposed to a fairly well-accepted regimen of ideas and disciplines.

But it's also been an attestation to the completion of a course of study, the value of which can be only partly located in the data exposure itself. The assumed total value, and that which never is reflected in a GPA but which is as highly valued (if not vaunted above all else), is the community of minds and bodies.

EDUCATING MORE THAN THE MIND

Higher education has never been purely an intellectual pursuit. One's collegiate experience educates and sometimes abrades the mind, the body, and the soul. Typically, at least in the well-known physical-campus model, the freshman is plucked from the childhood bedroom and plunked down in an alien environment alone with strangers. Despite well-intentioned orientation sessions, the freshman goes through a metamorphosis comprising crises in self-apprehension, social skills, hygiene, sexuality, and often no small amount of physical horror as well as physical pleasure. There is no question the person arriving for their second September is irrevocably altered from the version that showed up, perhaps almost tearfully, for their first.

Through these examples we can see that the expectation raised and largely delivered by the higher-education industry is demonstrably transformational. In prior generations this was a rarefied experience designed to meet the expectations of a privileged class. A degree from university meant entree to a world of refined possibilities utterly closed to the unschooled commoner.

At the same time American mythology abounds with tales of contrarians—of great successes achieved by the extraordinary, the brave, the tough, and especially the clever autodidacts who dropped out of school only to make enormous impacts on society. Often it's been these unconventional types who have driven the real innovations—probably the most recent example of which is Steve Jobs. But the bedrock brainpower of any leading nation is its army of educated minds, and the incorporated bodies thereof, that went through the experiences that made their educations complete.

Today, during a time of ultra-high cost, diminished institutional prestige, and the advent of digital alternatives, higher education may become for the first time in a generation a "maybe" on the checklist of items deemed necessary to success.[2] This is despite the fact the education industry seems to present itself as the very lifeblood of same.

RISE OF A NEW PEONAGE

The education industry in the last forty years has conducted an astonishingly successful campaign designed to drive a message of its value out to the millions. The generation that once revolted on the commons, that declared its elders and all its institutions doomed by corruption and sclerosis, ended up, just a few years later, the loudest crier for more and more and more education. Its members went from trashing the university to elevating it to the status of a necessary ingredient to success. The generation that came of age in the 1960s went on to build a nation of middle- and upper-middle-class über-parents who perhaps overnurtured, over-organized, and sought to overeducate their children in pursuit of a goal that Americans are almost bound constitutionally to pursue: happiness. Their children now have become parents themselves in many cases, and the trend has gotten even more pronounced.

We now have sub-industries in test preparation that coach not just the college-bound but also, in a most absurd formulation, the poor little rich (and often not-so-rich) baby bound for pre-K.[3] This sets up a comic/tragic scenario in which toddlers are robbed of their babyhood, railroaded into educational tracks at a tender age, already pursuing conventional success even as they have only just shed their diapers.

It has become accepted dogma that one needs a college degree if one expects any real chance at professional success. With the government as handmaiden to the student-lending industry, money has been offered (at low interest) that might cover the now-fantastical sums required by colleges to deliver their product, the cost of which, it has been argued, has risen in tandem with the availability of cheap funds—with the subsidy enrichment going right into the university profit centers.

Consequently, a league of educated young men and women has emerged as an over-leveraged debtor class that in large measure has compromised its hope of freedom and been locked into the shackles of mortgage-length financial commitments. The debt load has increased rapidly in recent years. According to an article in *Forbes* in February 2014, student debt on average has increased by 58 percent between 2005 and 2012.[4] Should it come a surprise that an over-stressed debtor class now becomes emblematic for "what not to do" for an even younger, more digitally inclined, less traditional generation looking for success?

For some of the least prudent and/or most needy among this generation of educated debtors, the load can become crushing.[5] While student debt is not a result of digital, the severity of it certainly serves to drive the next phase of digital destruction in the education industries. Those who today have paid hard dollars for a degree in a soft skill at a large, private institution that (perhaps knowingly) misled them into thinking it was somehow worthwhile would hardly question the need for a total overhaul of the pernicious system that has trapped them in an over-educated prison of penury.

The graduate debt crisis has laid bare serious structural flaws in our higher education system. A trepidatious new generation of knowledge-seekers has heard the horror stories from older siblings, cousins, and acquaintances. The day when even an upper-middle-class family might fund a quality degree program without any assistance now recedes in memory like freshman algebra.

Not to be denied information in an information age, and not willing to enter a condition of hyper-educated peonage, a younger generation may yet turn convincingly to digital.

Digital offers advantages in education that can be intoxicating for both student and school. Often for pennies on the dollar, a student can gain access to matriculation, courseware, and a legitimate degree in any of a thousand subjects. (Our discussion does *not* include the many sham "colleges" peddling nigh-worthless online programs in such as collagen-reduction therapy, nor the ultra-phony Internet-only schools known as "diploma mills" [apparently a $500 million industry],[6] any example of which might confer an "experience degree" based on attestation and, frankly, fraud.[7] Instead, we are in most every case talking about real courses offered by known and respected schools.)

YET ANOTHER GOLD RUSH?

A goodly percentage of institutions of higher learning today offer either complete or partial degree-oriented courses on the web and now (of course) on mobile. Some of them offer online classes for free, though not often for credit. Private companies like Khan Academy give away or sell courses on subjects ranging from engineering to financial services, often enough at the behest or with the assistance of corporations interested in a training regimen (or a public-relations effort) designed ostensibly to "educate" consumers.[8] In many cases, Ivy League–level courses can be audited online without cost. Specifically, an organization called Class Central advertises "free online education . . . from Stanford, MIT, Harvard," and so forth.[9] MOOC (Massive Online Organized Courseware) technology has become sophisticated and pervasive, allowing what feels like virtual attendance at a real school, including professorial oversight, lectures, assignments, feedback, class participation, and chat. Despite some current setbacks, it won't be long before streaming video and two-way audio will permit the full digital experience of what will no doubt be seen as a good education, and I am not here to suggest that is necessarily a bad thing. In fact, I am not convinced that digital necessarily diminishes education—but I am convinced, as I hope to demonstrate, that digital may well destroy the "higher-education industry" such as we know it today.

That said, and according to a *New York Times* article in December 2013,[10] online courseware has encountered some rough sledding, and some of it has been heaved over into the abyss. Many online classes were found to have astonishingly high drop-out rates, and graduates of a full course of online study have turned out to be rare indeed.

The digital student has more options than the analog equivalent. Courses can be selected based solely on need and interest rather than as part of a course of study (and typically not toward a degree). For those interested in digital careers, the notion that one might obtain valuable skills in a physical setting almost fades completely before the prospect of choosing only the knowledge necessary for narrow, careerist "certifications."[11]

At the same time, businesses in digital and beyond complain loudly that even traditional, four-year universities are not delivering graduates (job candidates) who know anything much that can help the business make money. According to an article in the *Huffington Post* in April 2014, "only 11 percent of business leaders . . . strongly agree that graduates have the necessary skills and competencies to succeed in the workplace."[12] Of course, these complainers ignore one of the main points of education, which, laudably, is not to feed candidates to industry, but rather to broaden the horizons of the individual.

A primary example of this putative educational shortcoming is where digital enterprises look for hires that are well suited to so-called left-brain/right-brain disciplines such as "digital content creation" and its close cousin, "content engineering." This notion assumes a requirement that a single individual can navigate both creativity and technology with equal skill. The content engineer will write well and understand software enough to deploy both in a sophisticated manner. The early incarnations of this would have been found in the world of desktop publishing, which leverages both editorial and technical acumen, and which is now the bedrock discipline of all print media. Its second incarnation was brought to fruition by the web developer who needed even more comprehensive skills and the ability to apply them even more nimbly in a complex, ever-changing environment.

His blessing, and the most liberating thing ever to smile upon print people, was the web-based disappearance of the *deadline*.

Today, the pace accelerates with interactive environments and a need to excel not just at content creation but also at content *optimization* based on data feedback.

Higher-education institutions have drunk from the same tankard. They envision greater velocity in delivering value with less of the friction associated with campus life. No doubt a number of institutions eagerly await the day when they can stop walking home fearful young partiers at night with private security teams and cleaning up after on-campus or near-campus bacchanalian rites [13] and dispense with all the vicissitudes of keeping apart the fleshly interests of faculty and student bodies (not to mention medieval-sounding constructs like "tenure").

That many universities now must deal with what seems—*seems*, I must emphasize—a pervasive culture of binge-drinking and even rape [14] suggests that the virtual classroom may offer significant virtues beyond what are possible when young men and women are put in close proximity unsupervised.

Like the more straightforward content industries before them, colleges and universities are taking bold new steps in cyberspace, hoping to gain advantage in the form of market share and eventual hegemony in a very lucrative education market as it evolves toward digital-only. Much as every senator (so goes the claim) sees a possible president in the mirror, it can be suggested in similar fashion that every university may be prone to believing it might triumph as the Amazon of Higher Learning. It's a zero-sum game, though, and there's just one Amazon.

TRAPPED IN A PARADIGM

A signal feature of the digital landscape is the near-absolute dominance of certain behemoths in a given market. This is both a lure and a trap for any hopeful entrant, but it is even more a trap for those who would dump on the market their valuables in hope of success via ubiquity while downplaying or undercutting the undocumented essentials of their business. They would only be following the music and the print industries down this dreary path to oblivion.

Yet higher education seems so directed. Education providers have extracted from the sinews of their complex offering the most measurable nutrients only (courseware), leaving the underlying *physical* tissue to languish and wilt. By this, I mean they stand to offer up the knowledge minus the experience. Like newspapers and musicians before them, they will have created a digital doppelganger that will eventually stalk their market and sap and destroy the essence of most providers while clearing a path of denatured absolutism for the few.

Amazon, the exemplar of digital marketing dominance, allows us to scry what may await the eventual winner of the race to digitize education. The warrior-named giant began in bookselling and now has seen many of its brick-and-mortar competitors wither and shrink from the marketplace.

Picture a roughly similar outcome in digital education. "Amazon University" (it does not exist, of course) could be an absolutely unmatched cornucopia of knowledge with a course for everyone and then some. No student would be left behind. Everyone might someday go to an Amazon-like university, and they'd probably be happy.

But much as we longingly recall the cozy bookstores of old, with the tactile pleasures of freshly inked and not-so-fresh tomes in our hands, the gazing at titles, the wonder at book covers, the perusal and head-scratching, the astonishing discovery, the chat with the owner, the comparison with other books of its kind with a real person who cares about the same things you care about, the running into somebody in the History aisle— much as we longingly recall it, we can only look back in reverie. With rare exception in exceptional cities, and even there less and less often, the above scenario is moribund, if not dead altogether. Gone is the unmeasurable pleasure in being bookish. It is replaced with the ability, yes, to buy any book, anytime, anywhere, and have it dropped off at your doorstep (and if you're bookish and not near a major city, this really works best for you), but in the end you've sacrificed something that involves your entire being and now only involves your tapping fingers and your wallet.

JUST ANOTHER TAB IN THE MENU

Amazon University, if it were to actually exist in a manner consistent with the rest of Amazon's offerings, would give you a degree and you would know a lot. But you would be only an extension of the wires and chips, the recipient of the datastream. You would have discovered little, or even nothing, on your own. You certainly would not have enjoyed the dorm parties. Nor the gazing and longing in class; nor the long walk to class in the rain. In short, nothing that makes up life itself. Digital, if it were to triumph in a currently dysfunctional higher-education system the way it triumphed in an unsuspecting book trade, would reduce the rich meal of a well-rounded education to the equivalent of a shallow platter of skim milk.

Digital . . . would reduce the rich meal of a well-rounded education to the equivalent of a shallow platter of skim milk.

Students are only behaving in reactive mode. Shocked by sticker price and goaded toward "marketability" and even "personal branding" by an ever more choosy job market, they gravitate toward what seems most advantageous. But they do so blindly and, as youth often can be, heedless of the consequences.

Without retrenchment on cost and a new focus on the real value of university attendance, digital, as always enabled by industry hubris as well as real structural challenges, will have, at some point in time not so long from now, destroyed education.

8

THE DOWNTOWN NEXT TIME: DIGITAL IS DESTROYING URBAN LIFE IN AMERICA

Certainly the American city can claim to have made at least a qualified comeback over the past twenty years or so,[1] but that comeback, at least in many second- and third-tier towns, is threatened by a number of factors including the onset of a more digital culture.

Only the youngest among us cannot recall when our cities were almost universally feared as killing zones where Dirty Harry duked it out and shot it up with punks, weirdos, and bums. Cities had fallen from a pinnacle, and hard. The American city of the immediate post-war era had become an icon of cultural progress and material success—perhaps undeservedly, given its later rapid decline. During the 1950s places like Cleveland and Detroit were peaking in population,[2] and their manufactures were sent out to a hungering world. But by the 1970s, cities were in free fall.[3] By the late 1970s even New York City, fresh off a bankruptcy scare,[4] was widely seen as a place to be avoided. It seemed that no one ambitious wanted to live there, drug bazaars were rife, and apartments were almost ridiculously cheap for the brave or foolhardy who would fain venture its needle-strewn wastes.

Perhaps not coincidentally, 1978 was the year I decided to move to New York City where I rented an apartment for an embarrassingly low sum. I had left the New York suburbs (where I'd grown up) and had been living in a city in the Pacific Northwest, where an artist I knew said he'd move to New York like I expected to, except that his childhood friend, who'd "done the whole artist thing" with "a hose for a cold shower" in a Soho loft, had been murdered there. Undeterred and confident, as a quasi-native of New York City (born there, not raised there), that there was enough street wisdom in me that I'd stand a better-than-even chance of not being slain, I headed back east.

My apartment was just around the block from the New York head-quarters of the Hell's Angels Motorcycle Club and its bearded, pool-cue-wielding captains. A high school friend moved in nearby and foolishly brought his car, which soon was stripped of every removable part and left sitting on cinder blocks. Homeless men (called "bums" at the time) warmed themselves all day and night around flaming barrels just a couple of blocks from my building. In the neighborhood where I worked during my first few months in the city, a six-year-old boy was lost and never heard from again. Only in 2014 did police claim they'd got a confession from his alleged killer.[5]

Many newcomers during that time came, saw, and left. Or just stayed away. But I enjoyed going to clubs where I saw the Ramones and Patti Smith, and no one was going to get me out except covered in a sheet.

Now the cities again have become paragons of upward mobility, and in the intervening years I moved to a different neighborhood in Manhat-tan where I could raise children without constant worry they'd fall prey to a miscreant. So I can attest to the success curve of urban America, having witnessed it from a decent enough vantage point.

Regardless of my own views, I think it is safe to say New York especially has been resurrected from its crime-ridden, malodorous tomb of yore to become what its recent and seemingly interminable mayor (Michael Bloomberg) called "a premium brand"[6] (even as he's been re-placed by a liberal firebrand [Bill DeBlasio] who talks of "a tale of two cities"[7]). Some say it may be the safest big city in Christendom.

Once again it seems the best and smartest flock there to flaunt their plumage, but also it seems to me not the same kind of flaunting as of old. Today, at least based on what I can discern, even dedicated urbanites are locked into a staring contest with whatever is looking back at them from their smartphones, and what was once the quirkiest urban landscape of all now seems like an open-air shopping mall full of chain stores and banks. Digital certainly plays a role here: the local bookstore is now Amazon. The shoe store is Zappos (unless it's couture). The newsstand sells mainly trinkets and gum while we browse the *Times* on an app. Never a happy place for supermarkets, Manhattan almost forces its residents to order food online (Fresh Direct is a favorite) and have it delivered.

Other American cities ascendant today are much smaller: San Francisco, with its thriving culture of all things digital (its outsized and not entirely well-deserved reputation notwithstanding), is one-tenth the size of New York; Boston, also a technology hub, is about the same size as San Francisco, and it is known not just for MIT but also for its egalitarian roots, the venerable and typically sold-out Fenway Park, and, generally, a highly educated citizenry. Seattle counts for something, too, because it really tries hard to be a happening place and sometimes even succeeds (being home to both Microsoft and Amazon cannot hurt); tiny Portland is likewise notable because it is a refined version of Seattle, and because you can clearly see a snow-capped mountain from downtown on a clear day. Los Angeles is part of the club because it is probably more of a success than people want to give it credit for. The sunny, water-impoverished megalopolis defies all categorization, creates more American export goods (movies and *lots of digital media*) than almost anywhere else, and seems not to care much what you think. Downtown Los Angeles, which for decades would have been more suggestive of an oxymoron than an urban destination, today boasts some fifty thousand residents,[8] almost all of them having arrived in the last decade. These are exemplary tales of urban success in the twenty-first century; there are others, but I don't have space to list them.

The attractions of the large, cosmopolitan city would seem obvious: continuous interaction with new and interesting people and things tossed together in a tumult of diversity, the stimulus generally of noisy ferment, access to major cultural events, an astonishing variety of foods and drinks, plus the availability of innumerable goods and services often not found in other places. These all constitute the near-irresistible lure of a big, important city. But, as I expect to demonstrate, this allure is made less relevant, and in some cases even *irrelevant*, by the nowhere-and-everywhere quality of digital life.

THE CULT OF URBANISM—AND ITS UNDERMINING

Some say we may have overdone the cult of urbanism. Desirability, especially in top cities like New York, Boston, and San Francisco, seems to have driven cost beyond the means of nearly any new arrival not willing to suffer almost biblical privations before hoping for success in the big town. I believe this overreach may yet prove a contributing factor to what some expect to be a coming decline in the long-term viability of these cities. Already we see a sad story written in the loss of smaller, more interesting shops and services to umpteen bank branches and national chain stores, even in the heretofore unique urban cores of these vibrant cities. And digital is always kicking at the foundations of urban brick-and-mortar, enticing us to "go virtual" and "order now" and otherwise consume bandwidth at the expense of a walk to the store for what used to be known as "the papers."

It has become almost fashionable for elder urban elites to proclaim the city *finis*. I cannot count the times I have participated in conversations with former urban bravehearts where it has been generally agreed upon that the cost of certain cities has become prohibitive; that they would not come to the big city now if young and adventurous; that instead they would move to a small, happy burg nearby where houses were still cheap and music could be played loud and not disturb a fund manager's sleeping toddler on the floor below, and, perhaps most importantly, *where broadband would make the distance from that overhyped urban core seem not that distant.*

A few years ago, downtown doyenne Patti Smith said New York City was "closed off" and that Poughkeepsie, New York, might make for a smarter choice.[9] Recently David Byrne (of Talking Heads fame) quipped he might rather be 120 miles upriver in Hudson, New York, than stay in New York City.[10]

It has become almost fashionable for elder urban elites to proclaim the city finis.

At the same time, some cities have been warped by their own re-branded success, we've seen the failure of second- and third-tier cities to remake themselves in the long decades following their initial collapse. Combine the departure of entire job sectors (partly but not entirely because of digital), unattractive housing, loss of public transportation, insalubrious weather, and the automobile to account for the gutted cores of cities like Flint, Buffalo, Binghamton, Scranton, St. Louis, and beyond.

Digital now plays a role in shaping and possibly destroying the long-term viability of even the most precious urban landscapes. Digital delivers a form of instant gratification and instant "presence" no matter where you are—which means you don't have to be "there" (or anywhere in particular) to meaningfully participate in what we once might have called "the fabric of urban life."

Serendipity, the happy happenstance of life heightened to an art in the best urban centers, has been increasingly diminished by digital. First, digital content, and ease of access to it via broadband, sophisticated software, and cloud computing, has at last become compelling enough to keep otherwise moderately adventurous types glued to their screens and off the streets. Binge-watching edgy television series on Netflix has become a rite of passage. And if you're on the couch watching *Orange Is the New Black*, you therefore are *not* out having sushi or a crafty cocktail in the company of like-minded strangers.

BATTLE OF THE CREATIVES

Instant virtuality, the same kind that saved us from the cubicle, has also made it unnecessary to *be* anywhere while working on a creative project (except perhaps for the digital film-shoot itself, increasingly [it seems to me] with action taking place against an urban backdrop meant to telegraph authenticity). Collaborative tools allow "workflows" to be shared across the globe,[11] and input can be logged and utilized from remote stations in a way that certainly seems astonishing enough to be "cool." For instance, an independent film community site like Stage32 can help a producer put together a team on different continents: a film editor in Mongolia, a sound guy in Halifax, a writer in Mid-Wilshire, and everyone Skypes. Adobe's Creative Cloud integrates entire categories of creative tools into a single-sign-on experience where one can "rent" (but can no longer "own") powerful digital creative tools like Photoshop, InDesign, and Illustrator, while allowing one to plug in digital analytics and data collection management at the same time. All of these sharing tasks can be accomplished from anywhere with a broadband connection, and the difference between that capability and the former need to be in the studio with your team in a fascinating urban landscape can hardly be overstated.

The cost of this radical change is high and the impact immediate. Gone is the geo-located community of creatives. Their tethers are now less substantial than ever and increasingly reliant on the largesse or the whims of publicly traded software or "cloud" companies that care not at all about the creatives but only about their bottom line (as well they should, lest their officers be sued by shareholders for bailing on mandated fiduciary responsibilities). Where once the bonds between the creative teams that drove urban culture were unbreakable due to proximity, they are now not much more sturdy than a moderately faint signal emanating from a wireless router. All it would take to destroy a project (or entirely disrupt a virtual "community") would be a prolonged denial-of-service attack, a change in ever-impossible-to-comprehend terms of service, a rainstorm in the mighty cloud, or any of a number of factors where *control of one's creative environment* has been almost entirely ceded to the *dictat* of the software giant.

We must also take into account the way in which the life of the creative type has been utterly disrupted by digital and only in a very, very few ways improved. Yes, the new creative loves the white, bitten apple and often is tuned in to the latest social media venue. But their actual ability to earn a nickel from their pursuits has been robbed. This ability to earn money on creative output has been much diminished by the actions of certain massive companies that deploy what is called "content aggregation" but which too often really amounts to unpunished copyright infringement. The ability to make money in the creative fields, ever fragile even in the best of times, has been diminished by the notion that while "content is king," it hardly matters *which* content, but just that there are areas of the browser screen (or mobile app) that have something or other on it such that the button we want to click is not the only thing on the page. Sadly, this characterizes, based on my own very unscientific survey, what passes for "content" on all too many sites on the web or mobile.

Writers of quality have no call on the publisher when persistent and (often) language-challenged bloggers can fill the same column inches with ill-constructed blather—minus payment. Media-critical cynics may have turned out to be right after all, insofar as the great volume of content available seems, in my opinion at least, to guarantee its mediocrity.

The public cannot be left blameless. Enabled by search engines and the ad-supported networks of content thieves,[12] the typical consumer happily reads or listens to or watches as much free stuff as he possibly can, and folks have become remarkably adept at gaming their way out of paying for any type of content they don't want to pay for.

Is it any surprise that the lives of creative people have been squeezed into the increasingly narrow interstices between high rent and diminishing sources of income? And that this ever-tightening grip is driving them out of town altogether?

I've already devoted a chapter to how musicians have been robbed. On a somewhat less dramatic scale, other creatives—often the pioneers of our urban landscapes—have also fallen on hard times at least partly due to digital. Journalism has been cudgeled in a manner described above. Filmmakers and documentarists are challenged to compete with random uploads on YouTube. And as the creatives often make up the best and most interesting part of the urban scene, they become the *rara avis* in a meadow of encroaching suburbanism in the urban core.

While we cannot blame gentrification itself on digital, we can see that its enabling technologies further weaken the need for community, drive increased pressure on cost (you can always hunt for entertainment that's either cheap or free online), and diminish the possibility for meaningful ownership of one's own creations, which, except for the plastic arts, are now almost always digital and easily appropriated by others.

MANIPULATED BY DIGITAL

Digital had at one time seemed as if it would improve our access to subjects we'd never otherwise have the facility to encounter. Who can forget the first time they went online and discovered they could browse the shelves of the British Library? We actually heard about these places from *other people.*

That was before the tyranny of the algorithm-perfected search engine. Before the great search powers like Google came to see their job as to guide us to what *they* think we want to see. According to an article by Graham Jones on the website business2community.com, if you "think you are making objective decisions . . . when you are using the web . . . think again [because] . . . you are being manipulated." Jones goes on to suggest that "Google is controlling your mind."[13] While this is almost certainly an exaggeration, it seems fairly plain that Google is controlling (or at least modeling) what you see in search-engine results.

In an earlier and more innocent encounter with digital, we might have hoped the sheer volume of data would give us breadth and depth unimagined in an era of paper and dog-eared pages. But digital is thin gruel compared to reality. We find much more of a random and enriching encounter walking down the street of any town or city—on any quest for goods or information that gets you off the couch. Random events find you in that place we still call "real life," and even today that type of real-world encounter—the narrow side street, the hidden curio shop—remains a compelling draw to the town or big city.

But inside your browser or your app, you're never going to see anything you've not been offered. The seduction that you are "searching" for something is pancaked by the fact that randomness is not part of any search engine's machinery. You are shown the expected choices only, and even in the best case, your choice is a purely digital choice. In no case do you walk into the Steppenwolf's Magic Theatre, nor do you interact as an entire being with any artifact you encounter in your search. Happy accidents, which often take place during physical searches, and which are more frequent in urban spaces than anywhere else, almost never take place in digital searches. In digital, the truly unexpected may forever elude you in lieu of targeted choices and pitches from sales organizations. At some point your world may shrink to the meager parameters outlined by the soulless *ordinateur* to which you have ceded your sovereign curiosity.

DIGITAL ESCAPE ROUTE

For many, digital offers escape from the mind-numbing banality of their prefabricated surroundings, and we can't blame computers for it. Many will argue that the American city, with its clutch of downtown shops and offices, died with the invention of the limited-access highway, and that, except for the top performers, these cities have been lingering in an undead state offering little except a tax burden to the surrounding counties to which their populations seem to have fled with almost manic alacrity. Digital cannot be blamed for the blinkered philosophies that led to ill-considered "empowerment zones," enclosed walkways, outsized traffic islands, potted plants, and so-called "street furniture" that was attempted during an abortive period of misconstrued modernism during the 1970s and 1980s.

Cities that fell victim to these tropes typically have little vitality left them anymore, and that is largely because they serve no discernible purpose, and certainly none that resembles what caused them to be built in the first place. Why, for instance, is there a Mansfield, Ohio (2000 population: about fifty thousand)? According to Ohio History Central, in 1888 "dozens of manufacturing businesses operated in the town, producing doors, brass objects, linseed oil, suspenders, paper boxes, and . . . cigars."[14] Today it seems a nice enough place, but in 2010 I spoke with a professor at the local branch of the state university who lamented that she could not sell her house for almost any price—she confided a fear that the home, not rundown, had, at least at that time, no market value. It may be argued that such a town exists today more out of habit than anything more economically or culturally dynamic.

For these places, digital, like the telephone and the television, becomes just another lifeline to a populace otherwise adrift in a sea of sameness and refuse, and it offers little incentive to fix up Main Street. There can be little question that the ability to order nice shoes on the web is a boon to anyone who must traverse nine miles of bad road to get near even a mediocre shoe store, and thus there is no emerging market for the local cobbler. Digital e-commerce has brought the era of easy-goods-to-the-prairie up to date. The world is delivered via UPS. You can be anywhere. Certainly it seems to matter less and less whether downtown thrives, when you can order exotic crystals from Shantung Province while reclining in your Barcalounger.

TOO MUCH OF A GOOD THING?

Yet even at the top of the urban pyramid, the great cities that seem now to thrive on digital culture are in fact being sapped. The drivers behind a generation-long reurbanization are receding. The flight this time is not to a leafy redoubt with a two-car garage, but rather to the even more tight-bound safety of a flatscreen. You cannot be harmed if you stay hidden behind your avatars in cyberspace, or at least not conventionally harmed.

Even in the great urban centers, an important emblem of inclusion is to be seen with a laptop at a cafe, with headphones and a cup of densely caffeinated beverage. The glassy look and screen-lit face have become *de rigueur* for the urban elite.

There's a place in Tribeca called Kaffe 1665 where it seems you might be asked to leave if you don't have a glowing white apple in front of you, and downstairs there's an inner sanctum that brings to mind a sort of digital opium den—it's dark and faintly mysterious, and the denizens are almost universally drowsy and equipped with a silvery laptop. It's as if they have all gone over to the modern-day equivalent of that bane of *fin de siècle* society, the "green faerie"[15]—under whose influence they might be painted by a latter-day Picasso, staring blind in the semi-dark, a small cup (and mobile device) before them and nothing going on inside.

There's a place in Tribeca . . . where it seems you might be asked to leave if you don't have a glowing white apple in front of you, and downstairs there's an inner sanctum that brings to mind a sort of digital opium den.

Walk down the main thoroughfare of almost any urban shopping district and you might expect to find the storied variety and ingenuity: the pipe store with all those meerschaums from Turkey; the hatter; the guy who perfected that cocktail everybody raves about. In many places you'll still find those things. But more likely you will find there what you found at the cynically manufactured mall: the pretzel kiosk, the national jewelry chain, the big box store, the store that sells sports regalia, the place where all the jeans and sweatshirts seem quite literally cut from the same cloth. And, of course, the bank branch.

GREAT (DIGITAL) EXPECTATIONS

Unique restaurants still thrive, but who knows for how long? Often they are like the mayflies of the urban landscape and are gone before you had a chance to try them out. And is it all just because the "rent is too damn high," as a recent New York City mayoral candidate insisted?[16] Or is it possible that "real experience" has already become such a specialized product that it is pricing itself out of common circulation? Perhaps just as bad in a different way, has digital had a role in creating expectations of ubiquity and conformity in the consumer in such a way as to destroy their healthy anticipation of anything new or different? E-commerce gurus have for years claimed that retailers "had better have the same experience at the store as on the web" and that "your website is the face of your small business."[17]

No less a person than Marc Andreessen, the founder of the first commercial browser (Netscape) and now a digital venture capitalist, has predicted that brick-and-mortar retail will die utterly not very long from now.[18] Perhaps he says so because he has skin in the game that it will die, rendering certain digital, e-commerce investments the more valuable. But there's a frightening sense that this may be in the cards, and that the results will be a new urban catastrophe.

THE DIGITAL TRIUMPH

When e-commerce fully triumphs, there will be no cunning shops, no big-box stores, no toggeries, no haberdashers, no wine shops, no malls, no movies, and perhaps no food markets except for a very few holdouts. And the urban elite will continue to stare at screens at cafes, interacting not at all with their fellows; the moms will arrange their small charges in their cushioned strollers while listening to a distant voice through earbuds; the entrepreneur will text his colleague in another time zone; the scent of fine coffee will continue to entice. But the essence of the old cafe, the notion that one might engage in conversation with a newfound friend, that one might relish a period of profound inefficiency, or pick up a stick of carbon and scratch it across a sheet made of wood pulp in an effort to create a likeness, or engage otherwise in a contemplative, even spiritually centered pursuit—these will be gone and shall be dimly recalled, much like the Library of Alexandria.[19]

What remains after the digital gutting of the urban scene will be the trappings. Not many will flee to the commutable split-level. Urbanites will stay in their lofts. They will, for a time at least, continue to perform efficiently as they generate value for the shareholders of whatever enterprise engages their talent. They will, for a time (but not indefinitely), go out to eat and drink and be merry. But they will be accompanied at all times by a tracking device in the form of a smartphone; they will be tethered to their digital life by invisible strands of streaming data; they will never be free of the demands of the job or their other distributed obligations. Original thought, stymied by a constant reminder that "the competition" is pulling incrementally ahead, becomes atrophied in an attempt to please the shareholders, or "the base," or even "the algorithm."

Worse, they may be unaware it was not ever thus.

Where the urban dweller is cocooned indoors with a tablet or mobile device, the dynamism of the actual city will have been destroyed. The urban rough-and-tumble, already diminished today by gentrification, will be eclipsed entirely by the allure of the frictionless encounter. Regional accents, long eroded by television, will disappear as people speak less often, and speak *much less* often to groups of people who grew up and live near them, and through whom a certain worldview is articulated in turns of phrase and sharpness of tongue. The desire to make real changes in the world, born of frustration with the vicissitudes of the urban jungle, will recede in the face of a desire to change merely the code base of an application.

But perhaps most important, digital will have destroyed urban life because the urbane, due to connectivity and collaborative technology, *will not have to be anywhere in particular* to be fully immersed in his or her community. The city is nothing if not a particular place. In a world increasingly virtual, the physical trappings are reduced to intriguing back-drops that might as well be part of a clever and well-rendered game.

REALITY GONE AMOK

We are witnessing the dawn of a technology called "augmented reality" (AR), as demonstrated by a product called Google Glass that, when worn as spectacles, introduces visual cues, data, and overlays upon the glasses themselves such that an "enhanced" version of "reality" is rendered for the wearer of said glasses.

Some digiterati today enjoy poking fun at those who wear these Google AR prototypes, calling them "Glassholes," but this won't last. As the data and the graphics become more and more stimulating, there's little doubt a new generation may adopt such augmentation as a natural extension of their perceptive selves much as we had long ago adopted such artifices as printing, radio, movies, and television.

The signal disruption of augmented reality is that it moves media intercession out into the constancy of the actual world. Where, even in an otherwise "natural" environment, the individual is no longer interacting with the physical space around him as much as the virtual amalgam created by the intersection of graphical information ("cool restaurant ten yards away!"), combined with data that may include facial recognition ("the man in the gabardine suit is a spy"[20]).

We've already seen hordes of empty-eyed commuters listening to voices via headphones in such a manner as to drown out auditory reality and ward off interpersonal contact. The eventual effect of disengagement with any *thing* (like one's surroundings) can often become a lack of caring about that thing—because it comes across as *incidental* rather than *essential* to the perceiving party. Augmented reality will take this notion and multiply it exponentially; not very long from now we can expect to see people walking about with headgear that obscures their eyes and ears and immerses them in an alternative reality only tangentially related to the one in which they find themselves physically. Engineering sophistication will eventually make the headgear less obtrusive and perhaps even imperceptible to the casual observer.

AR aficionados will navigate like the rest of us. But we will become icons on their inner screen. Life, for them, will begin to take on the characteristics of a massive video game. The lives and deaths and the welfare of those video icons (representing real people) will mean less and less to the user of augmented reality tools. And never mind that their every eye movement will be tracked and measured by someone, either in a digital marketing department or at a government agency. Wholesale disengagement with the actual town or city will become much more widespread than it is today, and urban life will be much poorer for it.

In a world overlaid with data *from somewhere else*, problems in the actual environment will be denigrated as less important than the trouble with a new version of software.

The undigital—lacking employable digital skills and linked to the rest of us only by an off-brand smartphone with a no-contract monthly plan—will be cast utterly adrift.

The city, fallen victim to the digital successes of its own creation, may begin to crumble as tax dollars falter, as fewer smart people need to be there and pay the price, and as more jobs become robotic. If this, or anything like it, comes to pass, then, just as the American city will seem to have gotten back its old mojo, digital, much as the automobile and the freeway did years ago, will have played a major role in destroying it once again.

9

OVERSHARING AND UNDERCOUNTING: DIGITAL IS DESTROYING RATIONAL DISCOURSE AND THE DEMOCRATIC PROCESS

Of late, the name "United States of America" seems to have become a misnomer. It is entirely possible that not since the Civil War era has the nation seen itself gripped by federal and state-level partisanship of such profound bitterness as we witness in the second term of the Obama administration. A salient example was the October 2013 "government shutdown" and near-default on American sovereign debt. Critics of the right say it was fueled by an ill-considered attempt by a small group of Tea Party acolytes to stop the government from operating, thereby taking down the world economy as a way of "defunding Obamacare."[1] Just one year later this already had come to seem a mindless farrago dimly recollected by even its perpetrators.

What role has digital played in the near-total breakdown of dialog and compromise that had for so long muddled us through the worst and the best of times in America? If digital allows legislators to send e-mails instead of engage in real-time discussion, to tweet instead of speak, and to participate in "dialogue" from afar—if they never sit down and have coffee in the commissary with their bitterest opponent—one might argue it has done a great deal of harm.

Of course, digital cannot be blamed for fueling many of the worst tendencies of anti-government nihilism, and these days that nihilism seems to come far more from the right than the left. Many will regard the nominally rightist Tea Party as less an organization and more of a rear-guard, scorched-earth tactical maneuver manned by an afflicted army of older, white Americans who wrongfully believe themselves the native blood of the land, and who perceive their crusade as a do-or-die attempt to rescue the nation from a multicultural horde of libertine layabouts. A more charitable assessment might suggest that they are merely living in the past.

But the charitable view is deconstructed by the argument that Tea Party adherents gain much of their strength through digital, and comparatively little strength through town criers with leather megaphones.

Digital has played a major role in the establishment of a so-called right-wing "echo chamber" characterized by self-reinforcing media permitting little, if any, competing data through its right-slanted sieve. It's true as well that traditional media outlets such as the arguably propagandistic Fox News, in league with right-wing "talk-radio" shows, have contributed to the single-minded mania exhibited by certain types of government-loathing extremists.

What's true for the red state denizens also applies to the blue. While not so much focused on getting yoga instructors elected to representative government, there are considerable cultural forces echoing to the "left" (although an old cabbage-and-pierogi socialist might never recognize it as having anything to do with "the left" of the twentieth century). There is a world of crystals, medicaments, shea butter, medieval-sounding decoctions, and energy channeling that finds expression in thousands of websites and online communities. Here the rigor of science is ignored as much as it is by the climate-change deniers at the other end of the political spectrum. In these precincts, one hears nary a voice to question "Is burdock root really a tonic, or is it more like a poison?"[2] People gulp the tea regardless.

But as much as digital has created blinkered communities among the kinder, gentler set, it is the bedrock technology of right-wing blogs that function, in risible fashion, as "original sources"[3] for generally incurious news organizations across the political spectrum. There are e-mail lists that blast out strident messages to a hungering audience; Facebook pages that foment virtual communities of like-minded politicos; and Twitter feeds that may seem to represent a cross section of the world, when more accurately they are just one flavor in the ambrosia of human experience.

In digital, everyone can be their own information curator. It allows the extremist (of any stripe) to construct an information cocoon that seems multidimensional, well populated, interconnected, and convincing, even as it might be utterly *un*connected to discourse not conducive to the presumed belief system. Via digital, even talk radio and television channels can stream to the most remote outpost via wireless and smartphone. Even the least connected humans can be logged in to a feed that finds them able to converse with other unconnected, untutored philosophical drifters, and often enough those who believe too much of what they ingest of finely honed and microtargeted media seem only to be looking for a hook to hang their political hat upon and somebody to blame for their lack.

At several dimensions of remove from the Tea Party, the Muslim extremist might as easily suffer from the same illusion of connectedness, dimensionality, popularity, and righteousness. How many bombers calling themselves "Islamists" have touted the Internet as their first entry into the catechisms of hate and destruction that characterize their activity? In 2014 a ghoulish gang called ISIS seemed to sting the world like a lightning-fast adder, with a so-called "social media strategy" that included posting actual beheadings on YouTube. Using both mobile and social channels, the black-hooded murderers reached out to no small number of Western-raised Muslims, even girls, who wanted to taste the danger, and they were able to entice many of these to leave the local food court and join them in an escapade of blood and pillage across Iraq and Syria.[4]

Digital can provide "reach" for the messenger and insulation for the recipient, and it can lend a false sense of coalescence to movements that are in fact small, fragmentary, and largely ignorant of fact. The extremist is free to construct a comforting chamber of custom news feeds comprising all of the voices that echo his or her suspicions, while enabling the total exclusion of news that doesn't fit.

THAT'S THE WAY IT WAS

In a less fragmented era, everyone "watched the news." It may have been largely pablum, and it may have been extensively subject to an implicit oversight serving the needs of a military-industrial propaganda machine, but it was, for the most part, uniform. A horrified nation watched at once as Walter Cronkite tearfully announced the death of President John F. Kennedy in 1963.

Network newscasters Eric Sevareid, David Brinkley, and latterly Tom Brokaw became trusted voices for all but the crankiest malcontents. They brought you the corporate-sanctioned view but also the occasional outlier or dissident, and there is no question that as mass media turned against the vicious folly in Southeast Asia we call Vietnam, it corroded the arguments to keep on killing and helped eventually bring an end to that tragedy.

In an era of mass media, many talk shows thrived on argument rather than reaffirmation. Conservative patrician William F. Buckley, as bright an intellectual light as the right has ever been able to claim, once in 1968 famously threatened to punch proto-liberal writer Gore Vidal for calling him a "crypto-Nazi" during a debate on national television.[5] Broadcast made it much harder generally to ignore a point of view not your own, because if you were going to watch the news, you were going to see whatever they were showing regardless of whether it matched the profile of your demographic.

Newspapers played their part in creating a cultural consensus, independent of whether this was a helpful or unhelpful construct. Everyone in Columbus, more or less, read the *Post-Dispatch*. The news was proscribed and shaped by a media elite, but, because our national roots are in free soil, it was never purely a propagandistic operation and there were always columns for muckrakers and naysayers. Controversy, even on the editorial pages, tended to sell newspapers.

But as we have noted already, "newsprint" is in desperate retreat almost everywhere.

We've not much discussed how digital is destroying television news, but television news, including cable news, is clearly eroding. Much of the news now comes from Internet sources that have supplanted reporting.[6] Fewer now watch any television, news or otherwise, than at any time in the past fifty years,[7] ostensibly as they switch to digital video snippets of cute cats, skateboard fails, massacres, and personally curated news feeds.

Digital permits the easy construction of one's own information bubble. Consider the amount of time the average digital citizen can spend with content on bookmarked websites, on Facebook with like-minded "friends," with Twitter followers, and, not to be forgotten, perusing the fairly inescapable e-mail lists that target the less sophisticated and generally older infonauts that populate the ranks of the politically conservative voter base. If you've ever been bombed with a much-forwarded list of aphorisms and barely disguised venom from Gramps, you can appreciate the extent to which the recipients of these digital circulars are held in thrall.

SLIVERS OF INFLUENCE

Digital is almost impossibly multifarious. Every splinter group, no matter how thin, gets its own website (or several) and, with a few deft content-management tricks, can be supplied with news sources and comment columns no less powerful in appearance than that of a major, well-funded publication. Many will call it the democratization of media, where the minority voice is loud and allowed. But the argument can also be made that digital has led to a Balkanization of ideas, and that our recent political and economic cliffhangers have, as a result, been rather too close in nature to the procession of Archduke Ferdinand through Sarajevo a century ago.

Digital has led to a Balkanization of ideas.

INFORMED ISOLATION

But loss of common cultural touchstones is not entirely due to self-selection. Some of it is due to targeting.

Not many Google searchers are as aware as they perhaps ought to be of the extent to which the search engine attempts to feed you what it believes are "relevant" results.[8] On the face of it, this sounds awfully convenient, even perhaps a bit flattering. "Personalized" search results can seem the digital equivalent of an especially intuitive research assistant who knows just which books will be most relevant to your argument. You say "Buneaux-Varilla," and he brings books not just about the Panama Canal but also about late nineteenth-century treaties in general and

Spanish-American political intrigue, and perhaps even treatises on yellow fever and transcontinental shipping.

Search engines want to do that, too.

Many people believe that search engines like Google, Yahoo!, and Bing (or at least the links they display) are the heart of the Internet. While their long-term impact can be debated, search engines have emerged as a near-indispensable component of digital information technology. When the 'net was still in swaddling, we all knew there were many, many more websites than we could possibly know about, and we could sense there was a decreasing likelihood that we could unlock the power of that information without knowing the addresses of these sites.

The earliest attempts at helping us navigate were actual *printed directories* of addresses that we could key into our browsers. On my bookshelf today is a curious volume called *A Guide to NYC's Silicon Alley*, published in the late 1990s *on paper*. It is full of company names, individual names, physical addresses, URLs, and e-mail addresses.

In a book called *Burn Rate*,[9] author Michael Wolff wrote that at some point in the early 1990s, his Internet company sold a list of e-mail addresses to a print media company for a fantastical sum because the buyer seemed to believe they were "buying the Internet." Such gross misconceptions about the power of lists were common those days among the overeager, uninitiated businesses that wanted in on the digital gold rush. Some would say the Wolffs of the world seemed only too happy to supply the gold-rush miners with blue jeans by the cartload.

The next attempt at providing a doorway into the digital dome were so-called "directories" that contained very long lists of links to subjects of every kind, and some of these became quite successful at providing linchpins for the languishing web hopeful. But most curated directories, since their upkeep required lots of (mostly unpaid) time and attention, became unwieldy and prone to rapid obsolescence as links "died" because the sites they led to had disappeared or changed addresses.

THE APOTHEOSIS OF SEARCH

Then, as the mythology comes down to us today, Jerry Yang and David Filo, a couple of students at Stanford, created a directory with a long, unwieldy name. They seemed not to take themselves too seriously and referred to themselves as "a couple of Yahoos" (after a race of sluggards in *Gulliver's Travels*). Soon the directory became algorithmic; by the mid-1990s, they had renamed their project, and Yahoo! had hit the big time. The Yahoo! engine would allow a person to type in a "keyword," and the engine, having been fueled by a database of links obtained by a digital "bot" that inspected and pulled data from as many websites as it could (referencing keywords in those sites), then linked keyword-relevant URLs correctly to a screen that would show search results. Yahoo! was the first globally popular search engine. Today it is still the second or third most popular site on the web, but well behind Google, which surpassed it at lightning speed in the twenty-first century.

The algorithm became the critical component of search. There were no "directories" until you asked for one, and it was now assembled for you "on the fly," as digital boosters like to say when something is being done by software very quickly.[10] And when you abandoned your search, the directory would cease to exist. It is possible that no two search directories of this kind have ever been identical.

Then came a company that seemed to specialize in giving away free software. Google, for a time, promulgated the tag line "Don't Be Evil." They don't talk about that anymore. And while Google did not invent "personalization," they brought it to a level of sophistication undreamt of prior. Ostensibly this effort was an attempt to provide more relevant search results, and, like Yahoo! and all other search engines, this wonderful service was provided for no money. Personalization would come to mean that at least some of the search results you saw were shown to you based on what you had searched for before. And then based on what sites you had visited. And then upon what you wrote about in your Gmail account.

Google, for a time, promulgated the tag line "Don't Be Evil." They don't talk about that anymore.

Google (along with Yahoo! and Bing) was sucking up all the data about you it could find. The fact that it took that data and sold it to advertisers is another subject entirely. In a darker manifestation, they also piped it to the NSA. But what concerns us here is that your search provider was not only most accommodating but also not very open to direct suggestion. Where you could tell your intuitive research assistant to stop making so many assumptions about what you wanted, the same could not be done easily with your search engine. The search engine shows you what it thinks you want to see, and there really is no way to change that.

Here is a case where you become trapped in your own information bubble. You're labeled in a manner unbeknownst to you, and you are fed results based at least in part on digital actions you've taken without realizing they might become part of your search profile. So when you type in the word "bacon," for instance, you might see recipes where your colleague might see health warnings—depending on your search profile. The current incarnation of this targeting mechanism includes what are called "suggestions" that purportedly save you keystrokes. If you type in a couple of letters, the search engine attempts to complete your search string from its massive database of possible requests. These suggestions are driven by somebody else's software deciding what to suggest, and they may in part be based on what you have already Googled. "Google," as we all know, is now a verb. This suggests how reflexive this activity has become and, further, how much we rely on it for delivering facts to us—almost never wondering why *those* facts and not other facts.

As this trend snowballs, it becomes entirely possible for biased users to stand a much smaller chance of seeing their assumptions challenged by data they had not expected to find. This is a far cry from going to a library or a bookstore and encountering books that say more than you were looking for on a given subject.

Serendipity, chance, and real-world exposure to new ideas are forsaken in the world of digital search. Your research assistant has become more than faintly authoritarian. You can ask for what you want, but you will receive only what's given. Worse, in an ad-infused online culture, your research assistant now emerges from behind an advertising billboard touting your favorite flavor of ice cream and gives you books that you are predetermined to see—and nothing else. Perhaps just as alarming, the results you see are often heavily influenced by intense "Search Engine Optimization" efforts by marketers to game the algorithm such that their results come up first. What you may believe to be an objective search for facts and truth is actually a sophisticated advertising gambit that combines targeting, pay-for-play, and sometimes exhaustive marketing efforts by content owners.

ISOLATION AND VIRTUAL VOTING

We may be tempted to suppress a smile when seeing pictures of voting that takes place in younger, less technological democracies, as citizens write down a name or place a preprinted card in a box and then ink their finger so they can vote just once. We imagine the vote counters smirking and puffing cigars as they crumple and toss votes belonging to the opposition candidate. It seems so easy to manipulate such primitive voting mechanisms! Not like our sacrosanct voting machines that are kept locked and guarded, and where tallies cannot easily be altered due to numerous fraud protections built into the hallowed vote-collection technology. Or at least this is what's comforting to believe.

New York City in 2013 hauled out its mothballed fleet of hulking steel voting machines for a mayoral primary[11] because the newer digital versions created "long lines and chaotic polling scenes in 2012, as well as problems producing complete election results." These camouflage-green bulwarks of democracy are like mini fortresses of electoral honesty, or at least they reek of probity and impregnability. They have levers and handles, and their bulk is frankly intimidating. Curtained off inside one of these, you survey the candidates, pull a lever, see a mechanically driven "x" appear next to that candidate's name (kind of like an old-time scoreboard), and hear a satisfying "clunk" that is the artifact of your decision. But that's not all! You can *un-pull* the lever and change your mind—ten times if you can stand the shouting of those behind you in line. And when you have done performing your duty, you take hold of a very substantial shank of steel bolted to a pivot at the bottom of the apparatus, and you yank it *hard* to actually record your vote.

There is no electricity involved in this method of voting. There is nothing virtual about your vote. The vote odometer is in there for real. Only a locksmith and a very serious and clever tamperer could successfully change those results undetected. Of course, there has been vote fraud in the past when these machines were near universal, and this was especially true in smaller elections, but the gears and levers inside them have over the years served democracy well.

Digital retires these clunkers like so many decommissioned turbo-props lying broken-winged in a desert scrapyard. In their place are not hanging chads but more likely some kind of scanning device or even a touch screen to record your voting intention. One might imagine that such a machine should generate a receipt just like a lowly cash register, but receipts are far from universal. According to an article in the *Stanford Report* in 2004, a local expert had called "electronic voting unreliable without receipt."[12]

Instead of that satisfying, vote-recording clunk that reported your vote using the old machine, the new, digital ones seem to do nothing. Your vote has been uploaded to the cloud—or saved on a flash drive. Your vote does not actually exist until an algorithm unpacks the voting file, decrypts it, and counts it electronically. The entire process is reliant on software. And the typical observer can have no meaningful way of ascertaining that any particular amount of votes were cast for any particular candidate. There is no record of the original voter intent outside "the code" and no way for a citizen to be assured by common sense or physical evidence that votes were properly counted. Anyone who is familiar with the many ways digital data can be corrupted by accident would have to be wary of digital vote-counting even if that were the only peril.[13]

The voting public must rely on the honesty of every person involved in the collection and counting of data. Many of these are entrusted with an essential responsibility based on nothing at all except that they work for a software company. The public further is forced to rely on a system that is much, much easier to hack and much more prone to secret tampering than a system composed largely of big, awkward machines that would need be broken into and, with a burglar's stealth and a watchmaker's precision, retabulated unit by unit.

With software, vote mistabulation can be planned in advance and be near-invisible to all but those intimately familiar not with voting or voting software, but rather with the very particular code associated with that particular vote-counting software. Often there are millions of lines of code, and hunting for a corrupting influence might be an almost insurmountable task[14] and certainly would not conform to the timeliness required in determining the results of a close election.

So when in 2004 the Republican-leaning Diebold company was said to have promised then-Ohio Attorney General Kenneth Blackwell (R-Ohio) that it would "deliver" the state in the 2004 presidential election, and when Diebold made the voting machines, and when the Ohio vote was close (and observed to be flawed) and then swung late for the Republican and decided the election in his favor, many suspected corruption. [15] The losing Kerry campaign may have known there was absolutely no way to actually count any votes, and some have speculated this led to his decision *not* to challenge the questionable Ohio results. He had no chads like Gore had in Florida 2000, hanging or otherwise. Diebold software was in play, and Diebold software was the beginning, middle, and end of voter clarity in the Ohio 2004 election.

Attributed to Groucho Marx is the illustrative question: "Who are you going to trust? Me or your own lying eyes?" Trusting that digital vote counting can be transparent and truly accountable is like that. No third party can verify honesty in digital voting. You are left only to trust Groucho.

MASS BALKANIZATION?

We've seen how digital facilitates ideological Balkanization. Of course, the Balkans were Balkanized before there was digital. They were emblematic of what was considered, in the mid-twentieth century, inexcusably backward. In addition to cultural atavism, they had no connectivity, electronic, physical, or otherwise—hence the insularity and infighting that characterized those nations in years past.

We have no such excuse, and digital has contributed to a form of ideological Balkanization such as we see today "from California to the New York island." [16] We have blown past the age of mass communication and its vapid sameness. We have moved to a new paradigm where every advertiser, rather than thinking in "big messages," now hopes for a one-to-one relationship with every prospect (even as this notion may well be nine-tenths blarney), and when communication can be both massive and unique at once, only mathematics and software can cope with the volume.

Much in digital's favor is the fact that the rapid dissemination of information to every corner of the globe makes it harder than before for secrets to be kept entirely from the populace. WikiLeaks and the downloads of Edward Snowden are powerful examples of the virality of classified information.

On the other hand, "the people" can no longer be counted on to agree upon any particular set of broad, well-supported facts. They are prone to falling in league with the proponents of cranky, easily accessed theories and half-truths that, by virtue of the power of electronic publishing, can seem (for some) every bit as legitimate and substantial as the front page of a highly regarded newspaper.

Digital has the power to empower the factional, and in a multicultural democracy this would seem an important consideration: You don't have to be mainstream to be in the news stream. Your small voice can be amplified to the whole world if the digital wind is right, and if your message is powerful enough. At least this has long been the idealistic claim of digitalists, and it may even be a real possibility. Factionalism already begins to undermine the nation's lead-footed two-party system, and if third and fourth parties ever become more than distractions, it will likely be at least partly on the strength of a digital backbone.

There is much good evidence digital has contributed to the fall of consensus. But it has also created a place for important new factions to organize and succeed without resorting to sly pseudo-facts or hectoring. Whether you have been a supporter of President Obama or not, it is difficult to deny that his campaigns deployed digital politicking early and often, and with obvious success. His ability to find every voter was facilitated by digital techniques. The communication of his message was accomplished largely through digital networking and voter micro-targeting.

But there are not enough examples of digital consensus-building in the real world. Instead, the memes that take hold (via Twitter, blogs, and YouTube, for example) are of belly-flops into the shallow pool; of forged birth certificates upon which hang the fate of the Union; of mythical "death panels" shanking Aunt Ethel in her wheelchair; of house cats in the commission of alarming misdeeds. We cannot blame digital for our own tendency to become buried in self-absorbed righteousness. Digital is a plow, and we are the planters.

The purposes to which digital has been put run the gamut. But too often (and, it seems, with increasing frequency), it becomes a tool to promote the narrow and damaging interests of prejudice and fear-mongering, and where accountability is needed, digital, as exemplified by the fungibility of votes that lack any physical trace, supplants trust with expediency. Sadly, it is also too often the tool of choice for those engaged in pursuits characterized not just by narrow obstinacy but also by broad dissemination. The manner in which digital has been put in service of an insistent, divisive cause leaves me wondering when we might see, if ever, a digitally driven mind expansion—when we might see digital contribute something more akin to evolution than to atomization.

10

BOOKS, BATH, AND BEYOND: DIGITAL IS DESTROYING RETAIL

We discovered something about ourselves we perhaps did not especially want to know with the advent of online bookselling—characterized primarily by Amazon. We discovered that, as much as we wanted to believe we were in love with the Little Corner Bookshop and its curmudgeonly owner, we were not *so* much in love that we would continue to buy books there at list price (or a few percent less) when those books could be had for much, much less at a place called "the browser" and delivered to a place called "the front door."

Our pocketbooks spoke loud, and the noise shattered the business model of the lovable bookstore and shuttered its welcoming portal forever. It turned out we were only too happy to forsake the comfy confines of the shop and the recommendations of a well-read proprietor for the algorithm that seemed to recommend (or at least facilitate) better than the human and his or her loving care for the subject matter—at what sometimes seemed (and sometimes was) an impossibly low[1] price.

Worse, we were happy to browse the actual books at the brick-and-mortar[2] shop and then, in shameless fashion, go and buy the book at the impossibly cheap discounted price offered by the online giant. In many cases, we opted for the e-book, which was *cheaper still* than having the paper book shipped; having done so, we were happy to tell ourselves that we were the greener for it. In a scenario like this, the borg has won big, and the carbon-based purveyor stands to have lost it all.

Recently a young digital entrepreneur in New York asked me when was the last time I bought something online that was *not* from Amazon. I had to think hard. I provided an answer that seemed accurate at the time, but in retrospect I recall now that the link to said retailer (of die-cast automobile models) had been found at the Big River of Small Boxes we call Amazon. The destruction of retail began with books, but it has rapidly grown to encompass pretty much everything. Business-to-business commerce is another matter and has also (d)evolved to a similar state but with different players and for different reasons.

I'm not here to bash Amazon, and I am a frequent customer of the same, but I am willing to use it as an example of the generally disseminated digital promise of superior value, as well as an example of digital's gnawing impact on the capillaries of commerce known as the stores in your neighborhood. For instance, how many neighborhood stores could operate while losing money the way Amazon typically loses money?

Shuttered storefronts suggest the answer is none. And while most people in the digital trades know the facts about Amazon's bottom line, few among the general public seem aware that Amazon continues to lose money every day even as its founder and CEO has become a billionaire. If you've been put out of business by Amazon, rest assured it was not because Amazon had figured out a model that actually worked. It is mainly because one of the most important goals for a company like Amazon was to put you out of business such that, eventually, it could control the entire market in your sector and force everyone else in the supply chain to play by its rules. In this model, the only way a company like Amazon ever repays dividends to its investors is by total domination, ultimately forcing providers to sell for less and buyers to pay more so that it makes money on what it sells (a heady concept in digital) rather than lose on every transaction.[3] Companies like Amazon thrive on the notion that investors will continue to have faith in its long-term plan to become either the sole provider or one of a very few providers in a given market sector (or "space," as digital entrepreneurs love to call them).[4] The long-range plan calls not for greater variety in the marketplace and more choice for the consumer, but rather for tight strictures on what you buy and where you buy it from.

THE SAD, STRANGE STORY OF INTERNET STARTUPS

Internet startups famously lose money in rapid fashion. It's an assumed part of the paradigm, and investors have called it "burn rate." Very few Internet startups ever become profitable, and nearly all that never become profitable close when the investors get tired of investing or when a buyer is found. Many of these startups today focus on the delivery of a service for free or nearly free (Snapchat, for instance, is a free messaging service). The goal, it would appear, is to get lots of people to use the service and collect their contact information for sale to marketers. And when the early investors want out, usually the buyer is interested not in the failing technology itself, but rather in the customer list.

The ultimate value of many failed digital companies lies in this so-called "customer base" (the one that was costing so much money to service with free technology). And, of course, the value of even a giant like Amazon is not its inventory or its distribution systems or its cloud services, but rather its *relationship with you as a customer*. The prevailing notion in the digital economy is that once a buy/sell relationship has been established with you, then, given the right parameters, almost anything can be sold to you through the same relationship.

The business model for digital profit assumes that one might achieve what is often referred to as "first mover" advantage, under which assumption the fact that one has entered the market before others and with overwhelming force makes it that much more difficult for a competitor to mount an effective counterattack. It also assumes that, after a time, the first mover will no longer need to subsidize its irresistibly low prices with investor cash. Once the field is deemed sufficiently cleared of consumer choice, and the first mover is more or less the only available source for the goods, then the prices are increased almost at will. The consumer, having played a part in immolating the rest of the market players, thus finds herself engulfed in the same conflagration where the crazy-cheap goods now begin to seem more and more unaffordable.

―――――――――――――――

The consumer, having played a part in immolating the rest of the market players, now finds herself engulfed in the same conflagration where the crazy-cheap goods now begin to seem more and more unaffordable.

―――――――――――――――

Arguably, this is the only meaningful endgame for a digital provider, but if there is a case where this has already succeeded as planned, I don't know of it. Failing the achievement of this goal (or actual profit), the digital provider will eventually run out of cash to burn, and it will disappear.

Digital enables the prospect of true market hegemony because *only via the global reach and ubiquity of digital* can the goal can be posited as even remotely achievable. According to this model, the final state is a market that has been blasted free of competitors and the one-to-one relationship with the customer becomes lopsided in favor of the digital provider.

In such a scenario, retail would be no exception to the rule.

SHOPS OF HORROR

How did the little shop on the corner become the little shop of horrors (for its owner)?

Many would rush to blame Amazon, but it is not Amazon's "fault" that the little shop became a horror—it's much more complicated than that. It's true that Amazon has played hardball against the competition and suppliers, but domination is never pretty as it's being prosecuted.[5]

Like most succeeding ventures, the Bezos juggernaut exploited significant weaknesses in the marketplace. In books, one might say that the business model was especially hidebound. Distribution models were arcane, and relationships were cozy. It was a multibillion-dollar industry that operated much more like an insider network than a business enterprise; in a demonstration of its relative insularity, the publishing firm Hachette only very recently adopted at its headquarters a format long ago adopted by almost every other type of company: that of the open floor plan and the cubicle.[6] Prior they had held to the now rather antiquated notion of offices where editors would do their work behind closed doors in a room not shared with others.

The explanation—not just about private offices but also about why publishing was different than other businesses—was always that products consisting almost entirely of intellectual property—such as books, which one might generously characterize as high-minded cultural events that defined the limits of an intellectual firmament—were just not the same as boxes of air-conditioners, and that there were qualities associated with books that were unquantifiable in typical business terms.

This may yet be true, but it relates much more to the writing and production of books, and very little to the merchandising and selling of bound paper with ink imprinted upon its pages. Still less does it relate to the distribution of e-books that have no physical presence whatsoever, are weightless, and which exist in a half-light between existence and the void. The physical manifestation of an e-book is thin indeed, consisting of the presence of electrical charges on an impulse-sensitive screen. Further, one does not really even "own" an e-book in certain business models; one merely rents the right to read it whenever one chooses, and on one device, as it were. Compared to the long-hallowed notion of book collecting (and the intoxicating allure of well-stocked bookshelves), there's not much romance in that.

RETAIL MYTHOLOGY

In order to understand the impact of digital on retail, we need to decommission certain myths about "art" and "being different" and "personal service" and "extensive knowledge" and about "being known and recognized." We can begin with books, because this was the first notable industry that fell not to nonpayment (like music), but rather to a *diversion* of payment from the local retailer to a massive, global, cash-negative effort to become the sole supplier of goods in its market.

How did the little retailer lose so utterly? Didn't we love little bookstores? Didn't we also kind of love bigger bookstores?

WHERE ARE THE WOMRATH'S OF YESTERYEAR?

What became of Womrath's, and Brentano's, and the enormous Coliseum Books in Midtown Manhattan? Gone to the harvest of unsustainable businesses. Today it is not uncommon for some communities to have no bookstore at all. Recently the City of New York had to step in to avoid closure of a Barnes & Noble in the Bronx's vast Co-op City, the only such store in a borough of well over a million residents. The Strand, on Broadway and 12th Street in New York, survives because it sells used books in the main, because it is enormous, and because it is pretty much the last of its kind in a city in love with the written word. We know what happened to Borders—the market-watchers blame its demise on poor decisions in real estate. Barnes & Noble expanded mightily only to find itself with a sucking wound where its Nook had hoped to thrive and, as noted above, is continuing to close stores quite noticeably.

Digital may not be at fault where a large bookseller has been unable to compete in a changing environment; instead, digital provided a new way of doing business that doomed those who cared not to try it out in earnest. The demise of the legendary Gotham Book Mart on West 47th Street in Manhattan was more a tale of real estate, questionable business decisions, and a general decay in the literary community that supported it—although some have argued that Gotham's (hardly unique) inability to make in-roads into digital bookselling must have played a role. Gotham had a sign that said "Wise Men Fish Here," and it was the bookstore *nonpareil* for the New York literary set from before World War II up until sometime in the 1970s. It survived into the early 2000s on a block that had been given over entirely by that time to jewelry merchants and gold buyers. This made for an incongruous sideshow on the way to the storied bookstore.

According to an article in the *New York Times*,[7] Gotham, looking for a more affordable storefront, moved into a nearby space on New York's East 46th Street where the landlord wanted to "save the Gotham." Then it turned out they could not pay the rent, which amounted to some $51,000 per month. Their collection of first editions and memorabilia was then bought by the landlords and later donated to Penn State, where it resides today as an academic resource. Might they have been saved had they "gone digital"? Nothing is certain, though it's safe to say they could not have done worse if they had.

MOM AND POP: NOT SO HOT

Many another smaller bookstore failed not just because it was inefficient and unwilling to see that there was an existential threat bursting forth in browsers worldwide. Here again, I don't want to lay heavy blows against neighborhood bookstore owners as a class. They had been as beleaguered as any small business owner and can be forgiven for not having had time to picture the big picture. The thrust of this argument is going to be more about how we try to escape from external versions of ourselves than it is about technology.

Let's call the non-chain bookstore, in general, a "mom-and-pop" outfit.

The mom-and-pop model connotes individuality and what probably amounts to some version of the so-called "small-town virtues" that seem to hold tremendous appeal to Americans generally. Among these virtues are friendliness, accountability, flexibility, local knowledge, recognition, and, perhaps most important, trust. And fine virtues they may be.

But one of the reasons the smaller retailer will have failed in selling what amounts to a mass-market good like a book is that they were too often *not especially good at it.* Also, I can report that, at least in my own limited experience, the local retailer tended to be rather unappealing in many ways. By turns suspicious, petty, arrogant, over-chatty, studiously quiet, and sometimes downright nasty, they would rarely embody the virtues we would prefer to ascribe to their benefit.

How often have you hesitated before going into a small shop for fear the owner would talk to you? It sounds mad, considering how we claim to value human contact, but talk to any number of local shoppers and they will tell you they have done so, and that they actually leave when approached by the owner or sales clerk. Certainly there's the fear of being gently coerced into buying something you don't really want; the cloying sense that you are being asked to contribute to a retail-survival fund against your will; or the suspicion that what the proprietor really wants is to talk or gossip or harangue. None of which sounds like a particularly good shopping experience.

How often have you hesitated before going into a small shop for fear the owner would talk to you?

So we have gravitated toward an Amazon because it is absolutely unlike that in every respect. Like many activities on the web (or mobile), it's relatively anonymous, or at least faceless, and there is neither pride nor guilt involved in any aspect of the transaction. We have discovered that what we really wanted was the book, not the bookseller. In fact, what we may have discovered is that we really didn't so much like the book-seller after all. That the scrimmage around the bookshelf and the cash register was really rather unpleasant and felt, in a way, just a little grimy, and the smaller the shop, the grimier and more uncomfortable.

Online retail saves us from the sweat and tears associated with our involvement with fellow sufferers. This is a powerful and overlooked strength of digital. It's why digital at its best is called "frictionless," because the friction is us. Ultimately, we would seem to desire a universe in which only we exist and in which every other thing in the universe serves our purpose. Right now, the frictionless domain of digital seems to provide an experience much closer to that than we might care to admit.

RETAIL FAILS

Despite their well-laid plans to put everyone else out of business, we cannot blame the Amazons of the world for the diminished state of retail today. Certain large retail operations just seem as if they cannot do anything right. A recent famous example is the department store JCPenney, an old but not very enviable name in retail that found itself with hundreds of underperforming locations catering generally to a price-conscious, not to say downscale, clientele. One day the CEO decided they would do away with the pesky and confusing gimmick referred to as a "sale."

The reasoning was that JCPenney would benefit if it could successfully make way upon the virtuous and common-sense path of having reasonable prices all the time. No "sales" necessary.

And who wouldn't want that?

Apparently customers didn't.

Sales dropped without "sales." It turned out buyers wanted to feel like they were craftier than they really were by "taking advantage" of sale prices, and they wanted to feel like they had a hand in their own economy by clipping coupons. Shoppers didn't find it especially appealing to engage in an honest exchange of goods. With sales plummeting, JCPenney went back to having sales just like everyone else. But according to its (public company) balance sheet, the company still has not figured out a way to make a success of the aging, irresolute brand itself.[8]

Digital commerce brands never have to deal with crudely constructed sales and specials unless they really want to. Instead, they are more likely to rely on widely available personalization and "retargeting" tools that seek to put the right offer in front of the right person at the right time. Digital commerce can change prices on the fly and offer different prices to different shoppers without any shopper knowing they're not paying the same price as the shopper down the block. At the same time, hybrid digital commerce companies (regular retail brands with websites) are told by digital retail advisers that they must offer price parity at the website and physical store.

At a recent marketing conference, one speaker noted that her grandmother "had better not be confronted with a different price at the store than she had seen online." It's almost as if the digital side sees the brick-and-mortar side of the same company as a burden that forces them to carry over certain unhelpful retail chestnuts like floor space and window displays and price tags and cashiers. In this paradigm, the digital-only retailer has tangible advantages over the tangible assets (liabilities) of the hybrid. Not only is its cost structure much less dependent on real estate acumen, but it's also unshackled from the need to coordinate anything between two vastly different operations.

AN "ONLINE" RETAILER OF
THE NINETEENTH CENTURY

Perhaps the most baffling failure of a brick-and-mortar giant in the age of digital is that represented by the still-estimable Sears. For those who do not know their retailing history, Sears got its start by supplying the frontier with all the comforts of home during the last quarter of the nineteenth century. Out of its massive warehouses in Chicago, Sears sent everything from petticoats to kerosene cookstoves to horse-drawn carriages to udder unguents out into the far reaches of what was then the rough-hewn American West.

Sears published, in an age when printed photography was prohibitively expensive, elaborately engraved and almost comically overdescriptive catalogs every year, and these were sent out among the millions at small, undercommercialized outposts on the plains, in the mountains, by rivers and glens and lakes, and in the depths of the forest. Deploying the resources of a growing transportation network and a good many intrepid carriers, the company sold, often on credit and with a generous return

policy, an unmatched variety of goods to a vast number of eager consumers out in the hinterlands. For many, Sears was the only source of
manufactured goods, even if its warehouse was as much as a thousand
miles distant.

This was the first instance of a major retail concern that created a
distribution system not reliant on pedestrians walking into a building
stacked with inventory. Except for the fact that it had no website, Sears
might as well have been digital. Everything was the same as a digital
retailer except for the servers and the html and the algorithms. Sears was
tremendous in its salad days and became one of the biggest retailers in the
world. Then, one day when the West was won, Sears decided to open
department stores across the land. And it became mighty in the realm of
mass merchandising, with locations in every municipality north of the
Mexican border and several to the south. As recently as the 1970s the
company was confident enough to build the nation's tallest skyscraper,
aptly named the Sears Tower, in Chicago. (It is now called the Willis
Tower after the real estate firm that bought it several years ago.)

Time has not been especially kind to Sears and its under-patronized
department stores. Today the big retail outlets are undistinguished, disor-
ganized emporiums where you can buy jewelry or hammers or children's
snow boots or earth-moving equipment just as you might have if you'd
been a prairie-bound shopper in 1891, and (based on my own visits to
Sears locations) said items are arranged often enough in a cheek-by-jowl
fashion that can at times seem either confusing or unsettling, depending
on the mix. For instance, it does not sit well to see the blades of a snow-
blower nearly touching the scarves and mittens meant for little ones to
play in the snow, but thus they might be arranged at Sears. Conversely,
digital retailers never need worry about some of the thornier challenges of
what is called "merchandising"—the propitious placement of goods in a
physical environment. The uncanny juxtapositions described above have
no equivalent in digital, though some have complained that digitally driv-
en "suggestions" can also be incongruous and even bizarre. Perhaps
worse is the manner in which Sears has attempted to incorporate digital
into its retail experience—a story in *CIO Journal* describes a harrowing
attempt to buy an exercise machine at Sears involving iPads, Bluetooth
pairings, disconnects, and frustration. [9]

But perhaps the most ironic factor in the failure of Sears in an age of
digital retail is that at one time it had *the same business model as a digital*

seller. More than a century ago, Sears created an online retail giant that happened to use paper and ink and coal and steam instead of silicon and electrons as a means of exchanging goods and information between distant locations. Today digital retailers still rely on petroleum products and rubber and steel to deliver the goods, and this part of the operation has progressed but little since the day of the Iron Horse.

But in the new dawn of digital, the institutional memory at Sears did not persist. It was not even the same Sears, Roebuck and Company of fame; now it was a hedge-fund polymorph called Sears Holdings. By the time digital allowed a rebirth of the catalog era, Sears considered its retail self a department store, not a catalog merchant.

It's questionable whether Sears can survive another downturn. Perhaps it ought to have gone digital when it could—but the catalog-centric Sears of yesteryear had already died and could not be reanimated for digital.

RETAIL HATING RETAIL

Sometime in the mid-1990s, retailers suffered a crisis of confidence that seems quaint in retrospect, considering the fact they ended up fiercely challenged by a robot competitor they could not have foreseen.

By 1994, retail had determined that retail was flagging. Year-over-year numbers for existing stores were troubling; chains were already ubiquitous. There seemed nowhere to expand. But what caused the rending of garments in the garment trade was the sense—based on research and a general sense of malaise—that people just didn't so much like shopping any more. Consumerism for the sake of consumerism seemed to have run its course. A population that had grown up on newness and freshness and planned obsolescence seemed to be tiring of the game, and many claimed they just didn't want to drive to the mall, park a half-mile from the store, trudge through slush, get ignored by bored shopgirls, pay too much, and lug the whole mess back to the car in bags for the long trip back home.

What was retail to do?

They tried specialty stores, because department stores were tanking. They surrendered to the proliferation of outlet malls, where elite brands would offer cut-rate goods in a Potemkin "town center" setting not far from a major population. They tried boosting private labels that would yield higher profit. They talked about focusing on service. And then came digital sneaking around like a pack of alien gremlins at the cash register; and digital grew into an earth-moving machine rasping away at the walls and foundations; and at last retail stopped talking about obscurantist issues like "rack appeal" as it was forced to deal with digital competitors that threatened to empty the mall out for good and all.

None of the big retailers present in the market during the decade of the 1990s turned out to have had anything much to do with the digital revolution. Instead, they watched and waited (Macy's, Saks, Sears, Nordstrom, Dillard's, and so on) as brand-new digital shopping centers started taking huge bites out of their already-riven hides in the late 1990s and on into the twenty-first century. Since having gotten a late start, many of these have invested heavily in digital and can boast significant online sales. But their hesitation suggests they missed out on the chance to dominate a new market that left them playing catch-up. While it's true that there's a reasonably successful Macys.com and a Walmart.com and a Gap.com, these are undeniably second- and third-tier players in a market they ought to have dominated.

DIGITAL SHARE OF THE WALLET

Internet retail in 2013 grew in the US by 13 percent, according to an article on Mashable citing a report published by Forrester, a company that tracks the digital economy. US digital shoppers spent $262 billion during this time, according to the same source. In Europe, it's up over 14 percent. By 2017, digital commerce will be fully 10 percent of all consumer spending in the US, and after that it becomes harder to predict. According to the same Forrester report, "Online retail's growth will outpace that of physical retail stores. . . . As a result, stores will continue to lose wallet share to web retailers."[10]

Statements like the above are likely to keep retail executives awake at night. There's only so much money in the national wallet. Losing share of the wallet is a rolling disaster for retailers, and happy news for digital.

In a 2013 ZDNet article about how digital will make malls into ghost towns,[11] author Jason Perlow says that in more than two hundred US shopping malls, vacancy rates exceed 34 percent, and that big-box retailers, with a large amount of mall exposure, are seeing sales decline at their locations. At the same time, he says, they must rent expensive retail space in a place with declining foot traffic.

Digital wins this battle also. Because digital is in fact made up of electrons and has no actual physical presence except for a herd of servers off in buffalo country somewhere (and warehouses in even cheaper places), they not only have very low fixed costs but also are not anchored to an anchor store in a mall already adrift. They can shift and change with market needs, can more easily survive downturns, can change their offerings in a more agile fashion, and never need worry about whether a real estate decision will go sour.

Perhaps most important, they don't even have to make a profit. They can lose money and still destroy traditional retail. Because they cast the magic fairy dust of digital before the eyes of eager investors; because they can with at least some sincerity say that they hope to totally dominate a market (with digital ubiquity, it's actually possible); because they can raise money in the public markets where traditional retailers are just hoping to survive another bad Christmas—because of all these reasons and more, digital is destroying more than just bookstores, record stores, any number of mom-and-pop shops, photography stores, copy shops, electronics stores, shoe stores, art stores, stationery stores, and toy stores. It's also destroying major retailers that, as a rule, were already struggling with the retail troubles that started in the 1990s.

No, your major shopping districts are not going to disappear in a puff of html. Despite everything, people still like to see and be seen in the places where people get seen shopping. Midtown Manhattan, Union Square in San Francisco, Chicago's Near North Side, and the Mall at Short Hills in Paramus, New Jersey, are not going to wither and wilt. As always, the very strong and the very special will survive and prosper. But these are the outliers. They are the 5 percent who excel and succeed despite market conditions.

But what about the countless half-empty strip malls across the land? The toothless downtowns where retail got started, left, came back, and left again? And what about their digital competition that ships right to your door and doesn't need to make a profit (for now)? Can all these retail environments wait it out until one day Jeff Bezos gets the unlikely call from the investment bankers that this is the year they have to turn a profit or the whole affair goes kablooey? In all likelihood, they cannot.

My prediction is that one day in the not very distant future, as a new generation matures having shopped online from day one, digital will account for more than 30 percent of all retail in the United States. The physical retail landscape will look very different then. There will be a few big-box survivors and a few specialty stores and lots of restaurants and the usual amount of supermarkets. But the millions of stores with little distinction, both large and small, will have laid down their burdens and come to rest in a quiet dust. And digital commerce will be much more the norm than the exception.

11

B2B AND THE PERILS OF FREEMIUM: DIGITAL IS DESTROYING THE BUSINESS-TO-BUSINESS MARKET FOR DIGITAL

Business-to-business (B2B) commerce is a world apart from business-to-consumer (B2C) commerce, as they are both known in digital. B2C is anything where a business is selling to a non-business. B2B is where business sells to another business, and, in digital, this can often mean smaller software companies peddling their digital wares to large enterprises and medium-sized businesses that are larger than the digital vendor. I've been involved in digital business-to-business sales and marketing for over twenty years, and much of this chapter is based on my own personal observations.

Google, Facebook, Microsoft, and Amazon (among others) are large enough to "make their own weather" and are largely immune to many of the perils described hereunder. But apart from these top-tier, very large digital product companies, the rest nearly all play a rather desperate game of one-upmanship and product positioning that often baffles the practitioner (buyer of digital products) at the target companies. Despite this, software vendors persist in engaging in purely dialectical ways to differentiate their products even when their products are unremarkable and not very different from several others in the market.

One of the ways they try to win market share is by giving stuff away, a practice sometimes referred to as the "freemium" model.[1] It's a one-step-ahead-of-the-hangman strategy, and they're forced to play because it's so very difficult to get anyone's attention, and harder still to get them to pay.

As far as I can tell, this model exists only in digital, and to date it has not affected industries like, for instance, dairy or exercise machines.

"Freemium" is a concept that somewhat resembles practices we've heard about in the heroin trade. First, you give the user a little taste. Then a bigger taste. Then, after they're hooked, you make them pay and pay. The only real trouble here is that digital products don't create anything like cravings on the part of the buyer, and, except for very rare occasions, there really is no "addiction." Still, digital (software) vendors in the B2B space like to think there is. They even use some of the phraseology we often associate with the underworld: for instance, they want to get the "user" "hooked" into a subscription model to their software. While the notion of getting a big company addicted to any particular solution is nearly fanciful, it does sometimes bear out when organizations review the cost of migrating from one platform to another and decide not to. Often enough, the organization pressures the vendor for steep discounts in order to keep the software, usually with no change whatsoever in the value received. Price is eminently fungible. The most important factor is to keep the customer at almost any cost.

"Freemium" is a concept that somewhat resembles practices . . . in the heroin trade.

Once again we are encountering a theme that seems to replay itself in digital: that you don't have to pay for using something of value. In any other industry, this would be for the most part impossible to support (witness the paroxysms within the music industry). No investor in a company that sells actual wingnuts would consent to giving the wingnuts away—because it would make the wingnut seem worthless, and no one would ever pay for it once he got used to getting it free. Nor could such a company last long spending money making things and then giving them away at a substantial loss. But the peculiar characteristics of digital make this possible, if inadvisable for most.

First, because digital investors are so very much interested in a "home run" where their investment eventually pays off a hundred-fold, they tend to allow digital vendors a long time in the batter's box. They will fund what in any other industry would be considered astounding losses and support dreadful balance sheets—until they won't. Then suddenly an under-funded company cuts staff, marketing, and service, and in the meantime it tries to look busy; frequently it talks about "focusing on core strengths" and being "all about growth." But this kind of activity is often called "circling the drain," and the outcome is usually certain.

Second, because once the money is sunk in developing the software, there is very little cost in allowing people to *use* the software. One of the most attractive things about digital wares is that they are endlessly replicable without any expenditure in materials whatsoever. Software that really catches on becomes a cash cow unlike any other property except perhaps a hit movie or a hit album in the days when people made hit albums. Most of the sunk cost is development. "Sunk cost" is another way of referring to money that had to be spent in order to have a product in the market, and it gets spent regardless of a customer base. Often, to establish a customer base, the software is then given away at no appreciable cost to the vendor and zero cost to the prospect or customer (there are operating costs to the vendor, of course, but they are not related to making software products).

This in itself is a ruinous tendency and speaks to both the desperation of vendors in a crowded space and investor expectation of vast profits to be had if the software becomes a "hit." So they look to build "footprint" and "market share" by giving away the goods so they can establish those critical buy/sell relationships we talked about earlier, hoping to later leverage those relationships into an exchange of real dollars once the product is deemed essential by the customer.

There are other rationales for giving away valuable software. Above, we mentioned "footprint," a term that refers to the user base established by giving the product away. The plan, when successfully executed, finds a multitude of nonpaying users who then reach critical mass, thereby making the software an industry standard. Many of the users in this case might be technical early adopters such as coders and developers who build other software using the software. There is no shortage of software that "lives on top of" other software in a symbiotic, not to say parasitic, relationship; there is software that exists mainly to provide translation or gateway services between two larger software products. In this niche we find what are called "APIs" and "plug-ins" that, as the latter name suggests, are connective software that allow other, larger, more complex software products to "talk" to one another and exchange information. And in an interoperable digital world, these are in fact essential parts of the ecosystem.

Investor excitement, entrepreneurial optimism, and an all-or-nothing ethos makes for plenty of software giveaways. Even software vendors that charge money to enterprises often have "free" versions that can be used on a small scale, with exactly the same features but with scaling limits (for instance, a mailing list in a personalization product might be limited to a thousand names). This represents a classic version of the freemium model: it's free up to a certain size limitation, and then a premium version must be bought at scale. Most of the time this model fails, but there are companies (like Salesforce.com) that have made it work. Google has made it work with its analytics tool, but it's such a tiny part of Google's business that it hardly seems to matter. In any case, it certainly seems a boon to the small businessperson that so much free computational power has been made available, allowing him to enjoy the computing capabilities of all but the most sophisticated, customized corporate systems.

Sometimes, larger companies give away some products because they know it's a "gateway drug" to a more comprehensive relationship. Adobe, which offers a complete suite of marketing tools that play a role in everything from content creation to measurement and personalization, recently began offering a digital marketing "tag management" tool for free. Adobe has an aggressive sales team, and it's likely that you'll hear from them if you start using their free tool.

Thinly disguising yet another level of desperation in trying to get paid for your technical wizardry is the notion of "open-source" products.

In my opinion, open source is one of the best ideas digital has spawned. It's certainly not *always* used as a ruse to try and get paid later. Many wonderful products have been built using open source, or freely available and totally open-source code, and almost all of them cost nothing to use. For instance, I am writing this book using Apache OpenOffice,[2] for all the world a fully functioning replica of Microsoft Office except that it costs nothing at all. Apache asks for donations, and it makes good sense to contribute. But there are no licensing fees of any kind, and no profit margin fueling high cost.

The World Wide Web itself is an open-source gift to humankind almost as astonishing as the gift of oxygen from trees. That squatters like

Google and Facebook have made permanent camp on vast, free, resource-rich digital territories is part of a land-rush mentality that has remade the world already. If the old leftist screed that "property is theft" could ever have meaning in the modern world, then it might have meaning where a free, unregulated protocol became overburdened with very closely guarded and very lucrative monstrosities like some of the vast social media networks that dominate today.

Open source has some powerful adherents. In 2007, the European Union endorsed open-source protocols, saying it was cheaper to work in an open-source environment than to run products by the likes of Microsoft.[3]

But open-source tools have another incarnation, and this is similar in nature to the freemium model except there's never a premium version. One of the ill-kept secrets of the software vendor business is that while it's difficult to make money selling enterprise-level software, it is possible. And the reason it's possible is because such software can be devilishly difficult to set up and understand. Therefore the vendor can sell plenty of professional services *around* the software.

Minus the jargon, this means "Dear Customer, we will, for a considerable fee, send our technicians to help you set up and use the software we built and sold (or gave away) to you." A less-than-honest version of the sales pitch includes long-winded hosannahs to the complete and natural ease with which one buys and then deploys the tool almost as if it were a car with a push-button transmission, only for it to turn out that the product is really more like a box filled with semi-assembled automobile parts and a link to online instructions.

Metaphors used by vendors where customers have become unsatisfied with their inability to get the complex tool to function include "they took a Ferrari and crashed it into a tree," without mentioning that the Ferrari arrived on site in several pieces. To stretch the metaphor a bit, it would seem as if the customer was asked to assemble the Ferrari, did so incorrectly, and then, somehow, smashed it into a tree.

The enterprise software landscape is littered with these wrecks and customers trapped inside. It's also populated by roving bands of mechanics who either fix broken software or, in a more intelligent manner, oversee the construction and operation of the software from the beginning and throughout its entire lifespan at the customer. Customers, for the most part, cannot do without these teams of experts, as their own internal staff are typically too busy with parochial tasks and internal politics adequately to be trained in the software. Moreover, the vendor would not long survive without taking in the hefty fees associated with these services.

Another telling anomaly that, surprisingly, is glossed over in many vendor financial reports is the actual revenue percentage associated with software sales vs. professional services sales. Many companies want to be highly valued as software companies, but because so much of their revenue is generated out of professional services, they really ought to be valued at a much, much lower multiple of revenue. So a high percentage of vendors in the enterprise space actually misrepresent what their companies do. They talk about software all the time and never about unsexy services. But it's the hard-slogging services team that generates a large and persistent source of revenue for the company. In fact, many of these companies are less software developers than consulting firms dedicated to the deployment of their own complex, often half-baked software products.

Perhaps the saddest part of this story is that the vendors' professional services are too often not really dedicated to making the product work so much as getting it to function minimally, so as not to cause an end user to call the help desk with a question that might be hard to answer. No shortage of mediocre or sub-par software installations have resulted from misplaced trust in vendor-based professional services. The customer often is better off having gone to an independent consulting firm with no loyalty to any particular vendor and that did not pretend to be a software company,[4] but vendors work hard to keep the consulting dollar out of the hands of an independent who, in addition to getting paid in lieu of the software company, might actually recommend another, better product.

Here we have described the destruction of the notion that you pay for something and then use it. Digital has created a business-to-business system where customers are trained to expect free software at almost every level; where honest work must be hidden behind walls of subterfuge; where the very notion that valuable products ought to cost money is relegated to a shadowy Hall of Antiquated Practices. Some say it's mainly fueled by investors who will encourage their portfolio companies to give software away until they either put everyone else out of business or have to go bust themselves. In any case, it is held to be a basic tenet of what's often called "viral marketing."[5]

It has corrupted the business-to-business software market to a degree perhaps unknown in any other market sector. Certainly mining equipment is never given away to create "footprint." Skyscrapers are not sold as "complete" when really a team of specialists must forever crawl through the air ducts making sure an impossibly complex ventilation system is not going to explode or spew noxious gas into living quarters. Ask any businessperson in any sound business *not digital* whether they would either give away a full-blown, mature product or trust one that was offered, and the answer is likely to be a fairly incredulous "no."

Non-digital businesses continue to deal with real things in the physical world. There are fuel tanks and heavy objects and rain to contend with, as well as actual things that people know they need and can't have without buying them. Digital deals with the unseen, the unquantifiable, the forever-replicable, the shifting, almost quantum nature of information, and it seems few (if any) of the rules of typical, physical commerce actually apply. The ability to give away free stuff is seen as an asset and a cudgel to beat the competition. A more or less fallacious belief that having many zero-dollar customers is inevitably a gateway to riches seems to be the rule, not the exception. In fact, venture capital looks to well-defined formulas to "value" companies they call "pre-revenue."[6]

Digital hopefuls will continue to build value and then give their wares away as if they were trifles, as if these might be random by-products that happen to have been produced in pursuit of some larger, grander goal of no great clarity except as lit by the reflection from a mountain of gold. As long as this model persists, and as long as customers enjoy either impossibly low or nonexistent costs because of larger strategies being played out, digital will continue to play a self-immolating role in business-to-business commerce.

12

DIGITAL HAS DESTROYED AUTHORITARIAN RULE (OR HAS IT?)

When the Twitter feeds from Tahrir Square in Cairo started to flood mass-media outlets in the West during the spring of 2011,[1] it seemed as if digital had found a political voice as profound as it was disruptive. Here was a just and urgent cause married to personalized technologies in a way that forced the mighty to pay heed to the wishes of the many.

Twitter, an apparently trifling technology that allowed people to post 140-character comments, had prior seemed to be the domain of silly self-promoters, charlatans, pop stars, wiseacres, and no small number of social-media marketers trying to make their brands relevant to a younger crowd. There had been little to suggest it would have any lasting effect other than to become a repository of inconsequential utterances that were also riddled with truncated words, impenetrable #hashtags, and smug little affinity groups, many with a text-only equivalent of a secret handshake.

But where smartphones with built-in cameras, text messaging, and fast connectivity became weaponized by a new generation of activists, they helped cause a political conflagration as the disaffected met with the forces of a monolithic, repressive regime in the main square of the most populous city in the Arab world. During the Arab Spring of 2011, in Cairo, powered by digital, a new dimension of dissent and political activism was born.[2]

An opaque government that depended on truncheons, water cannons, cattle prods, and endemic corruption met the anger of a yearning, tech-born generation, and the tools that gave youth instant and transparent and universal communication. These tools made the usual, brutal retaliation an impossibility. The light from a thousand iPhones banished the shadows in which government thugs might crush the movement. The outcome was made with equal parts revolutionary fervor and handheld global communications devices—and resulted in the fall of a longstanding regime that had enjoyed the backing of the United States.

A . . . government that depended on truncheons . . . met the anger of a yearning, tech-born generation, and the tools that gave youth instant and transparent and universal communication.

Twitter gave the protesters a cheap and powerful communication capability that superseded the expensive and closely guarded apparatus of staid newsgathering organizations and showed the world what revolution looked like in real time. The dissidents were able to alert thousands to take to the streets, to gather, to instantly share logistical information, and to crowd-source a raw form of counterintelligence. They were able to mass in Cairo's central square and, by the sheer amount of tweets and pictures, force their way onto the front pages of mainstream newspapers across the world.

Twitter-powered transparency prevented the Mubarak regime from successfully implementing its torment and repression, depriving it of the shadow and silence required to break the back of the opposition. Under the glare of live tweets from the battle zone, the regime was forced to deal with dissidents as if it held them in some kind of esteem. The back-alley engagement with piano wire might be transformed into worldwide embarrassment by a teen and her smartphone,[3] and thus began the pressure upon a regime to give way to what it otherwise would have characterized an unprincipled mob. With its Mideast ally exposed as an engine of repression and misery, with Mubarak's ethics, economics, and politics thrown into sharp relief before the conscience of a more liberalized West, the US government was compelled to withdraw support. Shortly thereafter, the long-time head of state was forced to exchange the palace and his privilege for imprisonment on the coast of the Red Sea. Meanwhile, a new power took his place.

Unfortunately, in the absence of any truly mature opposition, that power happened to be the military. Despite the fact that the military would be somewhat amenable to entreaties from their official supporters in the free world, this was still the army, and this would still be a coup where the army took over. It is possible that digital provided too ready a platform for an untested movement and paraded it forward too fast, too soon. As of this writing, the situation in Egypt seems to have reverted to a predictable form—Mubarak has been freed and cleared of all charges, and nothing suggests the Arab Spring sprouted much more than a few small shoots in half-shadow.

The muddled aftermath of a giddy triumph did nothing to deny the communicative power of a worldwide network with millions of mobile nodes. But the notion that digital had fueled a lurch toward fairness and democracy in a benighted part of the world was, if not extinguished by later events, at least significantly blunted.

WIKI POWER

When Julian Assange's WikiLeaks exposed atrocities committed by US forces in Iraq and Afghanistan,[4] the West was also put on notice that state secrets of the most explosive kind were not to be kept hidden any longer. WikiLeaks had already exposed massive banking frauds and secret spy rings that the Western powers wanted to quash, and one could sense the power of WikiLeaks by the reaction of the West.

That their dirt had been flung out upon the flagstones so incensed the liberal governments of the West that they hounded Assange into exile. He took refuge in the Ecuadorian embassy in London, where presumably he remains today, resisting arrest on what many believe are trumped-up charges of sexual harassment out of Stockholm.[5]

Where professional politicians wanted to brand him a traitor and a crank, many journalists and activists wished to lionize him as a hero in the digital pantheon. And while Assange himself proved a polarizing figure, his WikiLeaks creation proved a serviceable harpoon through gaps in the armor of several heavily laden ships of state.

The motive power of WikiLeaks was twofold: First, Assange himself was driven to provide a way for those in possession of sensitive, anti-statist materials to deposit them in such a way that no one, not even Assange, would know their identity. He believed his work to be mission-ary. He was determined that sunlight should brighten some of the darkest crypts of the freedom-touting states in a way intended to challenge their hypocrisy.[6]

Second, he was also a skilled hacker, which is like saying he was a good marksman. But whether you approve of his steady aim or not, his exposures were made possible *only because of digital.* Deploying power-ful encryption techniques plus the immediate global reach of the Internet plus a serious intent to illuminate musty corners of the dungeon, he con-jured a thunderstorm that struck the castle dead-on and maybe knocked a few bricks off its crown. Minus the power of digital encryption paired with the perfect, universal availability of data posted on the web, he'd have been faxing entreaties to newspapers, which in all likelihood would have been ignored by professional editors, and he'd have remained the equivalent of a lonely crank handing out leaflets in an arcade.

Digital enabled him to punch through the newsprint barrier. He took full advantage of bedrock digital characteristics that once, with what now seems rather a vapid insouciance, had been touted by early web cham-pions: "Your website is visible to the entire world!" We now have proof that is certainly the case, especially if your website features video of American soldiers hunting civilians from a helicopter like so many elk in a winter cull.[7]

And what the world would come to know stood to shock the Western powers like nothing since the youth movement of the 1960s. Their dis-comfiture could be measured in the loudness and pitch of their condem-nations. Perhaps the great surprise is their surprise. It was as if these captains of mighty states could not imagine that web pages could unfold all their worst secrets to the world. The power and speed of digital, they may have imagined, would only be used to promote either commerce or whimsy or conventional politics (except where criminals preyed on the greedy and the ill informed). In no way did they seem to anticipate that digital would bite them in a sensitive spot, and that the bite would be applied by such a meager outfit. They failed to understand that with the digitization of documents, photographs, and videos, these artifacts were, in digital form, inherently laid open to the transportability of biased electrons and their attendant ones and zeros. They did not imagine how the essential technologies that had enabled such comprehensive documentation might be the same technologies used to expose the extent of some of their rather brazenly recorded atrocities.

I'm not here to sanctify Mr. Assange. But I do believe he showed how digital, in the hands of brave and resourceful men and women, could be used to make information into a fearsome battery against the gates of entrenched power.

There are, of course, opposing forces at work in this drama, and the outcome cannot be certain. First, a crowning irony must be found in that WikiLeaks required the exposure offered by a newspaper (*The Guardian UK*) to really make its mark. Second, no amount of digital guile or prowess could protect Assange from the corporeality of his relatively comfy but nonetheless real imprisonment in the London embassy of Ecuador. Perhaps because of the subsequent pressures put upon his enterprise, WikiLeaks today seems diminished.

A third and perhaps most troubling aspect of the WikiLeaks affair is that, while governments seemed to rattle and quiver in the data typhoon that blew in, the general public continued more bedazzled by their new tablet and 24/7 access to thousands of movies than they were eager to nose around the nether regions of their own national governments. Here, digital almost certainly provided a form of nullification to the truths blasted free by digital. The banality of the silliest new mobile app trumped any sense of outrage that might have lit fires beneath an earlier, perhaps more idealistic (or at least less distracted) generation.

I submit that whatever bubble was burst by WikiLeaks was soon healed by the comfort of knowing your friends were on Facebook and your paycheck was direct-deposited and your debit card was accepted everywhere and all was right with the world. Or at least not so wrong as to suggest that one ought to link arms and stand for the truth.

SNOWDEN AND THE NSA

But another digital disclosure proved even more unsettling than anything that came out of WikiLeaks, and this time it pitted both big companies and little people against their own American security state. I will discuss the security state and loss of privacy in a later chapter, but here we will examine whether Snowden has had any effect on the strain of authoritarianism that runs through American government and especially law enforcement and security organizations.

By all available evidence, Snowden's digital document drip has, as politicians and pundits might say, "moved the needle," at least in a national debate about the limits of government control. Indeed, it seems to have met up with some strange bedfellows on the right where we might have expected more of them on the left.

Government in general is not very popular in the United States today,[8] excepting that part comprising the military, which, in a fashion that defies small-government logic, continues to enjoy a level of support almost as if it were extra-governmental and not an oft-misused and very costly *instrument* of "big government." Fortunately for Snowden, and perhaps all of us, the revelations from the NSA were not about military misdeeds but about a domestic surveillance program truly shocking in scope.

Most of us probably know already that Snowden worked at a private security contractor, and that he had access to at least some of the massive amounts of data that were being collected about American citizens presumably in the cause of anti-terrorism. One day he walked out with a pocketful of digitized documents and sent a few of them to the newspapers. He also hightailed it to Hong Kong. What ensued was the biggest domestic spying fracas in decades.

Big data, fancy algorithms, and connectivity combined with the NSA's natural tendency to seek information about everything, all the time, to create an ever-growing repository of nothing less than near total data collection of all digital traffic in the US and beyond. The NSA's counterpart in the UK mirrored the effort.

Americans, who apparently had a mislaid trust in their government's respect for their privacy, were genuinely astonished to discover the extent of the program. Outside of the security community, the facts were taken very poorly. Obama was no help at all to those who spoke out against the intrusion, though later he offered some milquetoast concessions. Nor were liberal senators quick to condemn the program, even though it had already been shown that the program has not stopped any terrorist attacks.[9] The loudest critics in Congress happened to be right-wingers like Rand Paul, who, in typical libertarian fashion, decried the program as just another example of government intrusion even as he conflated it with the president's attempt to bring health insurance to the uninsured.

Snowden claims he has achieved his goal: he exposed the program. It would be up to the rest of us to make of it what we might. And as a result, there have been numerous attempts to investigate the program, to rein it in, to quash it, to end it, to alter it, to put on the brakes.

The end is not in sight; the program continues unabated at this point, and it's unclear whether anything will really change. But Snowden certainly created an atmosphere in which it would be much more difficult for the agency to carry on with business as usual. The press is very much concerned, as are many large digital companies that have expressed their dismay.[10] It is yet to be determined whether the technology giants are serious about their concern or merely posturing in a way designed to keep people sharing personal information at their current furious pace.

Besides, there is nothing yet to indicate that the NSA is slowing down its data collection. And each revelation seems to confirm more and deeper privacy invasions that cannot be reconciled with a constitutional right of protection from illegal search and seizure.

Snowden changed the game, but he may not, in the end, influence the outcome. All we have is so far is protest.

YOU DIDN'T NEED A WEATHERMAN TO EXPOSE COINTELPRO

In an interesting and possibly related turn of events, in early 2014 we heard from a certain middle-aged couple as they finally came forth with an old story of anti-spy activity. They revealed how in 1971 they raided an FBI office and obtained documents that proved the extent to which the government had in the 1960s and 1970s been spying on domestic political groups opposed to the war in Vietnam. This operation was referred to as "COINTELPRO," and the program specialized in FBI efforts to infiltrate and spy upon what were then called "anti-war" protest organizations. Targets ranged from the Black Panthers to local chapters of Grandmas Against the War, and often the unsuspecting groups were successfully undermined, if not outright destroyed.

John and Bonnie Raines can no longer be prosecuted for the break-in due to a statute of limitations. They said they wanted to come forward to reinforce the importance of exposing unwarranted domestic spying. Their story made its way to the front page of the *New York Times* in January 2014.[11]

When they exposed warrantless spying then, it contributed to years of congressional oversight and an end to the domestic spying operations for approximately a decade—until the Reagan revolution, which aimed to roll back the clock on almost everything that had been accomplished by the left in the previous twenty years.

The Raines, now in their sixties, said they'd undertaken the task of exposing the spy ring because "no one would believe it was happening until it was proven."[12] A picture of them, as they are today, shows an attractive, silver-haired couple in what looks like a tidy upper-middle-class setting that might have been the home of any one of a million educated baby-boomers now with grandchildren and all the accoutrements of a life well spent. It is hard to reconcile this picture of smiling, sincere oldsters with the radicalized firebrands they must have been when breaking the locks on an FBI office back when Nixon was in the White House. These were brave, dedicated people, and the cause of liberty owes them a debt of gratitude.

They had to use bolt cutters. Snowden needed only a flash drive.

Does the US today have the wherewithal to stop its government from spying on its own citizens in a way that at least one federal judge recently called "near Orwellian"?[13]

It's tough to say.

But digital allowed Snowden to take away tens of thousands of documents rather than a handful of manila folders, and many would agree that the vast majority of the docs he took have not been made public. We don't yet know what has not been revealed, but we suspect it's going to look ugly in a country that prides itself on what it likes to call "freedom."

Has digital made it impossible to maintain an authoritarian regime? Not quite, it seems. But we are interested to see what happens next.

13

OBSESSIVE COMPULSIVE: DIGITAL IS DESTROYING OUR WILL TO CREATE ANYTHING NOT DIGITAL

I have a pet theory that different periods of history foster the concentrations of great minds in different disciplines, and I include the theory here because I believe that today the "Great Minds" are focused on digital. Perhaps my review is just a thumbnail assessment of pop culture through the centuries, or perhaps there is some value in its premise. Distinct cultural eras are often coincident with the rise of some technology or power struggle, as these two factors have often been the most surefooted rungs by which humanity levers itself out of the tidal muck and on toward a habitable meadow.

Allow me to explain what I mean by "Great Minds." It's a way of referring to those people whose nonmilitary achievements have made their works known and acknowledged centuries after they lived and died, as well as categorizing some of these closer to our own age (where I am taking some liberties with the time-based formula). Among these we would include Plato, Giotto, Shakespeare, Einstein, Freud, and Bob Dylan. There are many others, of course, and quite a few of smaller bore than the aforementioned, but this is the general caliber of personage to which I refer.

My theory suggests that Great Minds, without necessarily communicating as such, seem collectively to sense where they can find the best methods to express insights that often turn out to be earth shaking. And what they say and what they do in the expression of these insights is not always good for the status quo.

Great Minds . . . seem collectively to sense where they can find the best methods to express insights that often turn out to be earth shaking.

A MINI-TOUR OF GREAT MINDS THROUGH THE AGES

Here are some examples of the different ages and their attendant stars— including some sense of how they are linked to the technologies and power struggles of their times.

In the Golden Age of Greece, where technology was almost nil, the Great Minds focused on thinking about thinking. Plato, Aristotle, Socrates, Anaxagoras, Pythagoras, Archimedes, and the rest of this illustrious crowd brought us the foundations of Western abstraction. We became aware of ourselves with them and have separated from our natural state sufficiently such as never even to contemplate a return to a pre-Platonic myopia.

Rome built an empire at least partly because the Romans had invented paved roads and aqueducts. Culturally, they relied on the Greeks for gods and at least the foundations of social organization. Roman philosophy is relatively insignificant, but, in keeping with the exigencies of empire, its body of law has provided the foundation for our own.

During the so-called Dark Ages, the anonymous Great Minds gravitated to the abbey. The abbey concentrated both technology (stone buildings, vellum, ink, binderies) and power. From here they more or less ran society with oak gall, lambskin, and the cross, and they tried to preserve what knowledge they could with scant resources.

The Renaissance brought a blossom of painting, sculpture, and architecture, each made possible by new technologies like fresco, pigmentation, excavation, and the rediscovery of the arch and dome, as well as such navigational aids as the astrolabe, the compass, and the telescope. We know their names well: Michelangelo, Da Vinci, Galileo, Bernini, and a long list of Italian superstars now widely heralded as examples of superior genius.

They focused on what the latest advances in technology allowed.

The fruits stand in Italy and beyond today, and the more portable examples hang in great halls of culture worldwide.

It was also the age of discovery for Europeans: Cabot, Columbus, Magellan, and later Verazzano and Hudson. In search of nothing less than a New World, they sailed in boats that represented the latest in man's ability to put wood in water and float toward the farthest shores.

Closer to our own age, we can observe that during the early part of the twentieth century, the Great Minds gravitated toward the visual arts. Picasso, Braque, Klee, and others combined superior traditional skills with new philosophies and new imagery influenced by artifacts brought to their shores by trade with the East and with Africa, enabling them to explode "art" as it had been known for centuries. They tore it down and made it new again, changing our perception of what we were and what was observable about life. Leading a similar movement, Freud, at the same time, deconstructed the human psyche.

We can also say that, for too long, technology and opportunity have focused a certain type of mind on war and destruction, and in their despotic hands, technology has been put to the devil's work. We have two world wars as proof.

By the 1960s, the Great Minds turned again to music: the technologies of electrified instruments, hi-fi recording, radio, mass distribution of plastic ware, and, later, pharmaceuticals, fueled a musical output the equal of any great cultural explosion in history. The names of Elvis and the Beatles and the Stones and Hendrix and the rest of the pantheon created a body of work that may never be equaled for its raw power and timely influence. In parallel, while a generation was electrified by music, another kind of Great Mind, using the most advanced technologies of the day, successfully planted human boots on an alien astral body we like to call the moon.

FOCUSING ON DIGITAL

Today, and for the past twenty years, the Great Minds, such as they are, have been focused on just one thing: digital.

But this time, it's different. Where once the Great Minds shone out from an era of many concurrent accomplishments at least partly due to the fact people did not really know what other people were doing, today the GMs seem *almost interconnected*, and they seem focused, every one, on trying to create the next Facebook. It's as if they are all coders or entrepreneurs. They seem bedazzled by the power of algorithms and the fortunes to be had by using them to create a crowd pleaser.

If we can summon the notion of Great Minds one more time, we can say that they are not, apparently, focused on pop music in 2014, or, according to abundant evidence, fine art, the subconscious, outer space, [1] law, or electricity. To suggest they might be in politics would be, on its face, ludicrous but for exceedingly rare exceptions. In any case, it seems those within the most exalted ring of intellects today are all orbiting a digital sun.

We've certainly seen our share of benefits from their attentions to digital. E-mail alone might have been the only invention of the digital age, and we'd all have reason to be more than grateful. But by and large, and increasingly as time goes on, what we see is controlled by better-funded outfits, and this is not necessarily tied to the ultimate importance of the technology.

Too many in digital today are focusing on narrow, not to say hair-splitting, projects examining minutiae. They're focused on the numbers. To the extent that they focus too much on numbers, they're not trying to solve any real problems or come up with new ways of seeing or thinking.

Numbers guys are not inventors. I should know, because I have spent much of a professional life being a numbers guy in digital analytics. But I think of myself much more as a non-numbers guy, more in tune as an organism with analog.

If output is evidence of the efforts of us digital marketers, they are focused, for the most part, on deploying digital techniques to parlay trivial pursuits into billions of dollars. [2] Today this phenomenon is called, generally, software.

They have in the past created a panoply of amazing things we now take for granted: the above-mentioned digital-epistolary miracle, the PC itself, smartphones, tablets, and the IP phenomenon, thanks to the creators of Arpanet and Tim Berners-Lee.

But now they're just building Snapchat.

Snapchat, a company with no revenue and a list of subscribers, is a messaging service that deletes texts and pictures not long after they're sent. It is the very apogee of the ephemeral. And yet its owners famously turned down an offer of "billions" because they "thought [they] could do better."[3] Recently Snapchat was hacked, and its *raison d'être* (your missives disappear, in the interest of ensuring security) was compromised.

Some will say that Silicon Valley is the nation's primary engine of optimism and creativity, and not just for digital. But if that's the case, why is Atlanta the home of Rob Rinehart, who has invented Soylent, a drink that more or less replaces food. Rinehart claims that he's lived off it for weeks at a time. Perhaps we will all be lucky enough one day to enjoy its bounty, but so far he's not been offered a billion dollars for his potentially planet-saving idea (he has, however, raised $3.5 million).[4] In San Francisco a group backed by Bill Gates is working on a vegetable substitute for eggs[5] that they claim will make eggs irrelevant to the diet—but as far as we can tell, the investment is in millions, not the billions often lavished upon digital pursuits far less capable of rocking the world. And we've all heard of the synthetic meat grown in a European lab at great cost.[6] I would love to see meat growing on trees and spare our porcine and bovine friends a great deal of trouble by eating it. But where are the big investment dollars (the fake meat project costs 250,000 euros, or roughly 350,000 USD)? They're being invested in "communities"[7] based on digital gimcrackery, which are really nothing more than crafty ways to get your name on a mailing list and to figure out what ad to show you.

Every new thing in the world today seems based on digital and upon being networked. Technology infrastructure giant Cisco has recently placed print ads lauding "the Internet of things," where it is suggested, for instance, that prescription bottles shall be networked so they will give alerts for renewal. That seems nice enough, but one gets the impression they're doing it because they can, rather than because we really need it.

It's possible we'll have only begun to realize in 2015 the magical new capabilities that software in the cloud can bring, and that we are as justified in pursuing it with abandon just as we pursued gears and electrical current in years past. But too often, the focus on digital has created little but more stuff to do on a computer of one kind or another. Especially in the US, "technology" has become, for all practical purposes, synonymous with *digital* technology, or, as it was known when it was chiefly in the bellies of big companies, "information technology." Almost completely lacking is an entrepreneurial spirit focused on any endeavor not based on the bounty of Moore's law of computing power. [8]

A large number of Americans today will agree that our political system, mostly at the federal level, is a sorry excuse for government. They'll say nearly every major problem we have goes unaddressed as feckless hacks in government set about cudgeling one another in a ruinous Punch and Judy routine.

Yet where are the young idealists in politics? Where are those whose vision might stretch well beyond party politics and advance us once more such that we really are (and not just because we like to tell ourselves) the most admired nation?

They're not in politics. Instead, we might find them busy inventing animated massacre games. They're gathering data to create consumer "personas" for marketers. They're developing smartwatches and health-related electronic wristbands.

FIGHTING THE WRONG FIGHT?

Like it or not, the American carbon footprint is definitely of an elephantine nature, where that of even the Europeans (they who at cafes dispense paper napkins in what an American must consider comically parsimonious fashion) is perhaps the hoof size of a prized Angus bull. In underdeveloped nations, by comparison, the carbon footprint is like the scratch of a rodent. And except for the claque of climate-change deniers that careen the air-conditioned halls of their think tanks, pretty much everyone knows the ice caps are melting fast, huge storms are hitting hard, mangrove swamps are marching north to Saint Augustine, and subway tunnels are flooding with alarming regularity. And where are the great minds today in the battle against continued burning of dead dinosaur muck to light the pleasure dome?

By and large they are not focused on clean energy. Instead, they are organizing ways for you to easily order take-out online. Or creating platforms where you can complain about a hairdresser. Or (hopefully, at least) making it easier for you to find health insurance.

I love to drive, and I occasionally drive a gas hog from the 1950s, so I can hardly hold myself an exemplar of transportational correctness. But I also live in an area commonly known to transportation buffs as the

Northeast Corridor, that densely populated corner of the earth stretching roughly from Richmond, Virginia, to Portland, Maine. For many years, I was a regular rider of the New York City subway.

What is clear to anyone who must navigate the choked highways of this five-hundred-mile-long region is that its transportation is in dire need of an intensive upgrade. Also, there is density here more of a European nature than of a far-flung American type. And yet the train service here is piebald at best and, frankly, in the twenty-first century, maddeningly slow to the point where we ought to be shamed into action. But for what reason is there no consortium of young, brave, innovative minds at work to build a futuristic template of transportation that will be used for the next hundred years?

The reason—and I say this somewhat facetiously—is that they are building *virtual* railroad games that look very, very realistic but cannot carry a single passenger anywhere. Less facetious is the assertion that they are building screen-sharing technologies designed to keep people from ever needing to see one another and meet eye-to-eye to discuss an idea or two. They are tracking smartphones inside of stores so a big retailer can flash messages about Wheaties at you when you're in the cereal aisle. But as far as they are concerned, it's up to you to figure a way to get there and back.

Air travel has *devolved* since the first 707 came out of Boeing. No one, it seems, has devoted one hundredth of mindshare to the matter of moving heavy things quickly from one place to another, as they have done to making words and pictures dance across a tablet screen. They won't focus on speeding real people to new destinations because they're too busy mapping the world electronically so you can virtually tour a big city and even its major indoor venues without an airplane ticket.[9] Can all of these digital gew-gaws—smart-fridges and smart-clothes and smart-cars and smart-diapers—really amount to a hill of beans in this crazy world?[10]

The great minds—the smartest and most technologically advanced among us—have achieved much in digital. But their singular, faddish obsession with digital to the exclusion of nearly all other enterprise leaves us flabbergasted at the lost opportunity. Imaginations that once were bounded by the tracks of the stars are now focused on virtual spaces and facsimiles of a world that has come to seem, perhaps, too daunting for conquest. The apotheosis of the techno-geek is hardly a celebration of what's best in us but really a celebration of a very narrow, specialized breed of adept. They are particularly able to pull the levers and strings of a very particular and very limited type of engine that so happens to run on ones and zeros.

Our litany can continue as follows: Where are the great innovators in food science? Why is there no open-source version of biochemical science? Where are the great innovations in energy sciences? Can we really say these fail because they are crushed by Big Pharma or Big Oil? Would not the theory of creative destruction apply here as it seems to in the digital markets? We keep hearing that "the technology is already there" and that it's poised for a breakthrough. But we have not really seen the breakthroughs, and that's because some key ingredient is missing.

What's missing is the focus of great energies and great fortunes behind any particular idea that *isn't digital*. All the young minds have been called off to the digital wars, and many shall never return. They've become so enraptured by digital they cannot even act upon the suggestion of a great idea that reaches beyond the fingertips of the IP-driven robot. Specifically, let us ask what's become of Elon Musk's rather interesting proposal to whisk passengers from Los Angeles to San Francisco in half an hour. Who has stepped up to say they'll devote their considerable brain power to making this real?

To date, no one has.

It's too hard, perhaps. There are, literally in some landscapes, mountains to move. But how did we get here except to move mountains as needed? In the meantime, California's official "high-speed rail" project is not expected to be very high speed at all by comparison, and it has run into a hail of opposition from courts, community groups, and right-wing politicians who seem congenitally unable to like any form of transportation that runs on rails. My entirely unscientific guess is that it's probably worth less than Snapchat.

BUSTED IN BUSHWICK

Recently we've read about a worthwhile, non-digital, visionary enterprise in Bushwick, Brooklyn, that failed because, according to an article in the *New York Observer*, its founder and CEO, Richard Goodman, practiced a management style "which involved a lot of Silicon Valley–fueled jargon and conceptual strategies that were difficult if not impossible to implement."[11]

Silicon Valley–fueled jargon apparently works less well when applied outside the digital domain, where things like people, Dumpsters, cinder blocks, and bicycles get in the way of the continuing acceleration of Moore's law. So it might be suggested that 3rd Ward, an incubator for what have been called "makers" (and in the past would have been called "craftsmen/women"), failed at least partly because it was not digital.

Perhaps 3rd Ward can function as a cautionary example of the way cities have come roaring back only to stumble. It took an abandoned factory and turned it into a factory.

But it was a different kind of factory. Inside its walls people, perhaps not surprisingly, *made things.* Not digital offerings, but actual things made of wood and stone and words and bicycle wheels and electric lights. All manner of things from crafts to arts to things you might buy if you could find a place to buy them. There were classes and workshops and studios and filmmakers and artists and writers and teachers and cooks and carpenters and dreamers and students, and they all came to build stuff and to learn what they could from each other. It made money by selling what were called "lifetime memberships" for a couple of thousand dollars, which meant access to everything 3rd Ward could offer, for life. For a time it seemed to work and was holding its own.

Then its founder happened upon some folks from the digital world, and while we are not about to blame them for turning his head the wrong way, his head indeed seems to have got turned the wrong way, and he apparently started thinking of rapid expansion in the manner of white-hot digital companies with no revenue and lots of promise.[12] With a few bucks in his capital fund, he made some moves to expand but soon foundered, and then, late in 2013, the whole enterprise was closed, and the lifetime members lost their money and would not get refunds.

What's to stop us from wondering why a great non-digital idea that got the attention of digital investors was funded on a shoestring and then failed? The company raised a couple of million dollars in total. What was so wrong with it that it didn't raise twenty million or a hundred million the way any number of utterly pointless digital gambits have been funded?

Allow me to suggest the reason it didn't raise that kind of scratch was because it didn't scratch the digital itch. It was a brick-and-mortar ploy to change the world, except it was the real world, not a simulacrum of a real world bound by the limits of a tablet screen. It had buildings and people developing non-digital skills in those buildings and learning non-digital things. And while it was deemed interesting enough for a couple of digital investors (including the founder of Zappos), it was, in the end, just a dumpy little factory building in a dumpy part of Brooklyn with a few hipsters inside building stuff—or at least that's what the digiterati probably thought. In any case, the disparity between what this ambitious non-digital venture raised—a couple million—as opposed to what many very much worse digital ideas have raised—tens and hundreds of millions—goes a long way to show how digital saps the life from other investment tracks.

Did 3rd Ward deserve better? Maybe not. It's true the founder seemed mercurial and inconsistent (like lots of star entrepreneurs in digital). It's true he seemed to get distracted by the glitter of digital-entrepreneur stardust on his way to oblivion (he used some of his digital investors' money to buy a motorcycle and some fancy clothes), but if he'd been digital, he'd have been able to buy a Pierce Arrow and ten Brioni suits, and no one would have asked Question One. Instead, he seems to have overspent on a few small things, which, in the non-digital world, can break you. Because all the money is going to digital.

The 3rd Ward was a bold idea and intended to become a household name. But for a number of reasons, not the least of which was that it failed to attract but a fraction of the investment dollars of even a mediocre digital plan with far less to show, the bold venture failed. The factory closed, and the teachers went unpaid. It serves as a doleful warning to those who might try to build a new idea that doesn't rely on Moore's law for its economics.

GOOGLING TOWARD BABYLON

The engineer who, in an earlier, perhaps more intrepid era, might have pursued the bullet train, is now tucked away in a room with a whiteboard at Google, noodling away at another algorithm, coddled by free snacks and to-die-for architecture. We can imagine him ensconced in a self-congratulatory environment where the way our world staggers about half in stupor must seem an amusing prospect, taking place on the other side of the tinted glass.

If Americans seem proud of our computing prowess, it is most likely for a good reason. All of the latest inventions seem to come from our proud young entrepreneurs in various tech corridors. We may feel thankful they're building code instead of bombs, but let us not call them pioneers and let us not call them brave. The bravery comes into play mostly when they have to pitch VCs for millions funding a project with high hopes and no cash.

That said, it appears, according to Roger McNamee on CNBC, VCs are "partying like it's 1999 all over again,"[13] so perhaps it requires no courage at all to ask for money as long as you've got a bunch of subscribers. An article in the *New York Times* relates that "risk is being discounted tremendously,"[14] which, in my opinion, looks to be another way of saying that investors just don't care if they're plowing money into a loser, as long as they can unload it to someone else (by going public, for instance) before the roof caves in. Reading the above-mentioned article, I will admit I had to put the paper down and shake off the feeling we were headed for another meltdown. But I've been wrong in the past and have no wisdom when it comes to picking markets.

"Risk is being discounted tremendously" . . . is another way of saying that investors just don't care if they're plowing money into a loser, as long as they can unload it to someone else . . . before the roof caves in.

It seems greed is once again getting a boost from faster processors and more bandwidth. Too many smart people in technology, when separated from the realms of digital that consume their days and jolt their nights, present facades suggesting they're incurious, untraveled, apolitical, and not especially empathetic. No, they're not especially interested even in "changing the world" with a new and better chat service. Many of them seem to be mainly interested in one day going public and, without ever having turned a profit nor built anything of substance, becoming a billionaire.[15] It's what happens when the American Dream shrinks to the size of an electron inside a silicon microchip.

14

WALL STREET AS VAUDEVILLE: DIGITAL IS DESTROYING FINANCIAL SERVICES

Digital is enabling not just a wholesale transformation of the financial services industry—banking, the stock market, the mortgage-lending market and its bubble-blowing derivatives—but also the wholesale destruction of what's left of transparency and human oversight.

When the nation's largest bank pays a fine of several billions to the Justice Department in order to avoid further investigation of its morally bankrupt mortgage banking practices,[1] we can be reasonably certain that high finance has, at least in one very well-publicized case, begun to suffer from a condition of moral rot.

I am talking about the November 2013 deal that, according to *Business Insider*, hung on a call made by JPMorgan Chase's CEO Jamie Dimon to an executive at the Justice Department on the eve of a major expansion of the department's investigation.[2] Apparently, Dimon would agree to a record fine (that would dwarf the entire asset base of any of a number of other sizable banks) to make the muckraking stop. Except it really was hardly muckraking as much as it was a long-overdue and overly deferential review of the ruinous practices of a bank that had already proven it was indeed too big to fail.

Further analysis by the Justice Department determined that nearly every major bank in the United States engaged in major acts of mortgage fraud. While mortgage fraud is nothing new, this time it was based on the distribution of "mortgage bundles" as securities, and such bundling and distribution would have been impossible without digital algorithms and very rapid communication.

We've all become painfully aware it was the mortgage bomb that exploded the magazine of our economy, nearly sinking us to the gunwales except for an impossibly one-sided bailout. The bankers' staterooms got damp, and the ship of state righted the boat by dumping all the water down into second class—or at least it's a terrific temptation to think so. But we don't need to be feeling sorry for ourselves to recognize that, relative to the days before the boilers burst, too many of us have been slogging and wheezing and shivering inside blankets ever since those days of trillion-dollar gifts for the wealthy.

The bankers misbehaved, and many were even rewarded for it.

But there were others.

It was the million signatories on what were known as "liar" mortgages where income verification was seen as an optional fillip on the way to unsustainable "ownership" of a tacky McMansion. Unworthy borrowers got those mortgages knowing they hadn't the resources to support the payments. Maybe they expected to flip the houses and pocket a well-deserved margin considering the risk they'd just taken! These hasty gamblers bear at least some responsibility, even if they were unduly encouraged by lenders lacking a moral compass.

Some say it was the crime of the century, and they may be right.

And it was digital that made it technically possible to pull off the heist.

The financial industries, waist-deep in data and private information, went digital before most others. Digitally powered program trading, which I will touch upon, replaced for the most part the human calculations, instincts, and "gut" that drove the markets heretofore. Financial arrangements—often referred to as "products"—became increasingly complex in large measure because digital enabled them to become so. They became sufficiently complex that few financiers professed to fully understand what they were, how they worked, and who exactly owned how much of what and how much it would really be worth in a final accounting. According to Suleika Reiners of the World Future Council, "transparency is impossible as long as financial instruments are overly complex."[3]

Wall Street has long been accused of chicanery and obfuscation, and it has been blamed for having an outsized and unfair effect on our entire economy, including those who've never gambled at the Broad Street

Casino. And this reputation dates back well before the age of ENIAC and Turing and the lowly punch card. At the moment in 1929 when the clock of the world was halted, it was mechanical-electrical ticker tape that gave the gate to so many paper fortunes.

But by the mid-2000s, the notion of a stock exchange in a particular place with men vociferously trading on the floor had become more vaudeville than institution. The real action was taking place sort of no-where: there were servers and wires and microprocessors and fancy algo-rithms all communicating machine-to-machine, and math wizards figur-ing out how to build financial products so complex they could *only* be managed by digital.

The culprit financial instrument in the 2008 meltdown was known as the "mortgage derivative." Let's remind ourselves that the actual melt-down was of sufficient gravity that at least one presidential candidate, in the heat of a keenly contested election, decided to "suspend" his cam-paign and return to Washington ostensibly in order to keep the nation itself from unraveling.[4] His act may have been high theater, but the threat was no tap dance.

The nature of a mortgage derivative may be only moderately complex in principle, but its nature also requires the marshaling of massive amounts of financial instruments each with its own inner workings and moving parts. In fact, it requires many thousands (or millions) of these.

The mortgage derivative was based on the notion that mortgages could be bundled, valued, risk-assessed, and sold like a form of mutual fund. The trouble with this is that no human could comprehend the complexity of the product, nor even keep track of the manner in which any particular mortgage might have been bundled and sold or resold or partitioned; nor could any buyer know exactly how his or her product was collateralized. But it seemed clear the digital brains must know—or at least they didn't balk at being endlessly queried.

What made the 2008 meltdown both different and explosive was that these exceedingly complex products, bound together by constantly shift-ing calculations performed by computers based on algorithms, required a great deal of raw material in order to keep satisfied a hungry market.

The raw material of the raw material was the collective and individual ability of every mortgage holder to pay back a loan. In an era of fast-rising home values, this was no great burden. Many mortgage holders went out to refinance, take out some cash, and recommit to the bank for an even longer time. But in a slowing real estate market, the number of new and the number of sound mortgages began to contract at a speed that would prove catastrophic.

Worse, complex algorithms in the financial services industry had enabled the creation of yet another impossibly arcane packet of financial products called "credit default swaps." These essentially were attempts mathematically to mitigate (hedge) the effects of a drain on the value of any particular portfolio of financial instruments. Again, these were so complex, and had been sold and resold so many times so quickly, that no one could really assess the value of what they owned. The computer could ostensibly keep track, but the algorithm had not been written that could easily generate an actual value.

And this was more or less an acceptable circumstance until the bottom fell out of the market.

When owners of credit default swaps and mortgage derivatives had to raise cash in a hurry to cover some bad bets, they found they could not. An investment bank called Lehman Brothers fell in the political/historical equivalent of an instant. AIG, an enormous company that had relied too much upon digital gimcrackery to appear healthy, was next in line.[5] Many others, not far behind and equally beholden to values determined by complex digital calculations rarely (if ever) checked by a responsible human, waited in a collective cold sweat while their puppets at the Federal Reserve brought doomful news to Congress.

Having failed to do their own calculations, not able to perform anything like due diligence on a million mortgages, unable to comprehend the scope of their own exposure, far too reliant on the brainless brains of digital trading programs, they had gotten themselves well out into the surf before feeling the riptide.

Where were the arbiters of financial sanity? The true examiners of real exposure? Of the value of an asset against its risk of loss? If cross-table chatter is to be believed, at least some were enjoying an *amuse bouche* at Bouley in Tribeca (now moved to a new location), not far from the skyscrapers where they'd authored doom, and where the best thinking machines they could afford continued to reassure as if programmatically. Ostensibly they were at least partially mesmerized by calculations based on algorithms created in back rooms by "financial wizards" who in all likelihood really were only *math* wizards who knew how to build calculations so complex and so reliant on shifting data that no one was in a position to truly oversee what they were creating. To some extent, this was a self-induced self-deception and a scam, and, as all scams must, it came to an end.

The great debacle of 2008, from the chill shadow of which we only now begin to emerge, was forged in digital. Minus the computational power deployed to analyze and value and assess uncountable unique securities (mortgages), none of the bundling and buying and selling of these would have been possible. Without an unfounded trust that either the geeks or the software they'd written had somehow gotten it right, then the crash of 2008—the worst in several generations—would not have been possible.[6]

Digital is now more entrenched than ever. Traders on the floor, panicky as they might have been in an earlier age, now account for only a diminishing amount of trades in the market. The movement of millions of shares back and forth between funds of every stripe is accomplished in milliseconds by trading bots.[7] For a nanosecond, you own a stock. Then, because of the action of a "business rule" no one sees or understands, you don't. The stock's been traded. These market moves are facilitated by digital rules defined by programmers, and then they are left in what can be best described as a "set it and forget it" mode. No one knows what the robots are doing moment to moment.

As is perhaps not broadly enough understood, robots today lack what we would immediately recognize as common sense.[8] They are poor at dealing with outliers, rogue information, signs of unreason from other robots, or outright errors from trusted sources. They are uniquely prone to "panic selling," the roots of which are often left undiscovered.

As a way of preventing a robot-induced run, the stock exchanges have had to contemplate what amount to kill switches that, assuming a coherent human is within arm's reach of the right button, can stop trading altogether if there's some kind of wild sell-off for no discernable reason. On May 26, 2010, the Dow Jones Industrial Average plunged more than 1,000 points (9 percent) at 2:45 p.m., only to recover twenty minutes later. The blame fell to a combination of high-frequency traders (run by software) plus robo-trading of penny-priced "stub quotes" for illiquid but still-valuable stocks.[9] SEC Chairman May Schapiro said that "human involvement likely would have prevented" the crisis.[10]

Digital has been foundational to the creation of an impenetrable thicket of financial products made up of unverifiable assets and has contributed further to the risk of uncontrolled panic selling, based on nothing but calculations made without oversight and posing substantial risk of catastrophic failure. I fully accept that this will sound alarmist to some, but how many will care to deny we may be one glitch away from what could be a digitally driven, depression-triggering market plunge?

We may be one glitch away from what could be a digitally driven, depression-triggering market plunge.

CAPTAINS OF WAR, CAPTAINS OF COMMERCE

Must we accept the belief that captains of great fortune, with a world economy held like a bauble in their unsteady hands, would fain let it drop? Are captains with access to massively destructive weapons always careful and extra-careful in deference to the commonwealth? Recently it was disclosed that the warheads on all of the nuclear missiles in the United States arsenal were at one time armed with a code that had to be deployed before arming. The code was set to *all zeros*.[11] This was because nobody wanted to be caught struggling with a passcode as the Russkies were launching. And it was a code given out to everyone, just in case.

Is there any good reason to have faith that the financial markets would be so very much more conscientious than the men guarding us from mass destruction with weapons of mass destruction?

BUBBLES AND TROUBLES

But this is not the only manner in which digital has endangered the financial markets. Earlier I mentioned the case of an insubstantial company called Snapchat owned by a couple of bright young men who turned down an offer of billions of dollars for their zero-revenue company. The worst of it is not that they turned down the offer, but that the offer was made at all.

Silicon Valley, ever optimistic about digital, finds little that might trigger alarm in such an event. They even have a name for it. Companies like Snapchat are called "pre-revenue"—and many of them are sought after as extremely valuable properties for a variety of reasons that translate, if I am permitted to be at least tolerably *au courant*, into the phrase "because digital."

In a *Wired* magazine article in December 2013, Marcus Wohlsen suggests another tech bubble is inflating, and that he is reminded of "the dotcom bubble . . . when startups with no revenue spent millions on Super Bowl ads."[12] By November 2014 another "dotcom crash" seemed unlikely in the near term. But it remains true that because of the millennial dotcom crash, for years thereafter even faddish money steered clear of overvaluing companies with significant "burn rates"—which in itself is a flashy way of talking about a company that is losing money very, very quickly.

But apparently we have now fully healed the scars left from the Y2K debacle that had nothing to do with the expected Y2K debacle. And today, several companies, as they had in 1999, seem to induce a gleam in the eye of the investor and a rather spasmodic reach for the checkbook.

Early deemed a flop after it went public, Facebook shares have now vaulted to new heights even as profit remains elusive. Other passengers on the digital gravy train are well-known outfits like Twitter and Pinterest (private as of this writing) and not a *sou* in profit between them.

Yet, far from worrying that heated stock prices at many multiples of revenue and an infinite multiple of profit might create an unsustainable overhang, Valley investors scoff at the notion. They feel that these companies, many of which converge around the idea of building "communities" that allow them to cull data from users and resell it, have almost unlimited futures. But there is no suggestion that any of these companies is on the road to success in terms of actual revenue. In other words, they have no functioning business model. Putting it another way, and insofar as they are presenting themselves as valuable, they are scammers in the great tradition of scammers in the financial markets.

While disinclined to impugn anyone in particular, I find it difficult to imagine how anyone not a charlatan or a true believer could imagine companies with billion-dollar valuations and no revenue will ever deliver real value to their investors (except in a sale or public offering, which only passes the buck or lack thereof).

We're more comfortable these days labeling the run-up to the millennial dotcom crash as collective mania. And if we were to take an honest look at the very silly overvaluations of some companies today, why would we not say the same of the financial markets in 2014? One might be tempted to say "Who cares?" if some Valley billionaire loses a mansion full of chump change on a tech bet gone wrong. The trouble is that, much as a rising tide lifts all boats, a few big blazes where the flashiest boats all capsize tend to empty the harbor of all of its boats. Including the one you're piloting.

The collateral damage from the dotcom bust was substantial and damaging to everyone in the industry and many beyond it. I lost a perfectly good, small company during an ill-fated roll-up in 2000 and still remember the pain involved in shuttering that enterprise, even after it had enjoyed several years of profit and prosperity.

We ought to be much on guard that another digital bubble does not emerge, but today we are left with the real possibility that an unhealthy mix of digital plus unfounded faith in mailing lists can somehow be worth more to investors than the efforts of any of a thousand companies that build things and sell them and make real money employing real people.

DESTROYING THE BASELINE

With digital, none of the baseline metrics seem to matter as they do in the rest of the world. And perhaps it explains why digital and the financial services industry seem to have so much in common. Honest work, honest pay, and honest products seem held almost in contempt by the digital entrepreneur as well as many profiteers in finance. We can imagine that they guffaw at simpletons who strive to deliver something of real utility to the market and to construct a profit out of the enterprise.

That sort of homespun is not what digital, or the current financial markets, are about.

Digitally driven businesses, to an uncomfortably large extent, appear to be about creating something ephemeral out of nothing, hoping it catches on, building "buzz," and then cashing out without ever having delivered either a real product or a real nickel to the bank.

There are exceptions, of course.

But often enough it's up to the next owner to figure out what to do with a dog that might have been clad in ermine but that sure don't hunt. Often, that "next owner" is the public. And the public will then prance to the stock market minuet until one day the music stops, and if any member of the public is lucky enough or prescient enough, they will by that time not just have found a chair but also have left the ball. Of course, their leaving always depends on their ability to pass the dance to the next dancer, and the unlucky dancer faces ruin if there's no chair when the music stops. In 2008, it happened with big banks and mortgages, and the taxpayer (even if not a shareholder!) found herself slumped on the floor in a hall strewn with empty chairs.

Sadly, it may well happen again if we don't slow down the tempo, and soon. Because in digital, a company like Square[13] never has to say they made money on business operations.[14] But they are just one example of many—I've already noted where even Amazon still falls short of profit. Square and Amazon aside (I am not suggesting they are to blame), it's not a far distance between continuing lack of profit and a condition where you only have to make good on the confidence game, then pass the problem on to the next player.

My personal observation, based on all of the evidence presented above, can best be characterized by the following statement:

Due to an unprecedented combination of old-fashioned confidence games and digitally enabled, impenetrable financial products, *plus* digitally enabled, unsupervised ("program") trading, digital now becomes part and parcel of a serious threat to the stability of the financial markets and, by extension, the global economy.

15

INVADERS FROM EARTH: DIGITAL IS DESTROYING THE PROFESSIONS (AND MORE)

It might be almost too banal to list the jobs that have gone to Davy Jones's locker since the early 1990s. Remember secretaries? They were flesh-and-blood combinations of Google Calendar and e-mail. Unpaid interns bring the coffee now, but soon they may be replaced by cute Japanese robots. In New York City, many can still recall the unhappy visage of the token clerk and the epic rudeness that emanated from their battered underground lairs. They took your money and shoved tokens at you and made sure you knew they were hating every minute of it. I cannot say I miss the sullen token changers, and the digital card system now in use really works much better than even a polite token clerk ever did.

E-ZPass,[1] an automotive digital tracking system that I am sure reeks of Big Brother, allows subscribers to pay digitally at toll booths all across the Northeast and has depopulated toll booths from Logan to Harrisburg. Once in a while you see a sole toll-booth operator reading a book in an acclimatized booth while you zip past them with your E-ZPass pressed firmly against the windshield. I cannot think of anyone who doesn't think E-ZPass is the happiest thing ever to happen to a tollway. The days of getting backed up on the average turnpike because of a paywall have pretty much come to an end. And so have lots of toll-booth jobs.

I am certain that among a certain class of professionals, business owners, and other self-congratulatory types, we can admit to feeling badly about the loss of these jobs, but perhaps not as badly as we might. The booth-clerk position strikes us as among the most deadly dull of jobs, and psychologists might tell us we can only feel just so badly about losses that seem reasonably distant. Digital optimists would say those booth-dwellers (and routinely demeaned secretaries as well) have now gone on to become coders or bloggers, but there's never been a study to prove such dazzling career switches in any great number.

Most of us have been left unscathed by the loss of administrative, repetitive, dehumanizing jobs, and many of us may even feel a sense of benevolent gladness that certain humans have been freed from drudgery much as, in an earlier day, the proponents of motorized transport made the case that millions of weary workhorses were entitled to lives more noble than could be expected in harness. (I do realize how very incorrect it is to compare humans to horses, but correctness often leaves unsaid certain uncomfortable but very apt correlations.)

Certainly digital has not taken the work away from every man or woman in the labor force. Much of what people do today to earn money comes across as too *improvisational* as compared to what a robot or computer can perform routinely. Jewelry-making comes to mind. But even as these jobs remain, digital continues marching to new victories.

CYBORG, ESQ.

We've already seen very repetitive tasks, formerly performed by very bored humans, overtaken by digital performance devices. But the next wave of jobs to be attacked by digital will be of a different stripe altogether. The attack will bite deeper into the livelihoods of what we like to call the intelligentsia (or their close associates), including many of our most revered professions in law, medicine, and the arts.

The extent to which each profession will be affected can be established by the degree to which it involves rote research, review, and pure logic. For instance, much of the work in lawyering today involves extensive review of formally constructed documents, many of which deploy stilted phraseology and syntax unique to the courthouse. These programmatic documents become almost perfect food for digital consumption, and document-parsing software products[2] are already making certain types of attorneys and paralegals obsolete. For the foreseeable future, it's impossible, however, to see any danger to the experienced trial attorney. Her grasp of facts and a near preternatural feel for the intangibles of a case, plus, irreducibly, a need to appear in court, will continue to make the paradigmatic attorney indispensible.

But he or she may soon be surrounded more and more by computers and networked document-processing systems and less with paralegals, associates, and interns. Many say there is already a glut of young lawyers,[3] and digital only serves to make more young lawyers even less desired in the marketplace.

Laws may be complex but they are known entities and nothing if not well documented. Case law, the body of trial records that fill the firm's law library (now mostly digital, and enhanced by legal-research databases like LexisNexis), gives weight to the body of the law. Today's paralegals and young attorneys pore over these bodies of case law for long days and longer nights, looking for angles that will help the cause of their firm's client.

In all likelihood, however, this practice may not last. Because while it's true the legal profession has been slow on the digital uptake, it has not, as an industry, been a bulk buyer of foolscap, either. In an industry where, in the big cities, small armies of messengers would have raced from one end of town to the other bearing stacks of legal "originals" for signature, those messengers and their bulging briefcases have been almost totally replaced by e-mail attachments. So lawyers may remain digitally laggard in their businesses, but they're still moving more to digital than ever before.

Sophisticated databases of legal research[4] and case law already exist. The dusty law library is a relic. The Lincoln Building in New York City (a Jazz Age, brick-faced, sixty-odd-story behemoth) once housed so many attorneys in its warrens of small offices that it had, in the lower arcade (closed entirely since 9/11), a complete law library for use by any tenant lawyer. It's been gone for quite some time now.

Paralegals and associates pull up research from case-law databases and construct arguments out of digital templates of every kind. If we remember how codified is law, and how structured the arguments, and how large the databases and how sophisticated the algorithms and how fast the processors, we can see already that the role of the associate can be reduced to not much more than a concatenator of factoids and protocols.

Satisfying the least-contentious portion of the legal services market are businesses like Legal Zoom, a provider of basic, uncontested legal documents (wills and incorporations, for instance). It is important to note that using Legal Zoom is not the equivalent of hiring a lawyer and businesses like this do not offer what we would call "legal advice." Yet, in all likelihood, Legal Zoom and its competitors will find ways to build and guarantee more sophisticated legal documents for very low prices, and many run-of-the-mill firms, especially those providing the most routine services, will be forced to adjust their prices, if not their entire practices.

Price pressure is often driven by consumer choice; part of the choice in legal is enabled by the same blend of digital capabilities that have come to define the software industries. It's already the case that, except for contingency cases, many corporate firms have been forced away from the harrowingly expensive time-based billing and have begun to offer their large customers something akin to flat-fee pricing.[5] Digital only guarantees that law firms will continue to be forced into economies unimagined a generation ago. Rather than sacrifice a partner's share of the loot, many firms will empty out the cubicles and beef up on digital.

DOCTOR DIGITAL

As we enter the earliest era of what I will call the Age of Artificial Intelligence, we must be prepared for new surprises in workplace displacement. The notion of a nonhuman delivering packages to your front door may be astonishing enough, but what will happen when medicine, perhaps the most notable outpost of egregious price gouging in American life today, succumbs to price pressures brought on by digital?

Expect a strange new hospital full of helpers that move on wheels or leg pods. Not tomorrow. But the day after tomorrow, our children will, at some point in their lives, almost certainly be in the care of a nursebot. They will have their blood pressure taken *without* the guy or gal who now wraps the strap around your forearm and pumps the antediluvian pressure hose. They will have their bloodwork done by a sensitive machine that will have much better access to health records, genetics, and probability factors than pretty much any MD alive today. Diagnosis will come in the form of a screen rendering, a PDF, or perhaps a hologram. Robo-surgery will sprout right from the sci-fi screen and grow in the steel-and-composite operating room at the hospital.[6]

The day after tomorrow, our children will . . . almost certainly be in the care of a nursebot.

Somewhere humans will remain involved, probably in no small number. Sadly, it may already be the case that many health professionals are not much more than note-takers as they supply data to the medical databases, and that, instead of real observation, copying and pasting from the last check-in has become all too common—making the information in the information system useless and the entry of information a meaningless time-suck.

No doubt we are at least a few generations away from any kind of comfort with a health facility minus human oversight, though that is not impossible to imagine. But in the foreseeable future, while humans (doctors, nurses, orderlies, interns) will remain at least nominally in charge, there will be fewer of them, and except for certain celebrity docs who can carry a hospital with their reputation, many of them will be lower paid and lower skilled than today's counterpart.

In a *Forbes* article from 2012,[7] David Shaywitz posits that "technologists, investors, providers and policy makers" look forward to a day when "computers will become the care providers," and that doctors, nurses, and so on will become "like the attendants at Pep Boys, interfacing with . . . software driven algorithms."

By all indications, medicine as we know it today will soon be forced to come to accounts. In fact, with the slowest rise in health-care costs in decades upon us even now, some might say the adjustment has already begun. My prediction is that Big Medicine's massive, needless redundancies and inefficiencies (and institutional blindness) will, because of price pressure, come under insupportable scrutiny in the not-very-distant future. Assuming this reckoning takes place, digital stands to play a major role in corresponding with disparate databases, integrating data with diagnosis, and (with intelligent enough software) recommending not just one but several courses of action that the patient can (we hope) decide upon.

If Shaywitz turns out to be right, then I imagine tomorrow's health-care services may be carried out by a machine attended by a task-trained human, whose chief job may well be to make sure the gauges don't start blinking too fast and the dashboard doesn't emit smoke.

In his book *The Creative Destruction of Medicine*,[8] Dr. Eric Topol writes:

> This is a story about an unprecedented super-convergence. It would not be possible were it not for the maturation of the digital world technologies—ubiquity of smart phones, bandwidth, pervasive connectivity, and social networking. Beyond this, the perfect digital storm includes immense, seemingly unlimited computing power via cloud server farms, remarkable biosensors, genome sequencing, imaging capabilities, and formidable health information systems.

According to Rick Merritt in a 2013 article at *EE Times*,[9] Topol claimed in a Silicon Valley speech that someday "sensors in and around the body could enable real-time, mobile medicine tailored to the individual." According to Mr. Merritt, Topol went on to say that medicine had not yet "begun to leverage Moore's Law or low-cost gene sequencing, but . . . it will change healthcare forever." Today gene sequencing is at a fraction of its cost from just several years ago.

The opportunities for digital change—"creative destruction," if you will—in medicine are so large and so overwhelmingly requisite that it makes it rather a certainty that many of us will see the day when our doctor is really an algorithm.

This all sounds perfectly rosy and even very brave. But what about the people now performing medical services? What will happen to the doc we all know today? Having studied so hard for so long and with such dreams of wealth and magnitude; with the pressures of all the preceding generations of hopefuls behind him as he prescribes a pill for a pain and a scalpel for a clot; with his years spent in blue smocks tending for twenty hours at a time to the coughing, wheezing, dripping masses that roll in and out of his office and hospital rooms—will we still recognize him after the robots come in?

Chances are we may well recognize a good lot of them. But not as many as we do now, and they will almost certainly be more functionary and less well paid.[10]

The Pep Boys paradigm for medicine is powered by digital. Digital will make it more likely that nearly every doc will be like nearly every other doc, as they will all be looking at a screen to see what the great digital physician says. Of course, they will have the right to ignore the glitchy diagnosis and go with their gut. But by the time this scenario develops, medical attendants may not have the training, and may not possess the knowledge themselves, to go with any gut. And they will be forced, not by fiat but by need, to follow the digital dictat.

COMMODITIZING SPECIALIZATION

The melting away of professional positions in law and medicine can only serve to hasten the continuing disappearance of a viable middle class in the United States.[11] It's been said before that in prior recessions and in prior "productivity surges," it was the *labor* force that got hurt worst as jobs went overseas, were automated, or were replaced by software.

But now automation is reaching deeper into the realm of expertise.

It's not just motion that gets mechanized—it's also knowledge, nuance, and logic that are being turned over increasingly to digital. At the end of 2013 there was talk of the imminent launch of a computer that was capable of learning from its mistakes and coping with uncertainty.[12] As of this writing, IBM claims that its "Watson" machine, the computer that played and won *Jeopardy* a few years back, has been shrunk "from the size of a master bedroom to three stacked pizza boxes."[13] According to IBM, "Watson is a cognitive technology that processes information more like a human than a computer—by understanding natural language, generating hypotheses based on evidence, and learning as it goes."[14] Further, it is being offered as a cloud-based solution, which means its power can be "rented"; this suggests that artificial intelligence is about to become much more accessible than in the past.

As offerings like Watson proliferate, people who had felt secure that their expertise and specialization would protect them from being outdone by a machine will no longer have that security. In this scenario, they become the friction that software wants to eliminate, the weakness in the system, the overburdening cost factor that must be resolved. Knowledge workers and experts may face challenges from artificial intelligence, but the software entrepreneurs, their investors, and, as always, the wealthy in general stand to reap nearly all the obvious benefit.

What happens when non-digital professionals are rooted out of their professions and replaced by bots? Are we confident they'll all find a place to work and live and thrive even when their brains are largely redundant of an air-cooled cloud-server somewhere in the nowhere? There is some solace that in a digitally driven marketplace the public in general gets better pricing, if not better service. But in the long run, the depopulation of the professions seems like a long run to the bottom where prices are depressed and nobody has any money.

ROBOT NIGHTMARE

Many who hear of robots today may think back to popular stereotypes in which robots might range from frightening simulacrum (*Metropolis*) to goofball (*Lost in Space*) to hapless diplomat (*Star Wars*). Or they might imagine we had reached a pinnacle of robotry with the advent of automated production where disembodied steel appendages spot-weld fenders in a shower of sparks. But robots-to-come will most likely be far less folkloric in nature than their appearance in the media would have us believe, and certainly more mobile than an animated I-beam.

In late 2013 Google acquired Boston Dynamics, a firm known for its advances in military-style robots. Anyone tempted to think of advanced robots as clunky, kooky, indoor-type machines needs to dispense with those imaginings and picture something quite a bit more alarming. Some new digitrons resemble headless beasts that can walk in the woods.[15] They have legs like horses do and can withstand blows without toppling, and, in a test, one of the robots ("Cheetah") was able to "run faster than Usain Bolt" at over twenty-eight miles per hour.[16] One might argue they are bizarre enough in appearance as to beg comparison to the nightmarish figures painted by Hieronymus Bosch. I say they are unforgettable in appearance and are likely to haunt the dreams of a future generation of storm-tossed sleepers.

For the most part, the roving animatrons seem to be deployed as military pack animals, carrying mule-train loads over rough terrain— headless. One is tempted to send in an unsolicited note to the public relations division of the industrialists making the packbots and tell them to stick a fake head on these things so as not to turn us all into raving shock victims unable to cope with the sight of no-head thoroughbreds cantering among us.

While they are still largely experimental, digital quadrupeds can already climb a hill with more agility than many an aeon-evolved ungulate, and with the circulation of more than mere rumors of bug-sized robots[17] that reportedly can buzz in and surveil or even kill you,[18] we must face a future populated with flying, leaping, walking, stalking, administering, operating, notating, rubbing, scrubbing, temperature-taking nanobots that run on silicon rather than carbon. For those who pooh-pooh the notion that digital beasts and digital advisers will both become part of daily life, the future probably has, as it tends to have, a surprise in store.

A ROBOTIC FUTURE?

In his *Wired* magazine article "Better Than Human: Why Robots Will— And Must—Take Our Jobs,"[19] Kevin Kelly predicted that by the end of this century, 70 percent of the labor force will be robots, and that this won't be a problem because, ostensibly, we will have figured out cool new stuff to do once we don't have to do anything. He says:

> This postindustrial economy will keep expanding, even though most of the work is done by bots, because part of your task tomorrow will be to find, make, and complete new things to do, new things that will later become repetitive jobs for the robots.

But this kind of optimism may be ill founded. Of course, the more nimble among us will be just fine and perhaps even the better for a nation of botworkers. But to maintain the sunshine in his postulation, Kelly must ignore a range of middle and lower economic quintiles of the US population. Too many members of these groups struggle already to feed their families except with trans-fat-laden Whoppers. Too many can hardly read a news article halfway through, never mind "invent" anything.

Says Kelly, "You'll be paid in the future based on how well you work with robots. Ninety percent of your coworkers will be unseen machines."

I do not profess to know whether Mr. Kelly believes this is good, bad, or just a plain fact. But if anyone were to believe a robot future signals a new utopia, he had better start reading his science fiction a little more critically. There are lots of nightmarish future scenarios where robots really kind of suck.

I agree with Kelly that the professions will be laced with even more robots than are in employ today. Where today the robots sit on desks or remain attached to some control panel, soon they will become battery-driven, untethered, more independent than you might imagine they could be, and far more agile and specialized than all but the dreamiest mythologizers might have proposed a generation ago.

So, the attack of the robots is on. But it isn't going to be prosecuted with laser beams, and they are not going to be stopped by Terran bacteria. They'll be earthlings, and they will perform every type of job they can be made to perform. And that will include many jobs now performed by intelligent, educated humans in professions like law, medicine, and, as I hope to demonstrate, some of the more ephemeral pursuits suggested by teaching, writing, and the creation of that peculiarly human thing we like to call "art."

TEACHERS, WRITERS, AND ARTISTS

Full-on digitization is already a done deal in music. Sure, human musical artists are still in control. But they very often outsource creativity to past generations of music makers. Many of them sample endlessly, avoiding copyright prosecution by making sure their shoplifting comes in small bytes less than the legally allowable limit. Can you play the drums? No. But Ringo could. And you can pull his beats and loop them to create your own Magical Mystery Tour.

Somehow this lack of actual dexterity has come to seem an emblem of cleverness. And where in the past, a Phil Spector (now a godforsaken inmate) might have employed a real orchestra and a real gang of backup singers to produce his heady "wall-of-sound" sound, today a headless synthesizer that makes a Moog seem like a like a virginal is deployed to sample and dub and mix and squish and stretch and churn out deep, spooky tracks that employ no singers, no guitarists, no ivory-ticklers at all. In fact, with not much more technology than what a reasonably smart shut-in can deploy in his pizza-crusted bedroom, a musically inclined civilian today can create soundtracks that rival in complexity (if not in quality) what a Gershwin might have dreamed in a simpler and perhaps more illustrious halcyon.

And this is just the opening act. As musical originality seems further and further out of reach for most (and perhaps becomes irrelevant to a stultified public), we are becoming accustomed to entertainment that relies more and more heavily on automation. Led Zeppelin achieved an uncanny echo by recording in the stairwell of a mansion. We are told that Lindsey Buckingham sought new timbres by singing into a toilet. Today it's unlikely that a musician would even attempt to create new sounds personally in such a manner; in fact, it would probably come across as twee and quite unnecessary. Now, typically, they twist a few dials, draw down some sounds from the ether, and digitally weave them into something that passes for new. But weirdly, perhaps, much of it begins to sound rather the same as the same thing we heard last year or last decade. We await the arrival of the first (and we hope not headless) "band" made up of programmed musictrons cavorting on *Saturday Night Live* with a number-one track.

Writers can take small solace in the news that, so far, machines have not been widely deployed in creating paragraphs of informative or entertaining copy. The temptation is irresistible to compare the possibilities of digital scrivening to the legendary infinite monkeys with infinite typewriters ultimately clacking out a mindless *Macbeth*. But when billion-baboon brainpower is packed into a thumbnail-sized switching device, the possibility comes to seem less the absurd postulation and more a possible outcome of dogged digital programming.

According to Jamie Carter's 2013 article, "Could Robots Be the Writers of the Future?" published in *TechRadar*, "software that can construct sentences, analyse data and even put a 'spin' on a news story are threatening to make [writing] . . . very different."[20]

According to the article, a company called Narrative Science has created software called Quill that is a "synthesis of data analytics, artificial intelligence and editorial expertise."[21] According to the article, Quill has a patented ability to "reproduce journalistic 'angles' on a story." Moreover, Quill can create what is called a "bona fide" news story in "seconds."

But is it really bona fide if it's done by a non-bona-fide writer? I would say *no*, and, in the same vein, Carter says, "The concept of a machine being able to review consumer electronics products, apps and software, for instance, from a human user perspective—the only perspective that's relevant—is a concept that doesn't make any sense."[22]

Mark Coker, founder of e-book site Smashbooks, has said that "if Amazon could invent a system to remove the author from the equation, they'd do that."[23] If Google owns a menagerie of headless packbots and UPS one day can deliver by drone, how long will it be before the billions invested in digital make a writebot that is, for all intents and purposes, indistinguishable from a human writer of even considerable talent? Perhaps not that long.

Here is what we recently found on the home page of a company called Automated Insights:

> We Give Data a Voice™
>
> We personalize content in real time and at scale, writing actionable content for one user among millions. Our patented artificial intelligence platform transforms big data sets into actionable stories and insights written in plain English with the tone, personality and variability of a human writer.[24]

Perhaps not very long at all.

What Is a Teacher?

Writers are under threat as data busts its chains and gains its voice. Teachers may soon find themselves similarly challenged. We have already outlined the ways in which digital is destroying education, but we have not yet described the ways in which the actual *teacher in the classroom* may at some point be seen to have become extraneous, at least by certain groups not terrifically fond of teachers generally. Certainly teachers have fallen from a perch as has perhaps no other class of professional besides the politician. The keening of anti-teacher lobbies is incessant and may well be driven, in large measure, by the fact that teachers happen to be a reliable Democratic voting bloc. Kids, of course, have always "hated teacher" and cannot be counted upon to leap to the defense of that guy who gave them a C+ on a history exam.

But another reason why teachers today are embattled may be that too many teachers are not that good at teaching. But while they are bad at teaching, they may at the same time be very good at organizing into unions and making sure it's nearly impossible to fire them for incompetence. New York City's Department of Education features a so-called "rubber room" where teachers go to "work" when they are found in dereliction or while awaiting a hearing for same.[25] Thus, even a teacher who might have been caught in an unsavory circumstance, or proven utterly lacking in any ability to convey knowledge, is paid at full salary and is assigned to a location where they sit in a room not teaching. A teacher might occupy the rubber room for months or even years at a time,[26] billing the taxpayer for their time with every bag of Cheetos they munch before lunch.

That said, there are, of course, plenty of good teachers and some stellar teachers who impact young minds as perhaps few adults ever can. But even these teachers might be found replaceable with digitized teach-bots. And the teaching profession, unfortunately larded with more under-performers than can reasonably be accommodated in a straitened society, will be found at least partly to blame for the replacement of teachers with more standardized (nonvoting) versions.

Teacher Replacement?

Katherine Mangu-Ward, managing editor of the rightist *Reason* maga-zine, rhetorically asked herself, while speaking at a conference in 2013, if computers might replace teachers one day, and then said, "Dear God, I hope so."[27]

She was kidding, or at least seemed to think the suggestion was hu-morous.

As managing editor of a "conservative" sheet, she may represent a faction of what I call techno-libertarians: mainly anti-regulationists and supply-siders who seem to have become convinced that people just can-not get out of their own way and are largely incapable of solving any problem that doesn't involve a small hand tool or a spoonful of sugar. And that the only humans with any grasp of real problem-solving are trickle-downers, software engineers, and pioneers in robotry.

Ms. Mangu-Ward aside, there's a general lack of faith in humanity embedded in much of today's techno-libertarian cant that is both breath-taking and rather depressing. It's as if we were to suggest that the entire point of human pursuit were the happiness of humans but that humans could not be trusted to teach it, and that we had best turn over the entire enterprise to an algorithm and a sliver of silicon.

In this context, should we even be *trying* to replace teachers with computers? Unlike in the graphic arts, in education there is no equivalent to the lopsided comparison between hot lead typesetting and a PDF. Instead, we are talking about the awakening of the minds of those who must someday inherit this hurtling cinder we cling to in the void of space. And despite the dreary nature of too many schools and the lack of imagination displayed by too many unimaginative teachers (I disliked school when I was in it), it's not to suggest that software and flatscreens and one day an R2D2 will somehow manage to perform such an audacious task so much better than teachers do in 2014.

In my unschooled opinion, teachers have intrinsic value *as people*, and we need no other reason to leave them in charge of educating our young. Not too long from now the digital touts will say they've figured out a replacement, and the supply-siders will say they can't afford teachers anymore, and ex-teachers will, if they are lucky, pour your coffee at the rest stop until the day they can't do that anymore because robots never spill a drop and never complain and coffee will cost half what it costs today because there's no labor.

Or not. It's very possible that the push to replace teachers with algorithms will fall a bit short of saturation. Will parents and their children rally 'round those underpaid professionals who wield the hick'ry stick? Let's review for a few years, and at the end of the decade we will have a quiz.

Chips and Masters

Elephants paint with brushes on canvas in Thailand. The mahouts encourage it and sell the paintings to tourists who not only like the way they look (Franz Kline/Cy Twombley) but also who made them.[28] Some of the works come with a certificate of elephanticity. Pachyderm art is a small industry, and, like many artists, the elephants are largely unpaid for their efforts. Some of the money goes to protecting their habitat, a laudable effort that deserves every chance at success.

Chimps and bonobos also paint[29] but with less apparent interest and more spatter. Cats are reputed to paint,[30] but it is unclear if these are more the artifacts of feline encounters with paint than intentional creations.

Computers have been known to "create" what certainly satisfies a viewer as art, even if we cannot detect intentionality.[31] And people use computers to make art. At one time in my career I called myself a digital illustrator. Early attempts at showing my work encountered some flustered reactions, such as "How do you get art into the computer?" I am quite certain the art director thought my creations were the result of pushing a few buttons that accessed a massive database of images already resident in their final form inside the computer, and that somehow they had been put there by someone not myself. Later I got work *because* I was digital, but that is another story.

Will Computers Replace Artists?

Harvey Moon makes robotic drawing machines.[32] The machines "are created from motors and servos, while the drawings they create are defined by algorithms which determine the machine's movements and gestures."[33] In his Chicago studio he'll do things like use crickets to generate movement that the machines then turn into original art.

Much unlike what "computer art" might have seemed a few years back (Snoopy printed out in x's), and totally unlike the CGI magic we encounter at the cinema, these creations seem much more organic and unpredictable than what one might expect. Algorithms have come a long way. We now know that a few simple rules, compounded inside a programmed routine, can generate remarkably diverse results. And so it is with Moon's robot art.

Such is the concentration of force in digital today, and at such speed is the gallop of Moore's law toward impossible-seeming processing power and data storage volume, that it is possible we might one day see robots—without any discernable human assistance—creating works of art that we can in no way distinguish from that created by human masters. Can the day be far off when a well-balanced limb of composite fiber dips a brush into linseed oil, mixes exquisite colors on a real palette, and paints mindless but elegant creations on real canvas? Or uses new materials to 3D-print sculpted abstractions of a type similar to those that now confront us at museums of the modern?

We can at some point expect such creations to become all the rage, and, no doubt, a new class of art shall arise. Certain types of software engineers will create artware, and robots will create works that will hang in galleries, and human artists will perhaps come to seem more like artisans. Artists (and maybe elephants) will become members of just another class of competitor in a global, digitally driven art world.

DIGITAL DARWINISM AND MAN'S NATURAL STATE

It seems reasonable to suggest there really is very little humans can produce or provide that robots won't be producing or providing within the lifetimes of children born today. And there is no evident movement to support the notion that we must stop replacing people with machines. In fact, the greater force of enterprise is fully backing the wholesale replacement of humans in any niche in which robots might perform the work.

In a form of digital Darwinism, digital owners and investors seem to tout this replacement as entirely beneficial. That such replacement eviscerates the non-digital workforce seems to represent an aspect of not simply inevitability but also foundational goodness and justice.

Presumably our future selves will find new things to do even as every traditional occupation falls away to a mechanized army of doers. But before we look forward to a new golden age of inactivity, we must expect to weather a cycle of terrific societal upheavals as entire masses of ill-prepared people are displaced, replaced, misplaced, and left to wonder what they shall do with hungry bellies and idle hands.

In the past these upheavals have often taken the form of insurrection and, as Hobbes might have put it, "warre."[34] It seems not too audacious to suggest that without the traditional comforts of civilized pursuit (the pursuers having been replaced in large measure by unpaid skillbots), humankind stands at least a measurable chance of falling back into a state of nature in which life is "nasty, brutish and short."[35]

And in which the unblinking eye of the robocop is upon us.

16

FROM RUBYLITH TO SELFIES: LESSER PURSUITS DESTROYED BY DIGITAL

PRINT

Earlier I presented a case where digital destroys print media. But here I will refer not to the woes of print *media*, but rather to those of the now buried and forgotten industry called "printing"—until recently a tale of ink and solvent, of lead and of rubylith, of protractors and erasers. I know this story well, because I entered the field of commercial art and print production just as the days of India ink, rubber cement, and Bestine were drawing to a noxious and unlamented close.

Who today might guess that at one time in the twentieth century, glittering Manhattan may well have been the most densely *industrial* district in all the land?[1] And who might guess that a large percentage of that industry was engaged in putting ink on paper and binding it into magazines, brochures, and books? Today there are almost no printers in Manhattan. And the few printers left accomplish their product in a manner utterly divergent from the manner in which they accomplished it at mid-century.

I remember when a peculiar imaging language called Postscript[2] (developed by Adobe) freed the paste-up artist from the tyranny of rub-off typefaces and hand-lettering. It allowed for a scalable, perfect-looking typeface to be imaged on a digital printer with the possibility of infinite change at a vanishingly small cost.

Today the appearance of nearly every letter you see printed on paper (with the exception of hand-hewn greeting cards from a letter press) is governed by the algorithms of Postscript. Postscript may be one of the greatest inventions in document production since Gutenberg's press. It changed utterly and forever the manner in which printed words made their way onto paper. But Postscript was the virus that killed off the jobs of vast armies of paper-hatted printers and their harried, nearsighted, perfectionist compositors, replacing them both with a new, digitally aware artisan: the desktop publisher.

Desktop publishing probably deserves a history book of its own, and I haven't the space here to detail it. But desktop publishing is in every respect digital publishing, and digital publishing is immeasurably easier than non-digital publishing. Perhaps in no other industry has computing made such a rapid and total transformation. It's one of the few ways in which digital destroyed something truly unwieldy and replaced it with something that has been quite indisputably better.

PHOTOGRAPHY

Joseph Nicéphore Niépce lived well in Burgundy in the early nineteenth century, and he invented a form of light-recording that was not, at that time, called photography. Many today credit him with taking the first photograph (of rooftops from his estate window), but his name for it was "heliography." It involved the exposure of a sheet of pewter, coated with bitumen, to several hours of lens-focused light so as to leave an artifact of the photons upon the substrate. Certain other chemicals were later discovered to react chromatically under light, and thus when light struck the chemicals, an image was captured.

Photography flourished in the nineteenth century, but it became the communicative medium of choice in the twentieth century. We relive that period not by reading but by looking. We see dusk in a horse-drawn Old New York at Twenty-third Street in an Edward Steichen print. The Sultan of Swat trotting the diamond with the twig-legged swiftness of a Keystone Kop. American soldiers hoisting a flag at Iwo Jima. In a more advanced age, we all encountered the filmstrip shot by Abraham Zapruder in Dallas, showing the president of the United States getting his head blown off in broad daylight. A little later, we had images taken with (analog) Hasselblads during the moon shots. These were the pictures worth all the words that might be written, and they had a veracity that we all took for granted. Photographs were expected to be mute stalwarts of infrangible truth.

We laughed at the painfully obvious attempts at what was called "photo retouching" from a more innocent era. We knew it was nearly impossible to fake photographs, and motion pictures even less. Even the great moguls of Hollywood, sparing no expense, could hardly create any photographically false effect that did not also require at least a willing suspension of disbelief.

Today, almost no one believes photography is anything but a manipulator's paradise. Nearly every cinema monster today is digitally rendered from sophisticated 3D software, and they've become convincing in the extreme. This only drives home the notion that photography is not fact. It's no longer an *artifact*. Today photography is almost entirely digital, and almost any image can be faked (or at least substantially altered) by almost anyone with a computer.

Not a single photograph we see today can be relied upon as an accurate artifact of having captured light on a light-sensitive substrate; none can be relied upon as mute testament to a thing in the world. Perhaps only in horse racing is the "photo finish" unquestioned evidence of fact. Even the spectacle of a baseball manager kicking sand and furiously arguing against an "out" call at first base has been deleted by digital. Today, using a combination of digital video, remote viewing, and telecommunications to home plate itself, close plays in baseball are now often decided by a team of arbiters bunkered in a digital den somewhere in New York, and I don't mean Yankee Stadium. It may shorten the game, but it dramatically decreases the drama—without which, how much do we really care?

We had relied on photography as a window on the world, even if we knew that sometimes photographers would pull darkroom tricks to enhance or slightly alter an image. But we knew it was hard to do, and that, by and large, a photograph was authoritative, insofar as we knew there were those things in that place and that someone took a picture of it, meaning that it really happened in one way or another. Now we can have no faith at all. The veracity of photography has been destroyed by digital.

HISTORY

Try to imagine any attempt to understand the Civil War without trusting the veracity of the battlefield photographs of Matthew Brady. For many of us, photographs have sufficed as original documentation. This is at least partly because we knew they were awfully hard to fake. But photography is only a latecomer to the recording of history. We can also point to rock carvings, hieroglyphs, cuneiform, papyri, lambskin parchment, the illuminated manuscript, the printed book—in short, the entire spectrum of archival evidence that supports our sense of who we are and how we got this way.

Because of digital, today we stand to lose touch with tangible evidence and, thus, with our own history.

Digital content cannot be read or experienced by humans directly. It is nothing more than an array of electrical pulses generated by billions of switches a billion times over. And you cannot experience any of it without that very exacting machine called a computer.

Not much except brittleness and ignorance threatens the stones and papers of yesteryear. But digital is much less permanent and, more importantly, indecipherable except by computer.

Formats change. Computing systems change. Old digital artifacts don't just get dull, stained, scratched, and cracked. They become totally impossible to resurrect because there is no means available to read them, process them, and display them. Yet today there is no universal attempt at creating a permanently accessible archive of digital.

Years ago I created illustrations for magazines on a Macintosh computer. At first they were stored on floppy disks. Then they were stored on removable hard-drive cartridges called SyQuest disks, which for a time were an industry standard. Then whoever made SyQuest disks stopped making them, and there were no more devices that could read them, either.

This means that entire portfolios of my early digital work are simply lost. Not because I lost the disks, but because the technology for reading the disks is lost, or at least incredibly difficult to obtain—and this after less than twenty years.

If my own experience with SyQuest is any indication, we can only imagine the challenge of resurrecting data from a disk (or a cloud) that is hundreds, if not thousands, of years old. The data cannot be read by a human. And if the underlying technology is lost, it is very, very unlikely that it can be guessed at or reverse-engineered.

A DISTANT TRAVELER (ANALOG VERSION)

NASA launched the *Voyager* interstellar spacecraft in 1977—well before digital came into its own. *Voyager*, among other things, was to be a sort of interstellar ambassador, and it carried a "golden record" scribed with (analog) photographs, diagrams of our star system, outlines of humans, and, perhaps most whimsical of all, an intergalactic audio record. It continues to fly out into extra-solar space, carrying a golden LP made up of the same kinds of grooves they used to groove to in the 1960s and 1970s. It included a little diagram showing a needle and a cone. Presumably, a race of creatures elsewhere might spin up the sounds of Earth a million years from now, a trillion miles away.

We can make no such assumptions with digital.

Digital touts will say that all we have to do is make sure we've backed everything up. And that we should always move our digital assets to media that's readable on a current device. But it is not going to work in the long run, and by long run I mean after a period of more than, say, ten years. Most likely we are already losing part of our history in this manner. Except for a few vanity or academic sites that purport to preserve old websites,[3] what record do we have of the first few sites on the web? Are they not historically significant? Sure, many of them are being saved *somewhere*, and many more are hidden away on servers that no one accesses. But they have no intrinsic physical existence unless they've been printed out. One day the keepers may get restless and drop the preservation project, and these sites, along with millions of others, will be lost forever *without any hope of resurrection.*

What about other types of digital media? Is anyone likely to consider that there may in fact be historic tweets? Who is making sure these are even minimally archived in a manner fit for the ages? The Library of Congress is at least trying. It supports a program called the National Digital Stewardship Alliance, a public/private effort to preserve digital assets in suitable formats. Perhaps this will help stave off invisibility for a time. But the fundamental form factor remains. Once the chain of format upgrades is broken (and it will be at some point), the vast majority of our digital assets will irrevocably be lost.

Is anyone likely to consider that there may in fact be historic tweets?

Perhaps a concern with what we leave for the ages is of little concern to most, and it may even be the height of hubris to suggest that our future clans will care much or note much what we have done here today (deep apologies to Abraham Lincoln).[4] We can thank nineteenth-century English poet Percy Bysshe Shelley for a poignant review of the fate of even the greatest of physical memorials. In his "Ozymandias," a traveler in a desert waste comes upon a lone pedestal upon which is written:

> *My name is Ozymandias, king of kings:*
> *Look on my works, ye Mighty, and despair!*

The masterwork finishes with the words:

> *Nothing beside remains. Round the decay*
> *Of that colossal wreck, boundless and bare*
> *The lone and level sands stretch far away.*

With digital, we won't even have a colossal wreck. We will have stacks of oxidated storage media signifying nothing.

TOYS

According *Business Insider*, 2012 was the Christmas season when toddlers turned to tablets.[5] We thought it was cute on YouTube when the little girl tried to swipe a magazine as if it were an iPad.[6] To her, the magazine was a broken device and probably not very interesting. Children love shiny objects, and nothing shines quite like a smartphone or a tablet with a Retina display. Moreover, the method by which these devices are apprehended by children seems almost pre-verbal, and kids who are early exposed to them tend to learn where to find what they want not long after they are weaned.

Children love shiny objects, and nothing shines quite like a smartphone or a tablet with a Retina display.

Recently I saw a child strapped into a stroller, his little feet dangling in tiny shoes, navigating an iPhone to find the video he wanted, and then playing it. It's rapidly becoming a part of our basic human skillset to use a tablet. Poke, swipe, scroll. It's a new and wonderful paradigm that spans cultural divides almost as well as music.

If there's a downside, it's that kids don't want pull toys anymore. Or dolls, apparently. Or stuffed animals. Or toy cars, or action figures, or any of the wooden, rubber, plastic, or metal vessels that we have for decades assumed they have wanted and which they have accepted almost without question. Until now.

Retailers are reporting that toys are not moving much these days—but electronics are selling at lightning speed.[7] Anything with a screen and an interface will satisfy the digital diaper set, while Play-Doh and Barbie and Power Rangers and even remote-controlled widgets gather dust in warehouses waiting for a child to like them.

We thought that toys were both primeval and forever, but perhaps the era of the physical object is now beginning to fade. It's possible the flatscreen thing will pass, and that toys will come back as retro-cool (some, like the Easy-Bake Oven, already have). Or they won't. A generation or so from now, we will know for sure.

In any case, it seems we have passed another ambiguous milestone on the information superhighway. Kids don't seem to want all that touchy-feely stuff we thought they needed for healthy, mindful growth. They may need it, or they may not. But right now they are taking their cues from Mom and Dad, who cannot seem to look away from their own digital toys long enough to give the kids a hug. And the kids are learning, very quickly and completely, where the action is. It's there on the endless, ephemeral two-dimensional landscape of the touch-screen.

17

IT'S WORSE THAN YOU THOUGHT: DIGITAL IS DESTROYING PRIVACY

"Has the Internet Already Destroyed Privacy?" So asked *Huffington Post* in 2013. I might answer, "No, not yet."

But we are already stripped of so much privacy that we may hardly notice the point at which we are finally disrobed. A more cogent question might be "How much privacy do we really need?" The underlying assumption in this question is whether it is being asked in an open society or a police state. If the former, we may not need it that much, and we had better get over it. If the latter, then we must bar the door against warrantless intrusion and remote control.

First, let's examine the need for privacy in an environment where no one has any and where surveillance is difficult.

DO WE REALLY NEED PRIVACY?

We're culturally attuned to privacy at least partly as a bulwark against physical invasion. Long before we moved out of holes in the rock, our ancestors in all likelihood would have hung skins across the entrance of the cave so as not to reveal firelight to a night prowled by marauders. Log cabins in the wilderness provided a barrier against bears and unimpressed native populations. But an important byproduct of stacked logs was that even your fellow pioneer could not tell what you were up to inside the walls of your home. We grew accustomed to privacy as a natural condition in which we had the right to secrets.

It had not always been this way.

In an era before indoor plumbing or even the private outhouse, we had the public latrine. The Romans were fond of it, and we can find examples of their communal toilets in several ruins throughout the range of their empire.[1] In the fifteenth century it was common for a head of state to receive visitors while sitting on a toilet, and the Duke Federico da Montefeltro "had toilet facilities installed in his palace in Urbino, so his courtiers and visitors could sit next to each other whilst doing their call of nature."[2]

Soldiers in the field and refugees know that personal privacy is denied with little regard to propriety. And as distasteful as these examples may seem to the well plumbed, we hear little of the long-term ill effects (barring contagion) of this total abandonment of the private sphere.

This suggests privacy is a conceit. We can demonstrate that when none have it, it loses value for all. But the Philadelphia Convention saw fit to protect certain forms of privacy, as here in the Fourth Amendment to the United States Constitution:

> The right of the people to be secure in their persons, houses, papers, and effects, against unreasonable searches and seizures, shall not be violated . . .

Thus the US government is constitutionally barred from illegal search and seizure. But everyone else is free to do what they might to gather information about their fellow citizens without fear of having violated anyone's constitutional rights.

There's scant legal basis for a guarantee of privacy from one's fellows in the US and, I would wager, even less in most other countries. Certainly A. J. Weberman knew this when he went through Bob Dylan's trash in the 1960s when Bob Dylan's trash was deemed sufficiently fascinating to warrant study. Companies using digital analytics know this as they scrape from the web as much information about you as they can, while you slalom upon the surface of their digital assets.

INFAMY

Digital practices lead us to greater and greater exposure—much of it willing, some of it lacking consent—but always we find ourselves sharing more and knowing more about others. Consider the self-inflicted Twitter flameout of one Justine Sacco at Christmas 2013 as she boarded a jet to South Africa (witlessly tweeting something in poor taste about AIDS, Africa, and being white). In the time it took for her to fly away and land in Johannesburg, new Twitter hashtags had made her world-famous in a very bad way. She lost her job and became the victim of a gleeful hate-on-the-hater attack that went way over the top and *almost* made you feel sorry for her.

But if the above is any example, it seems lack of privacy online (and its close cousin, inveterate sharing) can too often entice cowardly jackals bent on vengeance. Perhaps nothing today stands for privacy invasion more than that heinous practice known as cyberbullying in which anonymous cowards make death threats to those victims, too often women, who have somehow raised their ire. The twin poles of oversharing and overt threatening can only make us wonder what we are likely to face when even the filter of a "send" button melts away; when our conversations might be billboarded,[3] our utterances parsed out of context by the millions as if we were all running for president of the United States; when digital dogs us into our homes, our beds, perhaps even our innermost selves.

The latest advances in smart-device technology suggest that devices like Fitbit will be able to tell when you're sweating or when you ought to take a nap.[4] Perhaps, in future, they will signal a robot to prepare a bath of warm salts. Or signal an advertiser to offer a discount to a spa. But as long as your smart device is on (and sometimes even when it's off), you're never entirely invisible to the grid.

Google recently bought Nest, a networked thermostat that will tell them when you're home and when you're not. Facebook says they have a technology that allows them to see what you have typed in a Facebook post *even if you decide not to send it.* Google's Gmail, in tandem with its G+ platform, may soon enable people on G+ to send you gmails even though you have never given them your gmail address.

Will universal transparency prove an antidote to brickbats? It may, or it may only provide a deepening ravine running right next to the trails we tread through life, waiting to swallow us as we misstep our way into an abyss of ignominy.

Universal transparency may only provide a deepening ravine running right next to the trails we tread through life, waiting to swallow us as we misstep our way into an abyss of ignominy.

NO PRIVACY, PLEASE, WE'RE MILLENNIALS

A recent article in *Forbes* suggests the kids just don't care, or don't even really understand, what the old folks mean by the word "privacy."[5] The article says that "seventy percent [of Millennials 18–34] . . . say no one should have access to their data or online behavior. Yet . . . 51% say they will share information if they get something in return." According to the USC Annenberg Center for the Digital Future, "Online privacy is dead— Millennials understand that, while older users have not adapted."[6]

Perhaps the millennials are right. In centuries past, entire extended families might find themselves living all together in one room. In Puritan America, courting couples, on nights when snow might drift upon the hearthstones, were expected to sleep in a single bed, separated by a "bundling board," or what amounted to a chastity plank.[7] Often this bed was in a common space shared by others, and the frequent appearance of pregnant colonial brides suggests the plank was not especially effective as contraception.[8]

"Privacy" seemed of little concern generally well into the nineteenth century. In 1890, Louis D. Brandeis co-authored an article in the *Harvard Law Review* that said, in part, "To satisfy a prurient taste the details of sexual relations are spread broadcast in the columns of the daily papers . . . [and therefore] the intensity and complexity of life, attendant upon advancing civilization, have rendered necessary some retreat from the world."[9] In a *New Yorker* article, Jill LePore says that "the defense of privacy follows, and never precedes, the emergence of new technologies for the exposure of secrets,"[10] and thus calls to privacy therefore "always come too late."[11]

Fifty years from now the notion that anyone cared to keep their doings curtained off from their fellows may come to seem quaint, dainty, and stodgy. And we can speculate that private information, accessible to all, will be kept at least reasonably safe in counterpoint by the ability of *everyone to see everything about everybody* if they cared to—but because transparency will be ubiquitous, it will seem insipid to have bothered looking.

Total lack of privacy may turn out to be a liberation from the tyranny of protections. Absurd behavioral rules will drop from the books; victimless crimes will widely be accepted as oxymoronic; vanity will become prudish. Insularity will give way to communalism. Everyone will be friends and enemies at the same time. Social strata will melt into a single pool of intermingled organisms out of which new forms might emerge. Or at least this would be the Panglossian view of a zero-privacy world.

Heedless optimism aside, there is an argument to be made that digital will have liberated us from our own isolation. If there is a human longing for completeness, it may be that we deploy digital as a rung to a higher state of consciousness and a further state of evolution.

All this assumes, of course, that sharing is universal and that information is not misused by the Powers to persecute the People. In a digital age, this misuse can become truly outsized.

EDWARD SNOWDEN, THE NSA, AND PERNICIOUS SPYING

Edward Snowden in 2013 claimed that his mission has been accomplished, [12] and good for him. I'm not sure what his mission was, or why he believes it's accomplished. But he does have the bully pulpit on privacy, and while he's not especially quotable, he at least has taken risks to expose some of the darker secrets of the secret-keepers (namely, the National Security Agency, or NSA) that use our tax dollars on digital techniques to spy on us. With impunity.

Naturally, this spy ring would ring hollow if not for digital. We know they are collecting everything and keeping it somewhere—and that somewhere is inside fifty acres of digital storage devices. We also know that even so-called liberal politicians have taken to either studiously ignoring or even defending the NSA's activities. [13] And a majority of Americans seem to find it an appalling turn of events. [14]

In a 2013 "Christmas Message" broadcast in the United Kingdom, Snowden said, "A child born today will grow up with no conception of privacy at all. . . . They'll never know what it means to have a private moment to themselves, an unrecorded, unanalyzed thought."

In December 2013, a federal judge declared the NSA digital megaspying program "almost Orwellian." [15] Later that month, another federal judge said, "Maybe not." Somehow it seems the massive spy program will never really go away and instead will only expand.

On this matter I cannot see room for much debate. I come down squarely on the side of the Snowden-heads who feel like he may well qualify for some kind of international commendation and (my idea alone) perhaps a Nobel Peace Prize. He has exposed a digital police state of a type that even the most cynical would hardly have imagined before his disclosures. The insulting responses from our elected leaders only make it seem that much more likely the program is nefarious and that there can be no guarantee whatsoever that it will not be used for ill at any given moment. Moreover, the fact that we know it's being collected necessarily has a dampening effect on even reasonable dissent.

How many young politicos are chilled by the notion that they may say something to someone somewhere that scuttles their chances of getting into office or, worse, invites further scrutiny and perhaps even harassment? And who gets to decide what constitutes dissent?

In the pre-digital days, the FBI's Operation COINTELPRO infiltrated organizations like the Black Panthers and SDS and Vietnam Veterans Against the War and others. Then they got caught fomenting crimes just so they could bust those they saw as security threats. The program was scuttled, [16] and a generation of espionage oversight made for grumpy spooks that got their wings again only with the ascendancy of Reagan-Bush. Perhaps it is useful to note that Vice-President George Herbert Walker Bush had once been head of the CIA.

Today they are demonstrably back at it, if indeed they ever stopped. A *New York Times* article in November 2014 suggested that any number of federal agencies are posting spies and moles all around [17]: as business-people, attorneys, protesters, and maybe even that guy sitting next to you at the bar.

Government Intrusion

Thus I draw the line on privacy at the point of government intrusion. It's one thing for people to shed their privacy from one another and perhaps expect the same from others. This is merely the will of the people, unprotected and untrammeled. It may be foolhardy, but it's a portion of free will, and many believe that free will is the foundation of humanity in humankind.

It's exactly the opposite, and nefarious in its very intent, to have a multibillion-dollar, secret, digitally powered, universal data collection scheme in full roar and accessible to a class of people whose very project is to pierce veils and undermine trust and ferret out secrets of every specie. The arrogant brush-off we've gotten from the liberal lights of the Senate and White House has only given us chills and forced us to accept that, when it comes to our fear of a police state, we can expect exactly zero protection from the left side of the spectrum (where we might have hoped to find it) and only a misguided, off-key attack upon surveillance from libertarians who link it with food stamps and birth certificates in a fashion approaching brain-dead. Institutional Republicans seem to have little comment on it, since it probably aids them not at all to find themselves in agreement with the White House.

No doubt the NSA will come under further scrutiny in the coming months and years, but to date there has been no real attempt to make it stop. It's certainly an interesting side note that while Obamacare was so poorly implemented at first, it seems the nation's spymasters have figured out how to use a keyboard and mouse quite effectively in pursuit of all data all the time.

SPYING AND ENTRAPMENT

Can anyone expect the total breakdown of privacy and the untrammeled infiltration of groups far and wide to *not be misused?* Does anyone really believe that the legion of men and women whose *job is to "stop crime" by entrapment* will not use this data to gull the cocklebrained into pathetic lunacies engineered by the state—and then bust them, claiming they've broken a spy ring?

Does anyone really believe that those who "stop crime" by entrapment will not use this data to gull the cocklebrained into pathetic lunacies engineered by the state?

I can recall a case in New York State not long ago when the FBI learned about some off-handed talk at a mosque and ended up "infiltrating" a few nincompoops who were taught to think of themselves as conspirators in a scheme to fire missiles at a synagogue. It turned out the caper itself was invented by the FBI,[18] the weapons were secured by the FBI, the money was brought by the FBI, and the so-called "jihadists" were led by an FBI informant who hectored them on jihad until they became incriminated enough to bust them on charges of terrorism. To such protectors can we send our unterrorized thanks.

We are told all of this is being done "to keep us safe." Indeed, there is nothing in a police state if not safety—for those already propertied, connected, or powerful. And in a country that has become so tilted economically, in which nearly all of us must have some fear of falling through a ragged or nonexistent safety net such as no other modernized population in the world needs fear, and in which social stratification is becoming entrenched, in which the concentration of wealth and its attendant power has become so stupendous as to beggar the notion of democracy, and (perhaps of equal importance) in an environment where digital powers data collection, storage, correlation, and reporting in an unprecedented manner, we now find ourselves told that our government is watching us everywhere they can and ramping up the effort. If this *sounds* bad, that may because it really *is* bad.

Billionaires might rest assured they're not to be victimized by government search and seizure as long as they stick to doing what billionaires do best, but anyone else might have a right to feel only provisionally protected by a Bill of Rights that seems to have become as outmoded as the quill pens with which it was scribed.

DIGITALLY COMPLICIT?

Let not the great Digital Kingdoms chide you that they are inalienably in favor of your right to privacy from government intrusion. Many of them, including Google,[19] Apple,[20] Experian,[21] Microsoft,[22] and others, are government contractors. These titans may caterwaul about the NSA and exclaim their shock and horror that what they helped the NSA do is actually what the NSA does, but it seems they are bound by law not to talk about it. It has been suggested they must be complicit, but today we can have no proof of that.

Perils of the Cloud

Nor can we say categorically there's a difference between information collected by the government and information collected by the private sector. Leaving marketing aside, let's take a moment to determine what sorts of liberties we forsake when placing all our faith and all our assets in the cloud.

The cloud, while making every smartphone a genius, also makes every computer a dumb terminal without it. Unconnected, we are nothing. We rely on universal broadband in order to support a digital existence. Remove this and remove our digital self—a virtual self that becomes more and more like a complete version of "us" every day. It's as if we had all decided to stop breathing air and submitted to a better version of oxygen that gave us additional powers but that we had to suck out of a straw. And while access to the straw was cheap and sometimes free, it was never to be guaranteed, nor suggested that it was a right. Yet we became so dependent upon the New Oxygen that we could hardly breathe without it.

We have essentially lost the permanent right to access our own stuff, because we have decided that for a few dollars a month it makes more sense to let someone else (Dropbox, Google Drive) keep it for us in the cloud. One of the very first concerns I had when getting my first computer was that storage media would become inordinately valuable and data backup a burden for the digital trailblazer. It still is a burden, but we don't really appreciate it because we've been lulled into thinking everything's okay if it's in the cloud.

But clouds change shape rather quickly and sometimes can look like angels and sometimes can look like ogres. The cloud is not a given. It's a package of unregulated and unruly services where we pay for a "service-level agreement" that ostensibly gives us the right to have "a neck to choke" (as the information-technology phrase goes) if something goes wrong. Small comfort that you can choke a neck when your life's work got lost because you missed a couple of payments. Or because the cloud company turned into a stormcloud and was blown out of business.

If I might offer any advice at all: Back everything up on your own. Storage drives are crazy-cheap these days. Certain things, do print them out. The sheet of paper has been known to come in handy as a carrier of information during blackouts if you have a candle nearby.

It pays to remember the cloud is not intrinsically private, no matter how many promises are made. The cloud is by definition a shared (and managed) space. And while there's no evidence Dropbox is dropping your files into an NSA box, it would be easy enough for them to do so, and perhaps at some point it might become mandated. Send it to the cloud, and you've spent your privacy.

Non-Privacy Goes with Non-Ownership

When it comes to software, it gets worse. Some of us may remember buying software at the computer store. It came in a box. Never could it be questioned that you could do what you wanted with it and that you could, in theory, own it forever and run it forever even if it became as antiquated as a typewriter.

The new paradigm is "no software." Many types of software today run on a subscription model. You pay by the month. If you are tiny, you pay almost nothing. It's quite a powerful concept, and once you are on it, you don't get off it, unless you stop needing that software.

Adobe now licenses its premiere products—Photoshop, InDesign, Analytics—in the same manner. I remember when Adobe Illustrator 1.0 came out. Botticelli's Venus was smiling out from the box top and it seemed that someone in software understood elegance the way Apple did in hardware.

Then came a tool called Photoshop that changed visualization in radical fashion.

Now Adobe says that these key software items can no longer be bought. Instead, they can be rented. For just a few dollars a month, anyone with broadband and a reasonably up-to-date OS can run Photoshop.

But what if you don't want your imagery parsed on Adobe servers? You haven't much choice anymore. Any advantage we might have had in the private ownership of a software license will have been lost to the hegemony of the cloud, and in the cloud we can be made transparent if the cloud-maker deems it needful.

More and more, the tools we spend our days and nights using, viewing, enjoying, and listening to are in the cloud, rented, controlled, and do not belong to us. A particularly nettlesome example is Apple's iTunes. Elegant and functional and world-beating it is, but it's also paternalistic and very strict about everything, even about the songs you may have believed you "own." In fact, you don't really own them, at least not in the sense that you own a vinyl LP.

There are iTunes device restrictions (for instance, you cannot, apparently, sync to more than three computers) that make it clear they are policing your use of content. Remember that, first, you had to buy the music. Then you were told that maybe you could not put that music you bought on that listening device.

One can imagine an earlier generation being told their favorite album had to be played on a maximum of three different stereo sets. The revolution would have been on.

The [digital] tools we spend our days and nights using, viewing, enjoying, and listening to are in the cloud, rented, controlled, and do not belong to us.

Security State Imperatives

Unless the NSA's massive data-collection plan is scuttled or at least cut to the bone, the prospect for privacy is not a pretty one.

Ever since the day when George W. Bush read of pet goats to kindergartners, we have been in thrall to the needs of what is sanctimoniously referred to as "the war on terror." Any suggestion that we should let our guard down is shouted down from every side as if it were tantamount to tacit support for terror. The notion of continuing threats continually justifies massive spying, and advancing digital technology makes more massive spying even more likely. And in a digital environment where eavesdropping is far simpler than ever before, you've got the recipe for a truly American version of the police state. I am fairly comfortable saying that much the same has become of our counterparts in the UK, and more's the pity. They had always seemed rather a sensible lot.

Common Sense

Common sense tells me that turning planes into missiles is easily thwarted by locking the door to the pilot's cabin, and made near-impossible by deploying a fair amount of both uniformed and undercover air marshals. But instead we have a huge army of bag-checkers and body-searchers that turn every airplane trip into a victim's course in command and control.

Common sense tells us that a smarter way of reviewing passengers—one that would not involve shoe removal and the confiscation of water bottles—would work much better than the sledgehammer approach we deploy today.

Common sense tells me that the government does not have the right to record all your phone calls and collect all your e-mails and store them under a mountain without some form of meaningful judicial oversight.

Common sense tells me that lower Manhattan should not feel like an armed camp with police towers and helmeted guards at regular intervals. And that you should not need to be photographed every time you want to see someone in an office building.

Common sense tells me that the smartphones in all of our pockets should not be sending digital signals to a central processor that tracks our movements as if we were in an episode of *The Prisoner*.

COMMERCIAL DATA COLLECTION VS. GOVERNMENT DATA COLLECTION

Right now some of the biggest retailers in the world are conducting what amount to deeply invasive data-collection techniques using your smartphone when you are in their store and sometimes when you're not. Some technologists boast they can sense the angle at which your phone is held, the speed at which it is traveling, its location, and its vertical movement. Such technologies can be used to tell if you're jogging, for instance, past a 7-Eleven. And if the analytics wizards work their wands well enough, you'll end up with an offer for a discounted bottle of Powerade.

That sounds like it might be okay if we are okay with being closely observed. The worst that can happen is that you see an annoying ad.

But with the same technology in the hands of a police state—where the definitions of "security" and "threat" might both arbitrarily be determined by an algorithm—we begin to approach the digital version of a Walpurgis Night where paranoia rules and badge-festooned hobgoblins try to trip you up with questions about your loyalties and your intentions.

I know this sounds awfully dire and even florid.

But I am worried that because we now are connected digitally as never before, and as we are still trying to understand how to understand digital in all its ramifications, and as digital has made almost a joke of privacy to begin with—because of these things I am worried we have crossed over into a foggy region of nuance and uncertainty where we are more or less unprotected from abuse.

It's digital, see?

The old rules are just getting in the way.

IT'S JUST TOO EASY

Spying used to be a kludgy thing.

There were tape recorders and mirrors, and even early James Bond hadn't much beyond a knife hidden in his briefcase. Deciphering and surreptitious targeting were more about books and unique typewriters and photographic memories than about a server and a watchful thermostat.

But digital has put surveillance on a higher plane. In the short time we've known about official universal data collection, how many of us have been able to stop and contemplate the catastrophe? Apple seems at least to be trying. They claim the new iPhone cannot be hacked. Nor, I have been told, could the *Titanic* have sunk.

But I have seen little else in the market meant to protect privacy, and much instead to compromise it. It has become so easy! A combination of sharing technology and sharing mindsets has produced what is called "the sharing economy," but I think a better name for it would be the "data collection economy."

The fact that it's easy to collect data does not necessarily make collection a bad thing. Marketers are collecting data all the time, and, in fact, I have been involved in the technology behind some of that data collection.

Much as I care little that marketers want to know how to sell to me more efficiently, I do believe there is a fundamental difference between TJ Maxx wanting to send me a coupon and the NSA wanting to put me on a no-fly list. I very strongly object to the high-handed, unconstitutional manner in which digital has been leveraged by Orwellian spy networks with a history of abuse.

I agree that freedom must have its limits, and that privacy is not an absolute. But this time it's different, because it's digital and digital can make privacy invasion so much more absolute that it threatens to destroy even the kernel of selfhood we all take home at night. Under constant surveillance we won't act like ourselves. At some point we won't even be ourselves. We will be putting on a big act and hoping to avoid the gill net of hypersecurity.

I take it personally that my personal privacy has been destroyed by digital.

18

MAYBE IT'S ALL BULLSHIT

Anyone who writes a book with a title like this one's had better be prepared to offer a debunking scenario well in advance of the critics.

First, let me suggest that I am aware of having failed, more or less, to sufficiently enumerate the glories of digital; nor have I devoted enough effort to describing how much we enjoy digital benefits. As we plunge blindly into a future bound hand and foot to digital, let's remember how we got ourselves bound.

It was love. A fiery, passionate, take-a-little-piece-o'-my-heart kind of love.

I was early enough in digital to recall hearing people ask me, "What is a website?" and "What is the Internet?" They tended to ask less with a sense of wonder than of trepidation, as if they had prepared themselves to hear the worst. In 1994 I met with an account executive of a large ad agency at his office and, after I showed him an interactive multimedia prototype, he asked, with what seemed to me considerable irritation, "Who is going to *pay* for all this?"

We do know today that billions have been paid by somebody to somebody else for whatever "this" is. However, the ad man was entirely myopic in the context from which he asked. He really wanted to know how it might ever amount to a dollar at an advertising agency or why an advertiser would ever pay for clicks and pixels. He seemed eager to end the meeting in favor of what I imagined would be a three-martini lunch, and we did not cross paths again.

In the beginning, folks resisted the wooing of digital. It was geeky, nerdy, not much fun. There were all those green screens and lots of typing.

Much seemed to change, and rapidly, with the widespread use of a graphical interface (Mac or Windows), and more rapidly still with even minimal connectivity. Not long after I e-mailed a friend "Get thee to a website," he excitedly told me he had "visited the Louvre." I was duly impressed. At a trade show I saw a plucky little product called MapQuest that purported to provide accurate maps of the entire United States, and I remember wondering how long it must have taken to create all those digital maps, and whether they'd be able to handle all that data going forward.

There was a sense of utopianism about digital, and perhaps a bit of overkill on idealism. The first e-mail ad campaign I remember hearing about (1994?) was of lawyers in Arizona who had sent e-mails to prospective clients. As I recall, the then-popular "chat rooms" lit up with righteous, anti-commercial fury. How dare they use this pristine new medium to worship at the feet of Moloch! It was as if someone had glued a bumper sticker onto a Stradivarius.

The first e-mail campaign I remember hearing about was opposed with righteous, anti-commercial fury.

Then digital became ubiquitous and went well beyond the web. And we began to realize what digital really meant even if it wasn't necessarily "wired," as the term was used then. We had anti-lock braking systems—computer-controlled micro-pulsing that prevented automobile brakes from locking and people from crashing and dying. We had electron scanners that allowed us to peer into the body in ways that made X-rays seem like daguerreotypes, and the results were reviewed on a digital monitor. We had massive amounts of weather-related data and had developed hurricane algorithms that gave us eyes upon nature's worst threats, saving lives untold. We had 3D imaging that helped us understand spatial relationships in ways never before possible, and 3D software programs allowed us to create prototypes in just a fraction of the time it had taken to sculpt clay or build architectural models with balsa.

Today it's almost more shocking to recall what we achieved *before* digital than to think of what we can now expect. Before digital became pervasive, we had guided missiles, radar, radio, television, moon landings, supersonic passenger jets, and nuclear submarines. Digital controls have made all of these more precise, less failure-prone, and much more upgradeable (except for the Concorde, which is on permanent hiatus).

That we can now carry all the music we love in our pocket is a blessing for which we had never dared hope, and we could hardly believe when we had it. Watching Netflix is an unalloyed pleasure. Buying hard-to-find items on eBay or Amazon has made us all connoisseurs of one thing or another.

All these advantages we now take for granted, and let us try not to forget how hard it used to be to do some of these bedrock tasks before digital.

PAST FUTURE

Futurism informs my approach to digital, and so it makes sense for me to suggest some sense of the future's past. We had in 1970 a book by Alvin Toffler called *Future Shock*, and it was a runaway best-seller. Toffler wrote of a project called OLIVER, an acronym for what began with the words "On Line Interactive." The OLIVER project would handle petty tasks like calendaring, reminding, remembering preferences, and organizing information. Then it would move on to allow the ordinary citizen to ransack the libraries of the world. It was speculated that OLIVER might even foster electronic communication. Further, it might determine what seemed to please us and try to give us more of that. Then OLIVER would plant "pleasure chips" in people's brains.

It was 1970! FM radio was considered an advanced format.

What Toffler missed was that OLIVER would become pervasive and come to dominate our culture—the world's culture—in a way we can hardly yet comprehend, never mind plan for.

One of Toffler's chief concerns was that it would be a bad idea to allow technology solely to be developed by "businessmen and engineers." Mr. Toffler may sound Soviet to us today, but he had been associate editor at *Fortune* magazine. His biggest concern was that we'd confront new technologies without preparation, and we'd therefore be prone to victimization.

Now we are completely in thrall to OLIVER (except, at least for now, for the implants). We've absolutely given over technology to anyone who wants to play with it and have totally failed to plan for any of it. And we are sort of doing okay, except for those of us who've seen our livelihoods destroyed or radically diminished in remunerative power. In that sense, he was right about victimization. But many of us would not trade digital for an unknown alternative, and we can say we've generally adapted quickly as we have always done. Going forward, I think any assessment of a digital future must factor in human adaptability as a key component of viability.

Digital has given us a lot to be thankful for. In many ways it has exceeded the dreams of the dreamers. But I did not name this book as I did because I think digital solves problems in every ramification, nor do I think adaptability will universally meet the challenge. I disagree with Toffler that "planning the future" will help, and I would suggest it's not really possible as a mid-century industrialist might have imagined it. Nor do I expect anyone to take seriously a suggestion that we "put on the brakes." It can't be done—it won't be done. Digital is the future, and the future is digital.

But digital is not a force for good, as many digital touts want to claim. It is a force. It is a force the way wind is, the way ocean currents are, the way nuclear power is a force. Most likely, as much as it has created, it has destroyed, and much that has been destroyed was better than what re-placed it.

[Digital] is a force the way wind is, the way ocean currents are, the way nuclear power is a force. Most likely as much as it has created, it has destroyed, and much that has been destroyed was better than what replaced it.

Let's ask ourselves a few questions on this topic:
Are we happier with Facebook than with cocktail hour?

Are we better off with a shallow keyword search than a trip to the library and a richer exposure to ideas in a serendipitous manner?

Are we better off with the government collecting everything we send digitally than with a more bumbling security apparatus that had much more difficulty spying on us?

Are we better off with Amazon being the only retailer that matters, and will we be okay when the stores are all empty and grass grows between the cracks of a hundred thousand strip malls?

Are we happier now that musicians and writers and artists today have even fewer ways of getting paid than before?

Are we looking forward to the day when we're outdone by a robot that learns from its mistakes better than we do?

Are we feeling like capital is well targeted at digital while highways crumble, forests die, oceans become acid, and class stratification comes to define our society in the US more than at any time in over a century?

That no one is capable of understanding the complexities of algorithms and their ramifications in dozens of bedrock industries?

That elections can be easily stolen?

That the word "community" now means "give me all your content for free so I can resell it for billions"?

That the most popular digital games focus mainly on gore-soaked warfare?

That digitally controlled drones drop bombs on civilians?

GOING NUCLEAR—AND COMING BACK

Let's think back to a time before the intriguing futurism of Toffler—to a time when another great new power was to bring an end to drudgery and care, would fuel and feed and speed the billions. I'm talking about nuclear. The Chernobyl-Fukushima kind. It could do great harm. It could do great good.

The 1950s were a time of paranoid optimism where we in the US knew we were ten steps ahead of the world and very worried about losing it all in a big radioactive fireball. We had fallout shelters, but we also had real speculation about the possibility of nuclear-powered cars. Many believed that electricity would soon be free because of nuclear energy.

One Cuban Missile Crisis, one Chernobyl, and a Fukushima later, nuclear is in the cultural doghouse. It turned out the techno-visionaries looking only at the wonderfulness of nuclear possibilities totally failed to acknowledge it might be doomed because of the ineradicable danger from radiation. It turned out nuclear reaction was not free. It didn't create something from nothing. It created deadly, long-lasting waste products. And we still haven't figured out what to do with the mess it made.

Digital has created more benefit with less mess than nuclear. But we need to review the seriousness with which a nuclear-powered future was propounded and by whom. Largely it was offered by advanced scientists and social engineers as a way to "change the world" and fix almost everything. But looking back at the history of nuclear, we can see how wrong they were.

I'm not predicting a digital Chernobyl. But I do believe we have come to believe our own propaganda to an unhealthy extent. We've been relentlessly assaulted by news and views pretty much unstinting in their praise of all things digital. For twenty years we have welcomed every new digital advance as a free gift from the science gods. Moreover, we have accepted the entire progression of digital businesses and the transformation of society as something as natural as the weather, to which it would be whimsical to object or even to question.

But when we are told that we "must give our jobs to robots," this signals a change where we now must beware losing ourselves to digital itself. It's almost as if the worldwide digital brain were beginning to wake into consciousness, and once it's with us we may not like what it thinks of us, nor what it wants to do with us.

At the outer limit of the development of artificial intelligence, digital and cognitive scientists grapple with things like "fuzzy logic," "serendipity" or chance, "mistake tolerance," "uncertainty," and what are often called "self-learning systems." Presumably they are hoping that one day they'll have created a genuine Insight Machine. It will understand irony, it will make funny jokes, it will generate original thoughts *and perhaps be able to act upon them!*

Within twenty years we can expect to see a quantum-driven, self-aware artificial intelligence that inhabits an attractive robot and is networked to a hive mind not much different from what today we call "the cloud." It will do what humans can do (at least as far as industry is concerned) and perhaps much more, depending on the software. And as we approach an age when we understand that DNA is software and that the "self" is somewhat an illusion, we will perhaps notice that the difference between our mind and a quantum brainiac may not be as much as we had once wanted to pretend. If you find Stephen Hawking an estimable observer, observe that he has said, "Artificial intelligence could end mankind."[1]

The argument is given that, no matter the pace of change, humans adapt, and that we will adapt to digital much as we adapted to the Ice Age, the Bronze Age, the Machine Age; indeed, it looks as if we have survived even the era of MTV. The corollary is that the machine age seems to have worked okay for us. That is, if you think the blitzkrieg was a ballet in tanks and jackboots, or if you think the Nobel Peace Prize legitimizes the destructive power of dynamite.

THE COST OF RAPID CHANGE

The past-adaptation argument leaves out a couple of important factors. One is that adaptation often includes enormous disruptions and high mortality. Another is that the onset of digital is far more pervasive than any of the above save the Ice Age and has happened much more quickly than, let's say, the Industrial Revolution.

In the days of the Industrial Revolution—the mid-nineteenth century—the world population was comparatively minuscule, and most of the world did not participate. Also, that revolution wasn't much a producer of comfort and ease until it was nearly over. The brutal work conditions invoke shock and horror today, and many of its early products were dangerous, dirty, and grossly inefficient. Someday the permanent underemployment of millions of capable, educated people outdone by digital *should* invoke shock and horror if we might summon the courage to look at it.

Digital goes hand in glove with a push toward economic efficiency and really seems to know no other paradigm. As with the Industrial Revolution, this one-dimensional focus is inimical to the commonweal and designed to enrich the few.

I need to register here a strong suspicion that class stratification may have everything to do with a manic focus on digitally driven wealth, while the drive for efficiency has put the mass of humanity into a tortuous economic decline. At the bottom of an economic system of things that "trickle down," the undigital find themselves suffering a slow drip of water upon their foreheads as if in a form of torture.

Many of those trapped under the weight of digital displacement will *believe* themselves digitally aware because they have smartphones and Facebook pages. But they are consumers of smartphones and products for Facebook, and apart from the immediate benefits offered by the device and the vanity page, they stand to profit little from any new efficiencies in the market. Many will probably not even know how proscribed their world has become. Instead, they'll recede further from economic independence and further from taking an active role in the world as they fiddle with joysticks and text people sitting right next to them.

TOMORROW NEVER KNOWS

Unless you're an owner, a shareholder, possessed of advanced digital skills, or already wealthy, you'll work harder in the near future, and longer, and get paid less because your company is cost-driven and digital keeps driving down prices. But you'll have more information about where to eat dinner than you ever had before. And when you go home, you'll show your "Pinterest" in your favorite movie and much more of your entertainment will be free or very cheap than ever it was before. But your rent won't go down because digital has no impact on the kind of brick and mortar you live in.

At the same time, your sensory inputs will be reduced in direct proportion to the amount of time you spend staring at abstractions on a bright rectangle. You'll have less time to develop your own thoughts because you'll spend less time without headphones. You will imagine, as media moguls encourage, that you are defined by your musical taste and that the music you select and the movies and shows you binge-watch are somehow *you*. But it's an outsourced you. Your Facebook persona, your Twitter account, your Pinterest pins, your bookmarked web pages, your apps, your iPod, your YouTube videos are all ephemeral projections that lull you into believing you *are* something when all you've really become is a throughput device that converts digital assets into cash.

Perhaps you will have saved a bundle on your education and done it on your own time because you "attended" an online university. You "took classes" remotely and had teachers that wrote to you and seemed to care and you earned your degree in less time, with less hassle, than it would've taken otherwise. But in all likelihood you'll have done this in isolation. You will have taken a droplet of vanilla extract instead of tasting the complexity of the vanilla bean itself. And insofar as the map is not the territory, you'll have become very familiar with the map but never tripped upon an unturned stone somewhere in the territory.

You may live in a cool part of town, but you'll spend less time idling in cafes planning a generational coup and more time consuming targeted information packets that exploit your personal preferences. Maybe you'll find a date online, but that seems a minor artifact. With a seventy-two-inch digital flatscreen showing your favorite movie, you'll be so enthralled you may not even need popcorn, much less the fuss and friction of an actual human companion.

Your investments, if you can afford them, will be managed by a robot, and this will include real estate, bonds, and other forms of "safe investments." If you're lucky, the robots won't fail to modulate their behavior when fortunes are made by cashing out before the crash.

Your tastes and your politics may feel like your own, but you'll continually be reinforcing your beliefs by digesting viewpoints from just a few sources, mostly digital and micro-targeted for folks who think the same way that you do. The digitally driven practice of "affinity marketing" almost guarantees you will always be given more of the same as what you already had.

But: *What if it's all bullshit?*

What if our love of digital, even if somewhat unrequited, is at least in some fashion a favorable exchange of electrons? I am thinking very long-term.

It's certainly possible that digital is the equivalent of agriculture in the evolution of the species. Agriculture allowed the race of men to populate much more densely than before, even as it turned predictable food into boredom and even serfdom. Some say agriculture was really the first command-and-control device in the history of the world; yet, until quite recently, it did not entirely forestall famine.

We worry less about famine today than at any time in history, even though great famines were occurring globally as recently as the 1960s.

We can also say that, until at least the end of World War II, we had a *famine of information.* Our brains hadn't enough data to make rational decisions, and we relied an awful lot on "gut." Some would say that "rational decisions" are only patch jobs on reptilian instincts we're embarrassed to admit.

But whatever the root of data-driven decisions, more data has given us a *sense of basis* for decision-making. We've come to trust information in almost unprecedented ways. We firmly believe that the more you know about a puzzle, the better your course of action will be in relation to the puzzle. The metaphor certainly bears out in a technocratic world. Battles are won and lost because of "intelligence" (e.g., "The tanks are disguised as mud huts!"). Data-rich digital controls allow tighter intervals between trains in busy corridors. Buildings take surprising new shapes because the data says the stressors won't take down the structure.

Data, and now its amped-up vehicle, digital, have combined in such a way that now what's often called "Big Data" is expected to help us solve problems we never knew we had and many that have plagued us forever and a day. On a somewhat whimsical note, a team of data scientists claims it can determine, having compared hundreds of examples for abstract traits and language construction, which books will be a success and which will be remaindered. No doubt we can expect books, films, music, facial characteristics, and everything that has a space-time coordinate to be sequenced and quantified in a similar way.

And perhaps, as we outsource all labor and nearly all data-based problem-solving, we'll enjoy the luxury of time to spend on loftier pursuits— to understand the cosmos, to penetrate cause and effect, to determine whether a disruption in the space-time continuum destroys free will or creates infinite universes. Perhaps we might even talk to the animals.

Some of us will find more time for lofty pursuits because of digital. But these will be people who understand the limits of digital and who won't merely accept the output as a real thing in the world, at least not real in the way an olive tree is real.

If we're to benefit from digital, we must question it at every turn much as we question every other "reality" presented us.

As almost any reader might have suspected by now, I'm not going to say the thesis of this book is all bullshit, or even part bullshit. Much of it is speculative, and the future may look very different from what I suggest. But I think I've been fair, and I also expect a fair amount of what I've discussed to actually take place.

The evidence of digital destruction is there if you want to see it.

Much of that destruction was deserved and has resulted in a general benefit.

But if you can agree with me that our future will include additional permanent unemployment due to algorithms, deeply intrusive surveillance, and even robots, and that a mandate to "find something interesting to do" (in an atmosphere of plummeting privacy) does not sound like an answer for a very large sector of society already struggling, then you would also have to agree that digital is going to continue destroying indiscriminately the good, the bad, and the undeserving. And that the future may end up looking lopsided and not very pretty.

Technocrats and digitally aware citizens will find ways to prosper, but this advanced demographic cannot account for more than 10 percent of the population at any time. The rest will continue to be on the receiving end of change, neither inventing nor getting more efficient, but continuing to consume in more and more wasteful and self-destructive ways while getting paid less and less in real terms—ending in what? I am not a believer in apocalyptic scenarios, but I do recognize long-term suffering must lead, at some point, to upheaval.

THE FRESHNESS FACTOR

This book is written in a time of very rapid change in the subject matter it covers. Digital flips itself on its head with alarming frequency. I've not often cited books as a basis for research because there are too few books about this subject to reference. I've instead cited magazines and newspapers because the digital universe tends to change "in real time," as some like to put it.

I have no idea whether, by the time you read this, the newest technology bubble will have burst or if it will have stabilized or expanded. No doubt something new and surprising will take place in digital between the time I am done writing and the time this book is published—we are moving that fast.

Soon it will be twenty years since I worked on my first website (total image load: 9K). Twenty years is enough time to say we've had a good look at the phenomenon I call digital. Twenty years gives us plenty of data to review and permits us to take a more mature look at digital as business people and as civilians. We need to review digital *without* a sense of wonder. We must evaluate digital on its merits and its outputs.

The time to do that is now.

19

DON'T READ THIS FIRST: SURVIVING AND PROSPERING IN A DIGITAL FUTURE

If you are about to read this chapter before you've read the rest, feel free. But you'll be missing most of the story.

Where I've spent eighteen chapters separating digital from its reputation, I will now make some suggestions toward securing a digital future in which we are perhaps even alive and well.

CUT DOWN ON DIGITAL

We are fat and getting obese on a diet of digital. We have allowed its empty calories to fill our cup, and we drink it deeply.

One day the first truly digital generation may look back and ask when they stopped caring for one another, and perhaps even why. The answer will be that it is not digital's fault but digital's effect: to simulate and stimulate, to cajole, amuse, and inform, and to inveigle its way into every cranny of life until all sense is digital. What then passes in physical and emotional space seems of less importance than what sound is plugged to our ear, what offer we must now take up online.

In order to combat this, the first and most important thing is *to reduce the time you spend doing things digital.*

This will remind some of the hard truth about dieting: eat less. But it is no less the imperative. You millions now content to stare at your tiny high-res screen even while in the company of other sentient beings must recognize a grave error in your proclivities. You are rejecting humankind for the cold comfort of a device full of rare earths and big data.

Put away the smartphone, and read a book printed on paper. Good hardcover books, by the way, make terrific gifts and better heirlooms.

Stop texting and start talking. Talking to real people in real time is much more challenging and much more rewarding than thumbing in your abbreviated utterances.

Find something real to do. Rather than an hour spent on YouTube, how about an hour of drawing with a pencil on paper? Or perhaps painting your house might be a good idea. Never mind that you can hire someone to do it. Do that yourself and come away slopped with paint and much the happier for the mess and the wonder of a final product actually real in the world.

Instead of binge-watching, how about taking a walk? Keep the earbuds stashed while you walk, and listen to the sounds of traffic and birds and the wind and the tiny monsters we call insects. It's bound to be a much more rewarding experience than sitting behind a joystick.

Some will say it's time to move off the grid: build a tiny house with no mortgage, engage solar panels and perhaps a wood stove, and sell dulcimers in the town square. This will work for a tiny wedge of the population, but most will remain in their apartments with their dogs and their prints of famous masterworks. They, too, will need to know what it means to disengage.

Any connection to real things and real people will suffice. Cut down on digital consumption, and try to remember that life has been rich and full and ripe with heartache since we first emerged from the darkened cave, and that we loved and hated without digital. Do not go quietly into that glowing flatscreen.

MAKE DIGITAL YOUR OWN

No amount of walking in the woods is going to make digital a minor factor in your life, and you might as well get used to that too.

Based on industry pronouncements, eventually everything that can be done by a robot or software *will* be done by a robot or software. It means that many jobs will either change radically or simply cease to exist.

I won't be the first to say it, but you can make digital work for you much more effectively if you recalibrate yourself from consumer of digital to creator of digital. For many, this means something like "retraining," and that sounds dreary and is no guarantee of success. But dig down one more layer, and you may find it isn't so intimidating.

Knowing how to build websites may eventually become a basic skill needed by everyone. Today you can take more control of your digital life by being able to build your own digital site and then perhaps help others build theirs. These days you don't even have to know html or "coding," as it is called (though it certainly won't hurt to learn how to code). Using a now universally deployed tool called Wordpress, you can avail yourself of an almost unlimited supply of free or cheap website templates and build the site using a GUI (graphical user interface) that writes the code behind the scenes for you as you go.

Having your own site is an entirely different matter from having a Facebook page, and while it won't be hooked into the social media network directly, you can do with it what you will, and can post likes to Facebook, tweet from it, and, of course, post your own content *and still own it.*

Not far from where I live there is a retailer in motorcycle parts that recently decided they wanted to plunge into e-commerce. Theirs is a very competitive industry, and shoppers never stop looking for the cheapest price, no matter what. The retailer will spend a fair amount of money building a digital storefront, but they will then have a platform from which to extract money from a digital economy rather than having digital rob them of sales and their livelihood while sitting on the sidelines. They will have used cloud-based catalog management systems and website templates. Even then it won't be easy—there will be marketing costs as well—but they are good businesspeople, they know their market, and they can look forward to a future where digital helps them rather than hurts them. Anyone with a small retail operation must consider making this move, or else risk extinction.

CODE IS NOT A SECRET

The next level of sophistication is rather a leap for most because it involves actually knowing how to write html, JavaScript, and analytics tags. Today these skills remain the charge of professionals, but these languages are tailored to a purpose and resemble very little the older, compiled software development kits that have ruled until recently. Learning these advanced techniques can make you indispensable in the digital world.

Perhaps most important, you can build functional tools that can build an income (or even wealth). Selling items online can go well beyond posting that old lamp on eBay—there are so many automated storefronts now that you can almost choose what you want to sell, hook up an e-commerce engine (like the motorcycle store), and get to marketing your wares or your expertise online without becoming an engineer.

Folks who have embraced this are able to generate a life of much more flexibility and freedom than folks who continue to plod away at a career whose future is crimped or outright threatened by digital.

TAKE A STAND

Politicians remain, typically, very much in the dark about digital, and that's probably a tragedy waiting to happen. Knowing little to nothing about the nature of digital life and even less about the technologies themselves, they cannot seem to grasp the important issues. Now it may be up to you to tell them what those are.

Tweet your congressman!

Let them know what you care about. Net neutrality? Privacy? Monopolization of retail? Digital education in schools? Open systems? They may not understand you half the time, but you can make it clear what issues might get your vote. Or perhaps go one step further. Last time I checked it was not illegal for a digitally sophisticated person to run for office—I am certain that among the millennial generation there are more than a few coders who might also become legislators.

JOBS THAT WON'T GET DIGITIZED

Despite the self-flagellation over "not having digital skills," as if it were in itself an economic death knell, there are many jobs that will not, in the foreseeable future, be subsumed into the belly of an algorithm. Many of these jobs are those done with your hands in places not factories.

What about landscaping? Robots are not going to get hired by your neighbor to build them a wonderful garden any time soon.

Construction is going to be manned by men and women for a long time. Especially in renovation projects, people are needed far more than computers. There are millions of good homes in America that could be turned from unattractive hulk into a Queen of the Neighborhood with some inspiration, some knowledge of drywall and tiles, and a willingness to get covered in paint and plaster.

Do you know cars at all? They often need fixing. We are not going to be getting our 2002 Mazda rebuilt by an algorithm. We are going to find someone who knows what is going on under the hood, and often enough we will pay them fairly well to use that understanding to fix the weird rattle or the scraping sound somewhere in the back.

Going to the greener side of life, think about solar power. The panels are getting much cheaper, and there will be a boom in this industry before long. Invest, perhaps, in a company that makes them. Or better still, open up a company that installs and manages them. This is both green and technologically advanced, and it requires actual humans to do the work. Much the same holds true for wind farms.

Also consider the arts. I wrote a chapter about how artists might be supplanted by robots, but that is a ways off. Making a great painting is still a skill possessed only by talented humans. Even in a ravaged industry, music itself is still powered by people, their voices, their instruments, and their words. If you've got the talent for art, music, dance, or anything that involves people going to look at what other people have done, now is the time to go for it. You won't have to worry much about an automaton taking your place any time soon.

But the most important factor in any of the above possibilities is a simple directive: *consume less of digital*, and gravitate more toward what requires your entire organism.

Downsize your digital consumption, and *increase* the energies you put into the rest of your life—even if you are a digital professional. After all, while we may adapt to digital, the more important concern is how we can make digital adapt to us. Use digital for what you find useful. And discard the rest.

Most of what digital offers the public is convenience, but convenience is not the definition of a life well lived. Get out of the digital comfort zone, and look for life in the breathing of good air, in the meeting of new people and good lovers, in the contemplation of essential matters, in trying to figure out what it means to be fully a human being on this unusual orb we like to call Earth.

I'm not asking you to hammer your smartphone and switch to carrier pigeons. I'm saying you should stick the phone in your pocket and leave it there until you really need it. And when you don't really need it, don't use it at all. Find something else to do. There are lots of trees that need trimming, drywall that needs raising, children to be hugged, and the more unfortunate that could really use your time and expertise to gain a foothold onto a better life.

Drop out of the ether and wake up in a world of struggling, sentient beings, much like yourself, trying to make it out of one day and into the next with dignity.

There is no such thing, save on an operating table, as a "last chance." But this would be a much better time than later to disengage where you can from digital, learn more about it where it can help you, and get on with a productive, fearless life not consumed by digital.

NOTES

FOREWORD

1. "This is everything Edward Snowden revealed in one year of unprecedented top-secret leaks," *Business Insider*, September 16, 2016

2. Cambridge Analytica, a political data firm hired by President Trump's 2016 election campaign, gained access to private information on more than 50 million Facebook users. The firm offered tools that could identify the personalities of American voters and influence their behavior. "Facebook and Cambridge Analytica: What You Need to Know as Fallout Widens," *The New York Times*, March 19, 2018

3. "Inside the hate-filled echo chamber of racism and conspiracy theories," *The Guardian*, December 16, 2016

4. "Aided by Palantir, the LAPD Uses Predictive Policing to Monitor Specific People and Neighborhoods," *The Intercept*, May 11, 2018

1. DIGITAL IS DESTROYING EVERYTHING

1. "Two Cities with Blazing Internet Speed Search for a Killer App," *New York Times*, September 5, 2014.

2. "Google Fiber Leaves a Digital Divide," *Wall Street Journal*, October 2, 2014.

2. CRAZY TRAIN:
HOW DIGITAL DROVE BIG MUSIC
OFF THE RAILS

1. "Gwen Stefani Launches Her Third Clothing Line," *People/Stylewatch*, January 6, 2014.

2. "Music Merchandise Goes Beyond the T-Shirt," *Fortune*, August 13, 2013.

3. "How the Internet Has All But Destroyed the Market for Films, Music and Newspapers," *The Guardian*, August 13, 2011.

4. "The Recorded Music Market in the US, 2000–2013," *Music Business Research*, March 21, 2014.

5. "What Is Online Piracy?" Recording Industry Association of America (www.riaa.com), October 10, 2014.

6. "Crime and Corruption: Recognizing Unethical Practices in the Music Business," *Music Think Tank*, April 7, 2009.

7. "Artists' Lawsuit: Major Labels Are the Real Pirates," *arstechnica*, December 7, 2009.

8. "Music Firms Target 12-Year-Old," BBC, September 10, 2003.

9. "The Unrepentant Bootlegger," *New York Times*, September 28, 2014.

10. Ibid.

11. Ibid.

12. "Lady Gaga, Jack White, Nora Jones and More: 10 Musicians OK with Piracy and Illegal File-Sharing," *Huffington Post*, February 9, 2012.

13. "2014 is the Best Year for Stadium Concerts in 20 Years," *Billboard*, August 22, 2014.

3. THE BEZOS BAUBLE:
DIGITAL IS DESTROYING THE NEWSPAPER INDUSTRY

1. "Washington Post Adds a National Tabloid Edition," *New York Times*, October 21, 2014.

2. "Paper's Would-Be Savior Now Faces Lawsuits," *New York Times*, October 21, 2014.

3. "Jill Abramson 'Still Not Entirely Sure' Why She Was Fired from the *New York Times*," *International Business Times*, September 14, 2014.

4. http://www.nytimes.com/times-journeys.

5. Many editions of the print version of the *New York Times* in 2014 featured full-page ads for gift items like antique radios, elaborate scale models, and framed photographs available directly from the company.

6. "WSJ's Digital Subscriptions Growing Even Faster Than NYT's," Mashable, April 20, 2013.

7. "Time Warner Opts to Spin Off All Magazines," *Wall Street Journal*, March 6, 2013.

8. Ibid.

9. "Death of a Small Town Newspaper," *Times Union* (timesunion.com), January 20, 2014.

10. Ibid.

11. "Charting the Years-Long Decline of Local News Reporting," *Washington Post*, March 26, 2014.

12. "The Scariest Thing about Print Journalism Isn't Print's Decline, It's Digital's Growth," *The Atlantic*, December 19, 2012.

13. "Display Advertising Clickthrough Rates," *Smart Insights*, November 13, 2013.

14. "Magazine Newsstand Sales: Read It and Weep," *NY Post*, August 8, 2014.

15. "Sit Back, Relax and Read That Long Story—On Your Phone," *The Atlantic*, January 21, 2014.

16. "The Future of Paper," *The Future of Publishing*, August 13, 2013.

17. "Americans Show Signs of Leaving a News Outlet, Citing Less Information," Pew Research Center's Project for Excellence in Journalism: The State of the News Media, 2013.

18. "Women and Social Media," *BlogHer*, March 12, 2012.

19. "Buy It, Try It, Rate It," Weber Shandwick (report), 2013.

20. "State of the Blogging World" (infographic), www.blogging.org, 2012.

4. THE BUSINESS CASE, OR,
WHEN DIGITAL DESTROYS DIGITAL

1. Judah Phillips, "Building a Digital Analytics Organization," *Financial Times Press*, 2014.

2. "Businesses Develop a Hunger for Big Data Analytics," March 2014, http://www.i-cio.com/strategy/big-data/item/businesses-develop-a-hunger-for-big-data-analytics.

3. "Why Nielsen Ratings Are Inaccurate, and Why They'll Stay That Way," January 31, 2011, http://splitsider.com/2011/01/why-nielsen-ratings-are-inaccurate-and-why-theyll-stay-that-way/.

4. Anna Li, "Nielsen Method for TV Ratings Missing Minorities, Young People," October 2013, http://www.poynter.org/news/mediawire/225876/nielsen-method-for-tv-ratings-missing-minorities-young-people/.

5. Rand Schulman, "Creativity without *Conversion* Equals Zero," April 14, 2014, http://www.clickz.com/clickz/column/2339586/creativity-without-conversion-equals-zero.

5. UNDIGITAL, UNEMPLOYED: DIGITAL IS DESTROYING THE JOB MARKET

1. "U.S. Textile Plants Return, with Floors Largely Empty of People," *New York Times*, September 19, 2013.

2. Ibid.

3. "India's Clothing Workers: 'They Slap Us and Call Us Dogs and Donkeys,'" *The Guardian*, November 24, 2012.

4. "My Summer at an Indian Call Center," *Mother Jones*, July 2011.

5. In September 2014, Alibaba "went public" on the New York Stock Exchange in the largest IPO to date.

6. "How Technology Is Destroying Jobs," June 12, 2013, http://www.technologyreview.com/featuredstory/515926/how-technology-is-destroying-jobs/.

7. "Coming to an Office Near You," *The Economist*, January 18, 2014.

8. "Jaron Lanier: The Internet Destroyed the Middle Class," May 12, 2013, http://www.salon.com/2013/05/12/jaron_lanier_the_internet_destroyed_the_middle_class/; Jaron Lanier, *Who Owns the Future?* (New York: Simon & Schuster, 2013).

9. http://www.statista.com/statistics/273563/number-of-facebook-employees.

10. http://www.statista.com/statistics/264122/number-of-employees-at-exxon-mobil-since-200.

6. THE LONELY SCREEN: DIGITAL IS DESTROYING HUMAN INTERACTION

1. http://www.shrm.org/hrdisciplines/technology/articles/pages/telecommuting-likely-to-grow-bans.aspx.

2. Ibid.

3. "When Working in Your Pajamas Is More Productive," *New York Times*, March 8, 2014.

4. http://www.forbes.com/sites/susanadams/2012/12/21/dont-get-caught-in-the-telecommuting-trap.

5. http://www.sciencedaily.com/releases/2012/05/120529144342.htm.

6. http://www.thegrindstone.com/2012/05/30/office-politics/isolation-among-telecommuters-a-myth-researchers-say-yes-my-experience-says-no-398.

7. http://techcrunch.com/2014/06/22/love-hacking-social-isolation.

8. Ibid.

9. Jay Rosen, "Facebook Has All the Power," *The Atlantic*, July 10, 2014.

10. "Facebook Terms and Conditions: Why You Don't Own Your Online Life," *The Telegraph UK*, http://www.telegraph.co.uk/technology/social-media/9780565/Facebook-terms-and-conditions-why-you-dont-own-your-online-life.html.

11. The FCC decided early that the Internet was not a utility, but rather an information service, and some say they mistook bandwidth for data, which has led to a cascading series of regulatory miscues, including what looks to be the real possibility we will see an end to "net neutrality" in 2015.

12. The Facebook terms-of-service agreement is reportedly about 14,000 words long, and to my knowledge the government had no say in composing it. It is a contract between Facebook and the user.

7. A GOLDEN RING, JUST OUT OF REACH: DIGITAL IS DESTROYING HIGHER EDUCATION

1. "The United States, Falling Behind," editorial, *New York Times*, October 23, 2013.

2. "Student Loan Problems: One Third of Millennials Regret Going to College," *Forbes*, May 22, 2013.

3. "The Latest Fad in Education Reform: Testing 4-Year-Olds," *Texas Observer*, April 14, 2014.

4. "$1 Trillion Student Loan Problem Keeps Getting Worse," *Forbes*, February 21, 2014.

5. "Crippling Debt Defers Graduates' Dreams," *Boston Globe*, August 25, 2013.

6. "The Truth About Diploma Mills and Fake Degrees," www.counterfeit degrees.com.

7. I once tested a hypothesis that scam universities existed by enrolling in one that promised an advanced degree based on "attestation" and "life experience." For a few hundred dollars I received what appeared to be a college

transcript describing "courses" and "credits" and a "degree" in psychology from an institution calling itself a university. I have never attempted to use this degree for any purpose. The university continues to send e-mails to me insisting that new regulations require that I get my degree "certified" by a party unknown to me, and I have several times asked the university to cease and desist sending me e-mails.

8. From "Khan Academy Founder Sal Khan Takes on Financial Education for Adults," *The Daily Beast*, April 9, 2013: "Khan Academy founder teams up with Bank of America on his next big project: teaching adults about money."

9. https://www.class-central.com/university/harvard.

10. "After Setbacks, Online Courses Are Rethought," *New York Times*, December 10, 2013.

11. http://www.onlinemarketinginstitute.org/course-certifications; http://www.learnmore.duke.edu/certificates/digital_marketing; http://www.google.com/onlinechallenge/dmc.

12. "A New Gallup Survey Says Colleges and Employers Disagree About How Workforce-Ready Graduates Are—Who's Right?" *Huffington Post*, April 29, 2014.

13. "Police in Riot Gear Respond to Crowd Near Keene State College," *Boston Globe*, October 18, 2014.

14. "The UVA Gang Rape Allegations Are Awful, Horrifying, and Not Shocking at All," *Slate*, November 25, 2014.

8. THE DOWNTOWN NEXT TIME: DIGITAL IS DESTROYING URBAN LIFE IN AMERICA

1. Alexander von Hoffman, *House by House, Block by Block: The Rebirth of America's Urban Neighborhoods* (Oxford: Oxford University Press, 2003).

2. Cleveland, Ohio, had a population of 914,808 in 1950, according to Wikipedia; Detroit in 1950 had a population of 1.8 million, according to the same source.

3. Cleveland in 1980 had a population of 573,822, according to www.city-data.com, while an estimate for 2013 from the US Census Bureau counts only 390,113 residents—a precipitous drop from both peak and 1980 numbers. Detroit shows similar declines.

4. "Ford to City: Drop Dead," *New York Daily News*, October 29, 1975 (after President Ford denied NYC a financial bailout from the federal government).

5. "Confession of Etan Patz's Accused Killer Finally Aired in Court," *Pro Publica*, September 15, 2014.

6. [Bloomberg's] "vision of the city as a premium brand," http://observer.com/2006/12/no-no-no-yes-the-mayors-curious-evolution-on-public-money-for-private-real-estate/#ixzz3IJ0grjvy.

7. "Bill DeBalsio Tells 'A Tale of Two Cities' at His Mayoral Campaign Kickoff," http://observer.com/2013/01/bill-de-blasio-tells-a-tale-of-two-cities-at-his-mayoral-campaign-kickoff.

8. "As of 2014 the population of the [downtown Los Angeles] district had grown to 52,400 residents," according to Wikipedia.

9. In 2010, according to the website Gothamist, Patti Smith, while speaking at the Cooper Union, said, "New York has closed itself off to the young and the struggling. But there are other cities. Detroit. Poughkeepsie. New York City has been taken away from you. So my advice is: Find a new city."

10. "Where [David Byrne will] go is a question he's unable to answer—'Join the expat hipsters upstate in Hudson?'" http://www.rollingstone.com/music/news/david-byrne-the-rich-are-destroying-new-york-culture-20131007#ixzz3IUoAE9dV.

11. Microsoft Outlook, JoinMe, and others provide virtual workspaces. See "LogMeIn's Join.me Can Now Record Meetings & Save Them to Cubby, the Company's Alternative to Dropbox," *TechCrunch*, August 19, 2013.

12. "New Study Shows Content Theft Sites Hijacking Online Ad Business to Make Hundreds of Millions in Profits," *PR Newswire*, February 18, 2014.

13. Graham Jones, "Search Engines Manipulate Your Thinking," May 21, 2014, http://www.business2community.com/seo/search-engines-manipulate-thinking-0882386.

14. http://www.ohiohistorycentral.org/w/Mansfield,_Ohio.

15. In 1890s Paris cafe society, the greenish liqueur absinthe (a.k.a. "the green faerie"), fermented from wormwood extracts and supposed to induce trancelike reverie and hallucinations, was widely seen as a societal ill. Its association with degeneracy played a role in keeping it outlawed in the United States until about 2007.

16. "'Rent Is Too Damn High' Candidate Is Back," *USA Today*, August 26, 2014: "Jimmy McMillan is running for governor . . . [said] The Rent Is Too Damn High Party."

17. *Forbes*, April 14, 2014.

18. "Retail Stores Will Completely Die, Says Tech Investor Marc Andreessen," *Business Insider*, January 31, 2013.

19. The ancient Library of Alexandria, believed by many to have contained a high percentage of all written pages at the time of its destruction, was burned or

otherwise destroyed in approximately the year 200 AD; many today lament what knowledge and history must have been lost in its demise.

20. A line from Paul Simon's elegiac song "America."

9. OVERSHARING AND UNDERCOUNTING: DIGITAL IS DESTROYING RATIONAL DISCOURSE AND THE DEMOCRATIC PROCESS

1. "Why Did The U.S. Government Shut Down in October 2013?" *Forbes*, October 3, 2013.

2. "Burdock Root Side Effects," *LiveStrong*, December 11, 2010.

3. "The Drudge Report Drives More Top News Traffic than Twitter or Facebook, Study Finds," *PBS News*, May 9, 2011.

4. "The ISIS Online Campaign Luring Western Girls to Jihad," *The Daily Beast*, August 6, 2014.

5. During their nationally televised August 28, 1968, debate in Chicago, Vidal called Buckley a "pro-crypto-Nazi." Buckley answered, "Now listen, you queer, stop calling me a crypto-Nazi or I'll sock you in your goddamn face and you'll stay plastered." See http://www.pitt.edu/~kloman/debates.html.

6. "Most Journalists Now Get Story Ideas from Social Media Sources, Survey Says," *Poynter*, June 21, 2012.

7. "TV Is Dying, And Here Are the Stats That Prove It," November 24, 2013, www.businessinsider.com/cord-cutters-and-the-death-of-tv.

8. "How Search Engines Operate," http://moz.com/beginners-guide-to-seo/how-search-engines-operate.

9. Michael Wolff, *Burn Rate: How I Survived the Gold-Rush Years on the Internet* (New York: Touchstone Press, 1999).

10. A high percentage of high-traffic websites today are made up of pages that are assembled "on the fly" by applications called Content Management Systems, which store content and serve it as pages that are requested by a browser. The chief advantage is that pages can be "personalized" based on certain criteria, and that the pages can also be updated rapidly without relaunching a site.

11. "Elections Board Rings In the Old, as Lever Machines Replace Scanners," *New York Times*, September 9, 2013.

12. "Electronic Voting Unreliable Without Receipt, Expert Says," *Stanford Report* (Stanford University), February 18, 2004.

13. "The Evidence," www.votescam.com.

14. I've been personally involved in a number of software implementation projects and can attest to the difficulty of understanding code written by others and the additional difficulty of "fixing" it without "breaking" something else.

15. "None Dare Call It Stolen: Ohio, the Election and America's Servile Press," *Harper's Magazine*, August 2005.

16. A line from "This Land Is Your Land," words and music by Woody Guthrie.

10. BOOKS, BATH, AND BEYOND: DIGITAL IS DESTROYING RETAIL

1. As is fairly well known in the business community, Amazon has lost money almost every fiscal year despite rocketing sales, in large part (as the data suggest) because of its very low—not to say impossibly low—pricing.

2. "Brick-and-mortar" is a pejorative used by digital business boosters in reference to those retailers who must rely on the antediluvian arrangement whereby they rent physical space in a choice location (a building—bricks and mortar), and then stock it with goods for the consumer to review and compare, and perhaps buy, at what are often unsustainable levels of cost driven by both rent and the cost of maintaining inventory.

3. Companies like Amazon say they make money on each transaction but lose money because they reinvest in the business, but that is of no consequence to the market at large: the net effect is that the company dominates while losing money.

4. As Amazon continues to post losses, some investors have begun to wonder if profits will be generated any time soon. In late 2014, the company's stock sold for about 25 percent less than it had in early 2014.

5. In 2014 Amazon battled with publishing giant Hachette over pricing and has stirred controversy by delaying shipment of or not selling Hachette books during the dispute; as a result, Hachette (plus hundreds of well-known authors) lined up against Amazon. In November 2014 Amazon and Hachette settled their differences, but the publishing market remains polarized.

6. "Cubicles Rise in a Brave New World of Publishing," *New York Times*, November 9, 2014.

7. "Gotham Book Mart Holdings Are Given to Penn," *New York Times*, January 9, 2009.

8. "A Strategic Mistake That Haunts JC Penney," *Forbes*, September 27, 2013.

9. "A Day at Sears Reveals Pitfalls of Retail Tech Implementation," *CIO Journal*, January 28, 2014.

10. "Forrester: U.S. Online Retail Sales to Hit $370 Billion by 2017," Mashable, March 12, 2013.

11. "E-commerce Will Make the Shopping Mall a Retail Wasteland," ZDNet, January 27, 2013.

11. B2B AND THE PERILS OF FREEMIUM: DIGITAL IS DESTROYING THE BUSINESS-TO-BUSINESS MARKET FOR DIGITAL

1. "Freemium is a pricing strategy by which a product or service (typically a digital offering such as software, media, games, or web services) is provided free of charge, but money (premium) is charged for proprietary features, functionality, or virtual goods" (http://en.wikipedia.org/wiki/Freemium).

2. https://www.openoffice.org.

3. "European Commission Report Endorses Open Source," ZDNet, January 15, 2007.

4. Disclosure: I am in the business of providing independent digital marketing services.

5. "The Six Simple Principles of Viral Marketing," *Web Marketing Today*, May 10, 2012.

6. http://www.entrepreneurship.org/resource-center/valuation-of-prerevenue-companies--the-venture-capital-method.aspx.

12. DIGITAL HAS DESTROYED AUTHORITARIAN RULE (OR HAS IT?)

1. "Tahrir Square Tweet by Tweet," *The Guardian*, April 14, 2011.

2. "Egypt Uprising of 2011," *Encyclopaedia Britannica*, http://www.britannica.com/EBchecked/topic/1756982/Egypt-Uprising-of-2011.

3. "What happened in Egypt in the last few years was that a lot of bloggers were just filming police brutality on mobile phones, and this is what caused so much uproar in the blogosphere." Interview with Evgeny Morozov, PBS *Frontline*, http://www.pbs.org/wgbh/pages/frontline/revolution-in-cairo/interviews/evgeny-morozov.html.

4. http://en.wikipedia.org/wiki/Iraq_War_documents_leak.

5. "Julian Assange Speaks of 'Leaving' Ecuador Embassy," *BBC News*, August 18, 2014.

6. "No Secrets: Julian Assange's Mission for Total Transparency," *The New Yorker*, June 7, 2010.

7. "Wikileaks Reveals Video Showing US Air Crew Shooting Down Iraqi Civilians," *The Guardian*, April 5, 2010.

8. "Congress Job Approval Starts 2014 at 13%," Gallup Poll, January 14, 2014.

9. "Pelosi, Boehner Defend Votes to Maintain NSA Phone Snooping Program," *Huffington Post*, July 25, 2013.

10. "Tech Giants Unite Against NSA," *The Hill*, December 9, 2013.

11. "Burglars Who Took on FBI Abandon Shadows," *New York Times*, January 7, 2014.

12. Ibid.

13. "Judge Richard Leon . . . blasted the NSA's practice of collecting phone metadata en masse as 'near-Orwellian. . . . I have little doubt that the author of our constitution, James Madison . . . would be aghast.'" See "Judge Says NSA Phone Surveillance Likely Unconstitutional," *Newsy*, December 16, 2013.

13. OBSESSIVE COMPULSIVE: DIGITAL IS DESTROYING OUR WILL TO CREATE ANYTHING NOT DIGITAL

1. As indicated by the two commercial rocket explosions in the fall of 2014.

2. "The 39 Most Valuable Startups in the World," *Business Insider*, http://www.businessinsider.com/startups-with-billion-dollar-valuations-2014-3?op=1#ixzz3J9r4VO8N.

3. "Why Did Snapchat Turn Down Three Billion Dollars?" *The New Yorker*, November 14, 2013.

4. http://en.wikipedia.org/wiki/Soylent_%28drink%29.

5. "'Artificial Egg' Made from PLANTS Backed by Bill Gates Set to Revolutionize Cooking Goes on Sale at Whole Foods," *Daily Mail*, http://www.dailymail.co.uk/sciencetech/article-2416808/Artificial-egg-PLANTS-backed-Bill-Gates-set-revolutionize-cooking-goes-sale-Whole-Foods.html#ixzz3J9uRmaQm.

6. "First Hamburger Made from Lab-Grown Meat to Be Served at Press Conference," *The Guardian*, August 5, 2013.

7. "More and More Companies Want a Piece of the Next Snapchat," *Harvard Business Review*, October 13, 2014.

8. Moore's law was posited in the 1960s as a relationship between time and computing power—roughly, that computing power would increase by a large percentage each year (compounding prior years) and that cost for same would at the same time drop noticeably. Hence many of the computing bounties we enjoy today.

9. http://www.google.com/earth/explore/showcase/3dbuildings.html#tab= skyscrapers.

10. Humphrey Bogart says in the film *Casablanca*, "Can the hopes and dreams of three little people amount to a hill of beans in this crazy world?" as Ingrid Bergman attempts with her husband to escape Nazis in Morocco.

11. "What Happened to 3rd Ward?" *New York Observer*, October 15, 2013.

12. "Before long, 3rd Ward was beginning to draw notice from other investors and local tech moguls, like Perry Chen, the co-founder of Kickstarter, who introduced Mr. Goodman to Joanne Wilson, the wife of the prominent venture capitalist Fred Wilson, and Tony Hsieh, the founder of Zappos." See "At Once-Promising Brooklyn Arts Center, Dashed Hopes," *New York Times*, December 12, 2013.

13. "VCs 'Partying Like It's 1999,' Says McNamee," CNBC, August 27, 2014.

14. "'Man, it feels more and more like 1999 every day,' tweeted Bill Gurley, one of the valley's leading venture capitalists. 'Risk is being discounted tremendously.'" —"In Silicon Valley, Partying Like It's 1999 Once More," *New York Times*, November 26, 2013.

15. "[VC firm] Benchmark . . . led a $13.5 million investment in Snapchat, the disappearing-photo site that has millions of adolescent users but no revenue." Ibid.

14. WALL STREET AS VAUDEVILLE:
DIGITAL IS DESTROYING FINANCIAL SERVICES

1. "The $9 Billion Witness: Meet JPMorgan Chase's Worst Nightmare," *Rolling Stone*, November 6, 2014.

2. "One Call from Jamie Dimon May Have Stopped the DOJ from Investigating Bankers for Fraud During the Financial Crisis," *Business Insider*, November 6, 2014.

3. "Towards the Mandatory Approval of Complex Financial Instruments," *Social Europe Journal*, September 22, 2014.

4. "Charting McCain's 'Suspended Campaign,'" NPR, September 25, 2008.

5. "The Lehman Brothers Hangover," *The Daily Beast*, September 10, 2010.

6. Excerpt from "A Colossal Failure of Common Sense," Lawrence G. McDonald, *New York Times*, July 21, 2009.

7. "The High-Tech Arms Race That's Causing Stock Market 'Tsunamis,'" CNN, August 13, 2014.

8. IBM announced in January 2014 that its *Jeopardy*-winning "Watson" computer could do more than find a needle in a haystack. It could, they claim,

"understand the haystack." But this type of advanced computing is not in wide use today.

9. "[High-frequency traders] began to quickly buy and then resell contracts to each other—generating a 'hot-potato' volume effect as the same positions were passed rapidly back and forth" (http://www.wsj.com/articles/SB1000142 4052748704029304575526390131916792).

10. "SEC Chairman Admits: We're Outgunned by Market Supercomputers," *Wall Street Journal*, May 11, 2010.

11. "During the height of the Cold War, the US military put such an emphasis on a rapid response to an attack on American soil, that to minimize any foreseeable delay in launching a nuclear missile, for nearly two decades they intentionally set the launch codes at every silo in the US to 8 zeroes." See "For Nearly Two Decades the Nuclear Launch Code at All Minuteman Silos in the United States Was 00000000," http://www.todayifoundout.com/index.php/2013/11/nearly-two-decades-nuclear-launch-code-minuteman-silos-united-states-00000000/.

12. "Will 2014 Be the Year the Tech Bubble Bursts?" *Wired*, December 16, 2013.

13. Square is a company that offers a device allowing anyone with an iPad or iPhone to swipe credit cards for payment.

14. "Back to Square One: Jack Dorsey's dazzling startup promised to transform the credit and finance industry with a sweeping, digitized vision of the future. After losing $100 million, has his company lost its edge?" *Fast Company*, June 2014.

15. INVADERS FROM EARTH:
DIGITAL IS DESTROYING THE PROFESSIONS (AND MORE)

1. According to the website www.e-zpassny.com, "*E-ZPass®* is an electronic toll collection (ETC) system that allows you to prepay your tolls, eliminating the need to stop at the toll plaza. The system has three components: a toll tag, which is placed inside your vehicle; an overhead antenna, which reads the toll tag and collects the toll; and video cameras to identify toll evaders."

2. http://www.capitol-digital.com. Capitol Digital claims to provide services "in all aspects of the EDRM (Electronic Discovery Reference Model), including forensic data collections, ECA (Early Case Assessment), Electronic Discovery processing, review, analysis, and production. We also provide additional essential services including document scanning (on-site and off-site), document coding, OCR, Bates labeling, media duplication, x-ray scanning and duplication,

audio and video duplication, printing, photo copying, trial exhibit board creation, and training for Summation and Concordance."

3. "A federal court has approved a computerized document review process that turns huge volumes of legal grunt work over to the machines." —"Attention Young Lawyers: The Grim Reaper Is Here," *The American Interest*, May 5, 2012.

4. The web page http://www.nyulawglobal.org/globalex/US_Fee-Based_Legal_Databases.htm lists several legal research databases, including LexisNexis, Westlaw, Fastcase, Loislaw, VersusLaw and others.

5. "Is This the Death of Hourly Rates at Law Firms?" *Washington Post*, April 13, 2014.

6. Listen to a discussion of the topic here: http://wgbhnews.org/post/future-digital-medicine.

7. "Turning Information into Impact: Digital Health's Long Road Ahead," *Forbes*, December 30, 2012.

8. Eric Topol, MD, *The Creative Destruction of Medicine: How the Digital Revolution Will Create Better Health Care* (New York: Basic Books, 2012).

9. "Digital Medicine Will Reshape Hospitals," *EE Times*, November 11, 2013.

10. "Serious health policy wonks will tell you that if you want to control health care costs, you will need to . . . shift a lot of work away from doctors towards lower-paid workers such as nurse-practitioners and physician's assistants, or those even further down the healthcare wage hierarchy." See "The Future of the MD," *The Daily Beast*, January 23, 2013.

11. "In the Future We'll All Be Renters: America's Disappearing Middle Class," *The Daily Beast*, August 10, 2014.

12. "Computers that Learn from Mistakes Coming to Markets in 2014," *Nature World News*, December 30, 2013.

13. http://www-03.ibm.com/press/us/en/presskit/27297.wss.

14. Ibid.

15. "A Closer Look at Google's New Robot Army," *Gizmodo*, December 14, 2013.

16. Ibid.

17. "Insect-Inspired Sensors Improve Tiny Robot's Flight," *The Scientist*, June 18, 2014.

18. "The government is pouring money into researching and developing artificially intelligent swarming robots, and the looming question is whether this cutting-edge technology will be used for good, or bring about a dystopian future of smart and lethal machines that could be used against humans." —"For Good or Bad, Intelligent, Swarming Nanobots Are the Next Frontier of Drones," *Motherboard (Vice)*, May 21, 2014.

19. "Better Than Human: Why Robots Will—and Must—Take Our Jobs," *Wired*, December 24, 2012.

20. "Could Robots Be the Writers of the Future?" *TechRadar*, April 1, 2013.

21. Ibid.

22. Ibid.

23. "[In] Mark Coker's '2013 Book Publishing Industry Predictions—Indie Ebook Authors Take Charge' . . . Coker noted that 'If Amazon could invent a system to replace the author from the equation, they'd do that.'" "Assault on Writers from Automated Software," *Huffington Post*, March 29, 2013.

24. www.automatedinsights.com.

25. "'Rubber Rooms' in New York Schools Cost City $22 Million a Year for Teachers Awaiting Hearings," *Huffington Post*, October 16, 2012.

26. "One Year on the Job, 13 Years in Rubber Room Earns Perv Teacher $1M," *New York Post*, January 27, 2013.

27. "'Will computers replace teachers? Dear God, I hope so,' says Katherine Mangu-Ward, managing editor of Reason magazine," *Reason*, April 6, 2013.

28. http://www.elephantart.com/catalog/funds.php.

29. http://www.zoosociety.org/Conservation/Bonobo/BonoboPainting.php.

30. Heather Bush, *Why Cats Paint: A Theory of Feline Aesthetics* (Berkeley, CA: Ten Speed Press, 1994).

31. "Algorithmic art, also known as *algorithm art*, is art, mostly visual art, of which the design is generated by an algorithm" (http://en.wikipedia.org/wiki/Algorithmic_art).

32. "Robot Art: Henry Moon's Drawing Machines," The Creators' Project/Vice.com.

33. Ibid.

34. In his book *Leviathan* Thomas Hobbes described the natural state of mankind as a "warre of every man against every man."

35. "Whatsoever therefore is consequent to a time of Warre, where every man is Enemy to every man; the same is consequent to the time, wherein men live without other security, than what their own strength, and their own invention shall furnish them withall. In such condition, there is no place for Industry; because the fruit thereof is uncertain; and consequently no Culture of the Earth; no Navigation, nor use of the commodities that may be imported by Sea; no commodious Building; no Instruments of moving, and removing such things as require much force; no Knowledge of the face of the Earth; no account of Time; no Arts; no Letters; no Society; and which is worst of all, continuall feare, and danger of violent death; And the life of man, solitary, poore, nasty, brutish, and short." Ibid.

16. FROM RUBYLITH TO SELFIES:
LESSER PURSUITS DESTROYED
BY DIGITAL

1. "In 1919, New York produced more than 50 percent of total national output in 12 lines of manufacture, and was competitive in many more." See *Slate*, January 23, 2014.

2. "History of the Adobe Postscript Format," http://www.investintech.com/resources/articles/pdfpostscript.

3. The Stanford Web Archive Portal stores legacy web pages from as far back as 1991: https://swap.stanford.edu.

4. From Lincoln's Gettysburg Address: "The world will little note, nor long remember what we say here, but it can never forget what they did here."

5. "Children Don't Want Toys for Christmas Anymore," *Business Insider*, December 21, 2012.

6. "A Magazine Is an iPad That Does Not Work.m4v," YouTube, https://www.youtube.com/watch?v=aXV-yaFmQNk.

7. "As Children Pine for Electronics, Traditional Toy Makers Face a Growing Tech Challenge," *Globe and Mail*, November 24, 2012.

17. IT'S WORSE THAN YOU THOUGHT:
DIGITAL IS DESTROYING PRIVACY

1. "Ancient Rome's Terrorizing Toilets," *Discover* magazine, June 18, 2014.

2. "An Expert's Take on Toilet History and Customs from Antiquity to the Renaissance," *Biblical Archaeology Society*, February 17, 2012.

3. "Facebook Just Made Your Private Messages Public—Here's What to Do," *MacLean's*, September 24, 2012.

4. "Hands On: Fitbit Charge Review," *TechRadar*, October 27, 2014.

5. "New Survey Suggests Millennials Have No Idea What Privacy Means," *Forbes*, April 26, 2013.

6. "Survey Identifies a 'Millennial Rift' Revealing New Views about Privacy on Social Media and a Willingness to Cooperate Online with Businesses," *USC Annenberg News*, April 22, 2013.

7. The bundling board was a large plank placed between the two lovers. See "Courtship, Sex and the Single Colonist," *Colonial Williamsburg Journal*, Holiday 2007.

8. Ibid.

9. Samuel D. Warren and Louis D. Brandeis, "The Right to Privacy," *Harvard Law Review*, 1890.

10. "The Prism: Privacy in an Age of Publicity," *The New Yorker*, June 24, 2013.

11. Ibid.

12. "For me, in terms of personal satisfaction, the mission's already accomplished." —Edward Snowden, *Washington Post*, December 23, 2013.

13. "The NSA Spies and Democrats Look Away," CNN, July 9, 2013.

14. "Major Opinion Shifts, in the US and Congress, on NSA Surveillance and Privacy: Pew [study] finds that, for the first time since 9/11, Americans are now more worried about civil liberties abuses than terrorism," *The Guardian*, July 29, 2013.

15. "Judge Questions Legality of NSA Phone Records," *New York Times*, December 16, 2013.

16. "Many of the techniques used would be intolerable in a democratic society even if all of the targets had been involved in violent activity, but COINTELPRO went far beyond that. . . . The Bureau conducted a sophisticated vigilante operation aimed squarely at preventing the exercise of First Amendment rights of speech and association, on the theory that preventing the growth of dangerous groups and the propagation of dangerous ideas would protect the national security and deter violence." —Final Report of the Church Committee on Operation COINTELPRO.

17. "More Federal Agencies Are Using Undercover Operations," *New York Times*, November 16, 2014.

18. "'Newburgh Four' Terrorism Case was FBI Entrapment: HBO Film," *New York Post*, July 20, 2014.

19. "Google CEO Larry Page has rapidly positioned Google to become an indispensable U.S. Military contractor." See "Google's Robots and Creeping Militarization," *The Daily Caller*, January 9, 2014.

20. https://www.apple.com/r/store/government.

21. http://www.experian.com/public-sector/risk-management-for-government.html.

22. "Microsoft GovCon Alliance strengthens solutions for federal government contractors." —*Community Dynamics*, June 16, 2014.

18. MAYBE IT'S ALL BULLSHIT

1. "Stephen Hawking Warns Artificial Intelligence Could End Mankind," http://www.bbc.com/news/technology-30290540.

INDEX